Studies in Contemporary Economics

Editorial Board
D. Bös G. Bombach B. Felderer B. Gahlen K. W. Rothschild

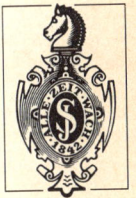

David Stern   Jozef M. M. Ritzen (Eds.)

Market Failure in Training?

New Economic Analysis and Evidence on Training of Adult Employees

Springer-Verlag
Berlin Heidelberg New York
London Paris Tokyo
Hong Kong Barcelona
Budapest

Editors

David Stern
School of Education
University of California, Berkeley
Berkeley, CA 94720, USA

Jozef M. M. Ritzen
Minister of Education and Science
Government of the Netherlands
Postbus 25000, NL-2700 LZ Zoetermeer
The Netherlands

ISBN 3-540-54622-7 Springer-Verlag Berlin Heidelberg New York
ISBN 0-387-54622-7 Springer-Verlag New York Berlin Heidelberg

This work is subject to copyright. All rights are reserved, whether the whole or part of the material is concerned, specifically the rights of translation, reprinting, re-use of illustrations, recitation, broadcasting, reproduction on microfilms or in any other way, and storage in data banks. Duplication of this publication or parts thereof is permitted only under the provisions of the German Copyright Law of September 9, 1965, in its current version, and permission for use must always be obtained from Springer-Verlag. Violations are liable for prosecution under the German Copyright Law.

© Springer-Verlag Berlin Heidelberg 1991
Printed in Germany

Typesetting: Camera ready by author
Printing and binding: Weihert-Druck GmbH, Darmstadt
42/3140-543210 - Printed on acid-free paper

CONTENTS

Preface VII

Introduction and Overview 1
Jozef M.M. Ritzen and David Stern

Job Training: Costs, Returns, and Wage Profiles 15
Jacob Mincer

Firm Financed Education and Specific Human Capital: A Test of the
Insurance Hypothesis 41
Michael J. Feuer, Henry A. Glick, and Anand Desai

On-The-Job Training of New Hires 61
John H. Bishop

Employee Training Programs in U.S. Businesses 99
Ann P. Bartel

Firms' Propensity to Train 135
David Stern and Charles S. Benson

Training and Employment Relations in Japanese Firms 153
Masanori Hashimoto

Market Failure for General Training, and Remedies 185
Jozef M.M. Ritzen

Nonmarket Failure in Government Training Programs 215
W. Lee Hansen

PREFACE

The papers in this volume were first presented at a symposium on "An Expanded Public Role in Job Training? The Issue of Market Failure in the Provision of Training." The symposium took place in May, 1989. It was sponsored by the LaFollette Institute of Public Affairs at the University of Wisconsin, Madison. Jozef Ritzen, then in Madison on leave from Erasmus University in the Netherlands, organized the symposium. Subsequently he became Minister of Education and Science for the Netherlands. He asked David Stern to finish the work of editing the papers for publication. All the papers have been revised in light of comments by discussants at the symposium, as well as subsequent comments by the editors and outside reviewers.

INTRODUCTION AND OVERVIEW

Jozef M.M. Ritzen
Erasmus University Rotterdam
Minister of Education and Science
The Netherlands

David Stern
School of Education
University of California, Berkeley

Two factors are contributing to an increased interest in the training of adult employees. First, there is the present high rate of change in the technologies embodied in products and in production processes. This enhances the negative effect of the undersupply of training on economic growth. Higher levels of training would provide a more fertile environment for technological change. The second factor is the aging of the population. Almost all industrialized countries have experienced a decrease in the birthrate in the sixties after a baby boom in the late forties and fifties. As a result, the average age of workers is increasing and will continue to do so in the next two decades. There is a good chance that, without increased training efforts, this will cause the rate of productivity increase to slow down, as older workers are likely to be less productive than younger workers.

Job training is the result of decisions by workers and firms. According to conventional economic theory, a worker may choose a certain level and amount of training in view of the potential future returns to be gained as a result of that training, and pay for training directly or through a decrease in wages during the training period. Or employees and employers may negotiate the terms of gainful employment and end up with agreements which are satisfactory to both parties. Job training can be part of those agreements as long as both parties see this to their mutual advantage. The financial returns to training for the firm or the worker are, in this view, the incentive for training.

What is wrong with the conventional view? Why not leave the job training of adult, employed workers to the private decisions of firms and individual workers? The first part of the answer is that there are empirical indications that the market for training does not work as it should. The little evidence we have shows that rates of return to the training of adult, employed workers exceed rates of return to other investments. So we suspect barriers in the supply of training which lead to underinvestment. Underinvestment is most apparent for workers who are older, work in small firms, and have low levels of formal schooling. The second part of the answer is that there are also theoretical reasons which make it highly unlikely that training of adult, employed workers would be provided efficiently by means of markets. Among the reasons are:

• Uncertainty. The financial returns to training are not certain, but risky at the time the worker has to decide whether or not to invest in training. For risk averse workers this causes underinvestment in training; creating a mechanism to pool risk could make everyone better off.

• Liquidity constraints. Workers may not possess the means to finance additional training out of current income and could be unable to borrow from financial institutions.

• Minimum wage legislation. This effectively precludes contracts in which minimum wage workers pay for their training through reduced wages.

• The existence of subsidized training for the unemployed which makes it attractive for workers to defer training until they are employed.

• Complementarity between general and specific training. Substantial turnover of labor reduces the payoff to general as well as specific training.

• Transaction costs involved in signaling to other employers the outcome of general training.

• Labor contracts which do not contain incentives for training.

• Unemployment insurance and transfers to the unemployed which facilitate the substitution of older by younger workers.

These arguments will be elaborated below, and in subsequent chapters.

Training can be provided in different forms. It can be made available within the firm, as on-the-job training or formal training. Or the formal education system can supply an education which is equivalent to the training. There are reasons to expect that formal education is often less efficient that training provided by firms. Workers learn more easily through a combination of practical experience and theoretical instruction. Firms usually have more recent equipment, have the experience in their use in production and can provide mentors for gaining practical experience. Also, workers are often more motivated for job based learning rather than learning in a school setting. And job based training is generally better connected to the knowledge requirements of jobs. However, formal education definitely can play a role in providing the theoretical instruction associated with training and sometimes the training can be so general that the formal education system can better provide it.

In this chapter we briefly present the case for an increased training effort in Western industrialized countries. This case is made on the basis of technological change and the aging of the working population. We then discuss possible reasons for market failure in training, and possible remedies. Following this introduction to the issues at stake, we provide a brief overview of the remaining chapters in this volume.

Technology and Demography.

Technological development is a driving force behind training. International competition requires firms to keep up with the Joneses in technology. Newer products and products made with newer production processes form an increasing share of the product market. In many cases it is new technology which allows the introduction of new products or production processes. This implies that the average life of products and of production processes will continue to decrease. Workers will experience during their lifetimes many different products and production processes. Once a new product or production process is introduced in a firm, the human capital of the workers receives a jolt downwards. It depreciates. Only training can ensure that the human capital stock is kept intact. Training is like rowing against the current. Once you stop you are dragged downstream.

The decrease in the average life of products is widely recognized. It should lead to more training by employers, except for the possibility that firms could instead refresh their stock of human capital by means of lay-offs of older workers and recruitment of younger workers when products or production technologies change.

In the next decades young well-trained workers will become more scarce. It will become more and more difficult to retain the human capital level necessary for successful technological competition by means of lay-offs of depreciated human capital and recruitment of fresh human capital, unless there is a substantial amount of selective immigration. The issue of constantly training the adult, working population will have to be faced.

A Failing Market

Let us now consider somewhat more in detail the theoretical reasons why we expect that markets are not going to supply us with the amount of training which is socially optimal. First we consider the financial risks involved. Then we turn to the role of liquidity constraints in the supply of training. Subsequently a number of other potential reasons for the training market to fail are discussed.

Risk. Training is a risky investment. The benefits derived for the individual from general training are rather unclear in advance. A welder who would like to know the benefits from a course in stainless stell welding or a machine operator who wants to know the benefits of a course on the operation of computer controlled machines will only have a vague idea of the benefits. The available information gives the probability distribution of the returns. The returns to the training could be high, but they might also be low.

Risk in the returns to training does not imply that no training at all will be chosen. But for cautious people who do not like to gamble, the amount of training chosen would usually be less than in case the returns were certain. This holds even if the expected value of the risky return is the same as the certain return (see Kodde, 1986; Levhari and Weiss, 1974; Eaton and Rosen, 1980). Cautious people want to include a premium for the risk they take when engaging in risky training. Or they would like to insure themselves against "the vagaries of wage rates". But insurance companies are not going to be involved in the insurance of human capital. Persons who are insured in order to receive a certain wage have no incentive to work hard or long hours such that they would not have to use the insurance. This is often called "moral hazard". Also it is likely that only those persons with low abilities are attracted to the insurance. This adverse selection would make it difficult to provide the insurance.

It is a well-established fact that markets are not efficient if there is risk for which no insurance can be bought, and if people are risk averse (Arrow and Lind, 1970). There is then a possibility that the results of the market can be improved upon by public intervention.

To be sure: investments by firms in specific training are also risky. But firms have more possibilities to pool risks than individual workers have. One might say that for the firm the risk in the return to specific training of one worker offsets that of the next worker. Also firms need not be as cautious as individuals, as they may be owned by stockholders who have stocks in different firms in such a way that their risks are pooled. In other words the riskiness of investments in specific training does not contain an invitation to consider public intervention in training financed by firms. In contrast, since individual workers have fewer means to pool the risk, a public role should be considered in support of training financed by individuals.

<u>Liquidity constraints</u>. There is also the matter of the availablity of loans for general training. The costs of training may be too high for the worker to pay out of savings or current income. At the same time there will be few facilities to borrow for investments in training, since such a loan does not provide the lender with a security, a collateral which can be sold in case of a loan default. This argument is less convincing for white collar workers as training is for them often relatively cheap. Liquidity constraints might be relevent, however, for blue collar workers.

<u>Minimum wage legislation</u>. For the group of young, blue collar workers institutional constraints like minimum wage legislation could also be an effective barrier to training, as employers cannot charge the costs of training through reduced wages for minimum wage workers.

<u>Subsidized training of the unemployed</u>. The existence of subsidized general training for the unemployed could be a disincentive for employed workers to participate in training while employed. However, it is rational

not to pay for general training while employed only if the benefit of the subsidy outweighs the income foregone due to the deferment of the training decision plus the income lost as a result of unemployment.

Complementarity between general and specific training. It is a likely proposition that general and specific training are complementary. For example, to acquire the specific knowledge of the foundry of axle-casks for trucks, one needs a basic understanding of foundry in general. Inherent in complementarity is that general training pays off more if it is combined with specific training, and that specific training is more profitable when it is done jointly with general training. Complementarity then means that employers will not invest enough in specific training unless workers have sufficient general training. The mirror image is that workers will not invest enough in general training unless they know that specific training will follow.

Complementarity in a world without turnover would imply a possibility for a contract between workers and employers such that employers pay part of the costs of the general training. This would be rational, because the general trianing provides a positive spillover for specific training. But when turnover is high, complementarity might lead to underinvestment in general training. Workers observe on the one hand that general training only pays off if combined with specific training. On the other hand, firms are reluctant to provide specific training, because of high turnover. Employers might want to hedge against the risk of early departures of workers from the firm by means of contracts in which workers only receive specific training if they stay with the firm for a specified period. However, a productivity which is commensurate with the specific training is not enforceable. As a result such contracts provide little support for employers.

Limited information. Employers generally lack information on the productivity gains which are made possible by much of the general training which has been completed in other firms. This information asymmetry renders general into specific training. A social loss is incurred, because of the transaction costs which are required to signal the importance of the general training to other employers than the one with which the training had been completed.

Contracts. In explicit labor contracts, wages tend to rise over the life time whatever the productivity development of the worker. Under the present condition of a high rate of technological change a decrease in productivity is likely to occur at a relatively early age, if workers rely solely on human capital acquired in their youth in the education system. But the labor contract does not reward general training of the worker. Contracts do not contain (enough) incentives for general training.

Unemployment transfers. Earlier we noted that firms may have secured an adequate supply of human capital through the substitution of older workers with obsolete human capital by younger well-educated labor. The existence of unemployment insurance or, more generally, of transfers for the unemployed has facilitated this process of substitution. This process is socially inefficient unless the costs of training of older workers are exceedingly high.

The process will also reduce the supply of and demand for general training. The time period over which individual older workers have to write off general training becomes shorter than it would be if lay-offs of older workers did not take place. In case of complementarity the knife cuts at both sides. General training becomes less attractive to older workers if they know that little specific training will be supplied.

The Public Role

The public role in training should be based on the reasons why the training market may fail: the riskiness for individual workers of investments in training, liquidity constraints, minimum wage legislation, subsidized training of the unemployed, complementarity, asymmetric information and inefficient contracts.

There are different means of intervention, which address different causes of market failure. Three kinds of intervention are mentioned here. First, the information asymmetry could be countered in part by making information more widely available. Second, the effects of minimum wage legislation on training can be countered by training wages for young workers with little education, or by subsidies for training facilities of such workers. Third, one can address the effects of risk, liquidity constraints, complementarity and contracts in a combined scheme. Two alternatives for the combined scheme are discussed, i.e. "inverse insurance" and "guaranteed wage increases with training".

Information. The information function would entail making information on the content and value of training more easily accessible to other employers than it is at present. It should be ensured that employers can evaluate the general training - or for that matter courses from the regular education system - which workers may have completed before entering the firm. One means to organize the information on training and education is to have some kind of accreditation. Training courses with similar objectives and similar content can be accredited if they satisfy certain conditions.

One of the most far reaching forms of accreditation is to admit only those courses for which final exams or other final test are being held statewide or even nationwide. Less far reaching forms of the information function involve the registration of courses and the collection of these registrations in a regular publication. This could again be done on a nationwide basis, or on a statewide scale. It is not always necessary to have a financial involvement in this information function from the government. It might be sufficient for the government to provide a stimulus. The information function could be also performed by private parties if they see means to appropriate the returns to the collection of information. For the Netherlands such a guide book for job training exists (Guidebook Adult Education, in Dutch; published by VUGA publishing company since 1981).

Information on the content and value of general training for employers also reduces uncertainty on the part of employees. They have now more reason to assume that potential new employers will recognize and reward the training they have received.

<u>Training wages</u>. Battle have been fought in different western industrialized countries over training wages. Trade unions have often objected against such wages because they view training wages as a reduction of salary. The assumption is that employers would reduce wages for minimum wage workers without providing general training. The solution for this quandary is very simple, as the experience in Germany and the Netherlands shows. In these countries training wages are only allowed if the training which is provided in the firm is approved by representatives of the trade union (as is the case in Germany) or by the government (Dutch system). The government also might subsidize the training, if it considers the training wage too low for a living. Or a subsidy for the training costs could be provided, as is the case in the Netherlands. Such a subsidy has a similar effect as a wage subsidy: it reduces the costs the workers have to pay out of the their current income and increases as result the net income.

<u>Inverse Insurance</u>. Liquidity constraints could be countered by means of public policy which ensures the availability of loans. A more effective scheme is inverse insurance. This looks very much like a student loan scheme in which the pay-back of the loan depends on future earnings (see for a recent proposal: Reischauer, 1989). It is more effective because it addresses not only liquidity constraints, but also risk. According to this scheme, every participant in training of a certain kind receives the same subsidy. Everybody who have completed that training also pays the same tax rate. But since the gains from training may differ between persons the amount of the tax paid differs between individuals. Ritzen's paper in this volume shows theoretically that such a scheme can engender a Pareto improvement because the risk of the uncertain return is in part neutralized.

Note that the Government does not have to supply any financial means for this scheme. It can work with a revolving training fund. The subsidies for training are balanced against the taxes received. Note also that the subsidy does not have to be the full amount of the investments in the training.

In principle, the scheme could be implemented by the federal or a provincial or a local government. But it could also be introduced by trade unions and organizations of employers within negotiated contracts, for example, on the scale of a sector or industry within a state or province or for the whole nation. Instead of a tax we should talk about a premium. In a contract, the scheme could become less individualized. For example, workers might be given paid educational leave for certain training courses and receive extra wages according to completed training, which are the gross average gains from training minus the premium.

Guaranteed wage. As an alternative to the inverse insurance scheme, the guaranteed extra wage scheme provides no subsidy for the costs of the training. But the training is certain to generate at least a predetermined wage raise. This scheme addresses risk as a source of market failure in training. There is now a subsidy for those workers who end up - after the training is completed - with less than the guaranteed wage raise. They receive from a fund a supplement on their wage such that the guaranteed wage raise is achieved.

The sources for the fund are the taxes paid by workers who earn more after the completion of training than the original wage plus the predetermined wage raise. These workers pay into a fund a tax out of the difference between their earnings and the minimum. It is - as with the "inverse insurance" scheme - a revolving fund in which the taxes finance the subsidies. The public intervention is mostly of an organizational nature.

As mentioned, inverse insurance and guaranteed wage increases are alternative schemes, not to be introduced jointly. The choice for one above the other must be made on practical grounds: which one is less costly to administer. In theory inverse insurance is to be favored slightly, because it also deals with liquidity constraints.

With these four proposals we have addressed several of the potential sources of market failure: risk, liquidity constraints, asymmetric information and inefficient labor contracts. The proposals are meant to stimulate reflection on the training of adulty, employed workers, rather than as the final plan. Further discussion of these proposals in in Ritzen's chapter later in this volume.

Overview of Chapters

These issues are discussed in greater depth and detail in the remaining chapters.

Mincer. In the chapter after this, Jacob Mincer uses direct data on training, which have become available in the past 10 or 20 years, to reanalyze questions addressed in his 1962 paper on the amount and profitability of on-the-job training (OJT). Depending on assumptions about depreciation of human capital and mobility of workers, the rate of return to OJT may be less than 10 percent or more than 30 percent. Given these estimates, Mincer concludes that there is "no definite evidence of underinvestment, though it clearly cannot be ruled out." He also estimates the amount of formal and informal OJT in the U.S. to be more than 10 percent of the total wage bill. Estimates of the amount of OJT based on direct survey information are about 75 percent of estimates based on indirect inference from wage profiles. Mincer concludes that OJT therefore accounts for most of the observed increase in individuals' earnings over their working lives.

One of Mincer's basic assumptions is that individuals who acquire general (i.e., portable) skills and knowledge through OJT must pay for it by accepting lower wages than they would receive in a job with no OJT. This assumption is based on a well-known and widely accepted argument by Becker (1964). However, the two chapters after Mincer's present evidence which contradicts that assumption.

Feuer, Glick, and Desai. In previously published work, using data on scientists and engineers, these authors have found that employees whose employers paid for some of their formal schooling did not obtain lower salaries in the process. Their explanation is that firms offer such benefits as a "hostage", so that employees will feel more secure about making their own investment in firm-specific OJT. In the absence of such insurance, employees would have reason to fear that employers would try to deprive them of a fair return on their investment in firm-specific knowledge and skill.

In their chapter in this volume, Feuer and associates conduct further tests of this insurance hypothesis. They find that, compared to employees who did not receive firm-specific OJT but stayed with the same employer, those who moved were less likely to have received firm-financed education, and those who had firm-specific OJT and stayed were also more likely to have received firm-financed education. Since firm-financed education is assumed to be portable, these findings are at odds with standard human capital theory, but they are consistent with the notion that firms pay for general training in order to induce employees to invest in firm-specific training, and to stay with the firm after they do so.

Bishop. Using data from the Employment Opportunity Pilot Project (EOPP), which collected the most detailed information available about OJT for newly hired employees, John Bishop also finds evidence that employees do not, in fact, pay for most of the cost of their own general training. In the months after being newly hired, employees' productivity rises much faster than their wages. This implies that employers are supporting the cost of training. Yet, according to employers in the EOPP survey, most of the training would be useful in other firms, so apparently employers are paying for general OJT. One explanation, according to other findings reported by Bishop, is that other firms do not recognize general OJT for what it is. This is the problem of accreditation we mentioned above. Employees may be unwilling to pay for their own OJT because they correctly expect that other firms will not recognize and reward what they learn.

Bishop finds the rate of return to OJT is very high, though it is lower on the margin for those who receive a great deal of it. Bishop's estimates are also not adjusted for depreciation or mobility.

Bartel. Ann Bartel's chapter presents analysis of another new data set on training by firms. Unlike the EOPP data, the Columbia survey analyzed by Bartel is not restricted to training of new hires. It is also linked to extensive financial data. However, the response rate was very low, especially on questions dealing with cost. Bartel's analysis is therefore limited to whether or not a given business unit reportedly conducts formal training for employees in each of seven specified occupational groups. She finds the existence of formal training programs is positively associated with a business unit's size, capital expenditure per employee, the ratio of research and development expenditure to sales, an index of sophistication of the firm's human resource policies, the existence of formal testing for new job applicants, the proportion of non-entry level jobs that are filled from within the firm, and (in manufacturing) the ratio of imports plus exports to total shipments. She also finds that formal training programs are more likely to exist for managers than for other occupations. She finds these results to be generally consistent with a profit-maximizing model of firms' investment in OJT. Therefore, while she admits the possibility that firms may under-invest in OJT, she judges that this conclusion is not clearly warranted by her data.

Stern and Benson. After a review of economic theory and empirical studies, David Stern and Charles Benson find that basic theoretical questions remain open, and that available data are not sufficient to provide precise quantitative answers. Instead, their chapter focuses on case studies of certain firms that are investing heavily in OJT. They find that these firms are in the process of transforming their method of operation to become more learning-intensive. This entails not only the transfer of knowledge and information from some individuals to others -- what is conventionally meant by training -- but also the discovery of knowledge and information that no one knew before: what could be called on-the-job research. In order to support this kind of flexible, learning-intensive production, firms are integrating OJT into the work process itelf, using mechanisms such as pay-for-knowledge and "doing by learning". One of the organizational preconditions for learning-intensive production seems to be a commitment by the firm to try to protect workers' employment security. Market failure may arise here because there are theoretical reasons to believe that provision of employment security by one firm creates positive externalities. Therefore, one way in which government can prevent under-provision of OJT is through macroeconomic policy that promotes employment stability. Other policies include promotion of counter-cyclical training, literacy training on the job, and accreditation of what employees learn from OJT.

Hashimoto. The link between employment security and OJT is also described by Masanori Hashimoto, in the context of Japanese firms. One hallmark of human resource management in large Japanese firms is the practice of job rotation over a long period of time, which produces what Hashimoto calls "intra-firm general" skills. These skills make the workforce more flexible and contribute to employment security in the face of changes in product demand or new technology. The existence of employment security also encourages senior workers to train newcomers without fear of being displaced.

In Japanese firms, training includes not only investment in technical skill and knowledge, but also "investment in information reliability." Joint consultation, consensual decision making, and quality control circles are mechanisms for this kind of investment in teamwork and trust-building. Technical training, investment in information reliability, productivity growth, and employment security are all mutually reinforcing.

<u>Ritzen</u>. If employees have to pay for their own OJT, they can be expected to under-invest. That is the conclusion of a theoretical model presented in the chapter by Jozef Ritzen. Under-investment is expected because the payoff to training is risky, and most employees are assumed to be risk-averse. Liquidity constraints may also contribute to underinvestment. Evidence that under-investment does in fact occur is found in the fact that OJT is concentrated on younger workers despite rapid obsolescence of work-related knowledge and skill; it is also concentrated on employees with more formal schooling despite evidence of no higher rate of return for them; and it is also concentrated in large firms.

Ritzen proposes two alternative schemes to bring about a more efficient level of investment in OJT: "inverse insurance" or a "guaranteed wage increase". These have been summarized above.

<u>Hansen</u>. In the final chapter, Lee Hansen offers some cautionary advice about governmental intervention in training. He reviews the history of training programs sponsored by the federal government in the U.S. The success of these programs has been debatable at best. Furthermore, these programs have not been clearly based on standard economic definitions of market failure, according to Hansen. He reviews these definitions and examines their applicability to job training. One of the arguments is that specific and general training are inseparable, so that if firms under-provide general training they also will under-invest in firm-specific training. Although Hansen finds this contention "interesting", he rejects the premise because he assumes that workers will pay for general training through reduced wages, and therefore firms will not under-provide it.

Hansen goes on to discuss possible reasons for "nonmarket failure," i.e., inefficiency by public agencies that are trying to correct alleged market failure. Nonmarket failure may occur because the benefits of training programs are not clearly defined; training providers may substitute their own self-interest for the public interest; new programs may conflict with old ones; public agencies may be captured by powerful political groups; they may invest in the wrong kind of training because they do not have perfect information about future demands in the labor market; and public programs tend to be inflexible in the face of changing conditions. Even locating publicly subsidized training in workplaces can be problematic, according to Hansen. Wise public policy must balance the risk of market failure against the equally real risk of nonmarket failure.

A Basic Question

These diverse and sometimes conflicting contributions are a sampling of current theory and research by economists on the issue of OJT. We will not attempt to draw any simple conclusions. However, it seems useful to focus on one question that runs through several of the chapters, and which is basic to conventional economic analysis of OJT. That question is: who pays for general training?

If employees pay for their own general training, then market failure may arise for the reasons explained in Ritzen's chapter: employees under-invest because they are not willing to take an uninsured risk. The problem, then, would be to create better incentives for employees. (This would also apply to any part of firm-specific training that is financed by employees.)

However, if employees do not pay for their own general training, then there may be a very different kind of market failure. All the available data indicate that employees do obtain a payoff in the form of higher earnings after they have received general training. But if they do not pay for it, or if they pay for only a small part of it, their rate of return is very high (it approaches infinity as their cost approaches zero). If employers are absorbing the whole cost or almost all of it, their rate of return will be considerably less than the rate of return for employees, unless the productivity gains from general training are a large multiple of the wage gains paid to employees. Since the social rate of return is, by definition (in a competitive product market), an average of the rates of return for employer and employee, the employee's rate of return is likely to exceed the social rate, while the employer's rate of return falls below it. Therefore, it will be the employer who lacks sufficient incentive to invest in OJT if employees do not pay for it. After all, on the face of it, employees are being paid while they are in OJT, so why should employers provide more than the merest minimum necessary? This is the very common-sense view that Becker's argument rejected.

Given market failure of this sort, one way to correct it would be to make Becker's argument true in fact: i.e., make it possible for firms to "sell" general training to employees as Becker supposed they do. The problem, as discussed in Bishop's chapter here, is that employers apparently do not give full credit for each other's training, even if the content is judged to be quite general by the firms that are providing it. Some form of accreditation would appear to be necessary. Formal apprenticeship systems provide this. The Office of Work-Based Learning in the U.S. Office of Labor has recently conducted studies to test the possibility of developing such accreditation for OJT outside formal apprenticeships.

Becker's argument that employees must pay for general OJT is so logical, and has become so comfortably familiar, that many economists will hesitate to give it up. As mentioned, the analysis in Mincer's chapter assumes Becker's argument is true. Mincer does acknowledge in a footnote that there is no direct evidence for it, but he mentions three kinds of indirect evidence. (1) Barron, Black, and Lowenstein (1989) found more screening for jobs where new hires receive more training. Mincer, as well as Barron et al., interpret this to mean that more able individuals get more training, and since more able individuals also can command higher wages, there is no observed negative correlation between training and wages. However, Barron et al. have no actual measure of ability. Furthermore, if ability is multidimensional, it is practically impossible to demonstrate that jobs with training pay less than jobs without it -- holding constant all relevant dimensions of ability. (2) "Training affects negatively both quits and layoffs." This does not imply that workers pay for training, since they would presumably try to protect their human capital against unwanted job separations even if it they acquire their training at no cost to themselves. (3) "Initial wage gains in job changing are (non-spuriously) negatively correlated with wage growth during training in the new firm." This indicates that workers who move to a new job may obtain their monetary reward either in higher initial pay or higher subsequent wage gains, but not both. Be that as it may, this finding does not imply that the compensation package is any smaller if the new job includes OJT. In sum, this defense of Becker's argument is not decisive.

Readers will make up their own minds. This volume will have served a useful purpose if it engenders more serious discussion of this question, and its implications for public policy.

In concluding this introduction, we also want to underscore another major theme in several of these chapters. Learning in workplaces is not only a matter of taking time out from production in order to participate in classes, receive informal instruction, or watch other people work. It also includes problem-solving and continuous improvement in the production process. To stimulate all these forms of learning may require systemic change both within and between firms.

References

Barron, J. M., D. A. Black & M. A. Loewenstein. 1989. Job Matching and On-the-job Taining. Journal of Labor Economics 7(1): 1-19.

Becker, G. 1964. Human Capital. New York: National Bureau of Economic Research.

Eaton, J. and Rosen, H.S. 1980. Taxation, Human Capital and Uncertainty. AER, Vol. 70, pp. 705-715.

Hirschleifer, J. and Riley, J.G. 1979. The Analysis of Uncertainty and Information - An Expository Survey. JEL, Vol. 17, pp. 1375-1421.

Kodde, D.A. 1986. Uncertainty and the Demand for Education. Review of Economics and Statistics, Vo. 68, pp. 460-468.

Levhari, D. and Weiss, Y. 1974. The Effect of Risk on the Investment in Human Capital. American Economic Review, Vol. 64, pp. 950-964.

Reischauer, R.D. 1989. "HELP, A Student Loan Program for the 21st Century" in Laurent E. Gladieux (ed.), Radical Reform or Incremental Change. New York: College Board.

JOB TRAINING: COSTS, RETURNS, AND WAGE PROFILES

Jacob Mincer
Columbia University

Abstract

Using information on time costs of training and gains in wages attributable to training, I computed rates of return on training investments. The upper range of estimates based on several data sets generally exceeds the magnitudes of rates of return usually observed for schooling investments. It is not clear, however, that the difference represents underinvestment in job training.

Two methods were used to estimate total annual costs of job training in the U.S. economy, for 1958, 1976, and 1987. The "direct" calculation uses information on time spent in training and on wages. For 1976, costs so calculated amounted to 11.2% of Total Employee Compensation, which is about half of the costs of school education. In the "indirect" method, training costs were estimated from wage functions fitted to PSID data. In 1976 the direct estimate amounted to between 65% and 75% of the indirect estimate based on the wage profile. This result is consistent with a human capital interpretation of wage profiles.

The estimates indicate a slower growth of training than of school expenditures in the 1970's. Substitution of schooling for job training is a likely cause.

This report is based on work sponsored by the National Science Foundation, grant SES-8921357, and in part by the Office of Educational Research and Improvement, U.S. Department of Education.

I am grateful to Lalith Munasinghe for research assistance, and to David Stern for editorial comments.

1. Introduction: Background

The emergence of job training as an observable—albeit still a fragmentary one—has the potential of filling some important gaps in the empirical analyses of human capital investments and of related wage structures. It enables us to pursue questions which were not amenable to research in the past. Thus, while a vast literature, accumulated over several decades, contains a wealth of findings on volumes and on profitability rates of educational investments, corresponding estimates of job training investment could not be constructed. Instead, growth of earnings over working age, known as the "experience wage profiles," was assumed to reflect returns on workers' investments in the labor market, especially in job training. Indeed, a first (and last) indirect estimate of on-the-job training costs by schooling level and in the aggregate was obtained using this interpretation nearly three decades ago (Mincer, 1962).

Job training was used as a latent variable not only in analyzing shapes of wage profiles but also in the study of labor mobility, or turnover. In particular, turnover and slopes of wage profiles were linked in a hypothesis according to which training affects both: On the assumption that some degree of firm specificity usually attaches to on-the-job training, we may conjecture that, on average, the more training a worker receives, the more it tends to be specific to the firm. Consequently, with more training the worker's wage profile is steeper and turnover slower. This "duality hypothesis" was proposed in a paper coauthored with Jovanovic in 1981. In the absence of empirical data on job training or learning, the duality hypothesis provides insights into labor market behavior, as was shown in that paper as well as in a more recent study (with Higuchi, 1988). The latter compares wage structures and labor turnover in Japan with those in the U.S. The negative relation between slopes of wage profiles and labor turnover is shown to hold across industrial sectors within each country. Much larger investments in job training in Japan were adduced to generate both the steeper Japanese wage profiles and the much stronger attachment to the firm in Japan.

As usual, the absence of direct information leads to a proliferation of theories. Thus, the lack of direct evidence on job training stimulated the development of alternative theories that attempt to explain upward slopes of wage profiles as devices to economize on costs of supervision (Becker and Stigler, 1974; Lazear, 1979), or turnover (Salop and Salop, 1976), or as consequences of job sorting or job matching of new hires (Jovanovic, 1979).

The recent growth of information on job training in several data sets has led to empirical studies of the effects of training on wage growth.[1] In my own work, information available in the University of Michigan's Panel Study of Income Dynamics (PSID) was brought to bear on the duality hypothesis. Job training magnitudes were explored as a factor in wage growth and in labor mobility in a National Bureau of Economic Research (NBER) Working Paper (1988): Using information on timing and duration of job training among PSID men, I found negative effects of training on turnover and positive effects on wage growth in the firm and over longer periods transcending tenure in one firm. The positive correlation between general and specific training which explains these results also explains the apparent paradox that, despite wage gains in moving, frequent movers' wages grow less in the long run than those of less frequent movers.

Another effect of job training which has been observed is the reduction in the incidence of unemployment among workers who receive training. This is a corollary of the reduced turnover, as close to half of firm separations involve unemployment. Finally, there are two important observations bearing on the determinants of job training: (1) Workers with more years of schooling are more likely to engage in job training,[2] and (2) more training is provided in industries in which technological progress is faster.[3]

The potential significance of these initial research accomplishments is of a high order: (1) They indicate that human capital analyses of labor market behavior based on proxies for post-school training hold up when direct measures of such training are used. (2) The documented link between training, schooling, and technological change directs attention to the sources of demand for human capital and to its role in economic growth.

As we reach better, empirically based insights into the effects and determinants of job training, it is necessary to return to a task that I attempted in an indirect fashion in 1962: to estimate the extent and profitability of private sector job training, this time based on direct, albeit imperfect information. Although

---

[1] See section 2 below.

[2] All studies described in section 2 found this positive relation. See also the data in the Time Use Study shown in Table 3.

[3] See Lillard and Tan (1986) and Mincer (1989).

precise estimates cannot be hoped for, given the quality of current data and the conceptual complexities, orders or ranges of magnitude are feasible, and should yield insights into important issues.

This is the primary purpose of the present study. At a time when concern is raised about the quality of the American workforce and statements about underinvestment in human capital abound in public rhetoric, an attempt at comprehensive estimates of volumes of investment and of their profitability is a prerequisite for public discussion. Another objective of this paper is to compare the directly estimated magnitudes of training investments with indirect estimates obtained from wage profiles, as was done in the 1962 study. Such comparisons can help in gauging how much of the growth (slope) in the wage profile is attributable to observable training processes. If the magnitude is significant, a link between the direct and indirect estimates can be used to infer changes in training investments over time.

2. Data Sources and Related Literature

Direct information on the incidence, timing, and duration of job training is available in several data sets. The information represents responses, mainly from household surveys, to questions about formal or informal job training or learning in the firm or outside the firm during the preceding year. The questions are phrased differently in the various surveys, both in detail and in degree of subjectivity. Nevertheless, the elicited information makes possible qualitative and quantitative estimates from which a degree of consensus may emerge.

The available data on job training suffer from poverty amidst plenty. Table 1 indicates both the proliferation and the shortcomings of the data. Although concentrating on one consistent source of data would provide single-valued results, I attempt in addition to draw on results based on various data sets to gauge a degree of robustness, if any.

Table 1
Information on Job Training[1]

Data Set	Coverage	Incidence	Duration of Spells	Duration in Hours
CPS	1983 survey All workers Cross-section	During current job	Not available	Not available
PSID	Question on current job asked in 1976, 1978, 1985 All males	Dates estimated within current job	In months	In a separate 1976 survey
NLS Previous Young Cohort	A number of periods Young males	Variable survey periods	Not available	Not available
NLS New Young Cohort	A number of periods Young males	Over 3 years	In weeks	Not available
EOPP	Young male new hires at low wages 1980-1982	Within 3 months after hire	Within 3 months	Available, incompletely

[1] Available and utilized in the references. More information and broader coverage may exist in the data sets.

The PSID, an annual survey of about 5,000 households, provides usable information on job training for about 1,200 male heads of households in 1976, 1978, and 1985. The information covers the length of time of training required during the current job, as well as its learning contents in 1976.[4] Information on intensity (hours per week) of training is available in a supplementary time study of PSID workers by Duncan and Stafford (1980). The PSID data have been analyzed by Duncan and Hoffman (1978), Brown (1988), Gronau (1982), and Mincer (1988a).

The National Longitudinal Samples (NLS) surveys covering several thousand households conducted at Ohio State University contain annual or biannual information on job training for two cohorts of young men (aged 14 to 24 in 1968, and 14 to 21 in 1979), and for mature men (aged 45 to 59 in 1968). The new (1979) cohort of young men contains information on the duration of a spell of training. In-house training reported in the 1968 cohorts has been studied by Lillard and Tan (1986). The new young cohort has been analyzed by Parsons (1986) and Lynch (1988).

The Current Population Survey of the U.S. Census, the largest periodic sample of US households, contains the incidence of training in its March '83 survey. The data have been analyzed by Lillard and Tan (1986).

Finally, the 1982 EOPP (Equal Opportunity Pilot Project) is the only survey of employers (about 2,000 in 31 areas). It provides information on hours of training of new hires during the first three months on the job. These data have been described and analyzed by Lillard and Tan (1986), and Barron, Black, and Lowenstein (1989) and reanalyzed by Holzer (1989).

In my work with the PSID (1988a), I compared year-by-year wage growth of workers in the 1976 firm in periods with training with workers and periods without training. The effect of a year with training on wage growth in the 1976 job was 4.4%, using the 1968-82 annual PSID surveys. No other variables had much of an effect on wage growth, except for a small negative effect of prior experience.

---

[4] One question asked was: "On a job like yours, how long would it take the average new person to become fully trained and qualified?" This question followed another about training prior to the current job, therefore intending to measure training attached to the current job. Another usable question was whether the current job provides "learning which could help in promotion or getting a better job."

The effect of training on wage growth was greater (9.5%) at younger ages (working age 12 years or less) than at older ages (3.6%). The difference reflects greater intensity of training among young workers, as is shown in the Duncan and Stafford (1980) time study (see Table 3).

The findings that wage growth decelerates with age because training does, and that no other variable appears to affect individual wage growth, indicate the importance of job training or learning in producing the typical upward sloping and decelerating wage profiles over working lives.

The same conclusion is reached in a study by H. Rosen (1982). Using the 1976 PSID data, Rosen divided the sample into two groups: workers who received training during the year and those who did not. (Cross-sectional) wage profiles were steep and concave in the first group, and very flat in the second. This suggests, once again, the importance of job training or learning in creating the typical shapes of wage profiles.

As with the PSID, all the studies based on other data sets found positive and significant effects of training on wages and on wage growth.

Barron, Black, and Lowenstein (1989) use the EOPP survey of over 2,000 employers located in 31 areas across the country. They measure training in hours spent in training by new hires and by their supervisors and co-workers during the first three months of employment in the firm. The mean training hours were 151 in the three months. They report that in a two-year period, training raised wages by 15%, or 7.5% per year. It will be recalled that a year of training in the PSID raised wages of young workers, whose average age was about the same as the new hires in the EOPP, by 9.5%, and by 3.6% for workers who, on average, were 15 years older, and who had correspondingly smaller intensity (hours per week) of training. This is also consistent with the 9% effect per year found by Brown (1988) for new hires who had no previous training.

Holzer's (1989) reanalysis of the EOPP data yields a smaller wage growth effect of 4.7%. Lynch (1988) uses the new young cohort of the NLS. Here information is available on all training spells of recent male entrants into the labor force during the 3-year period 1980 to 1983. She finds that wages of young workers with job training during the year rose by 11%, while an additional year of tenure without training increased wages by 4%; the net effect is therefore 7%.

Lillard and Tan (1986) also find significant effects of training on wages in the CPS and in the 1963-1980 young cohort of the NLS. In the CPS (their Table 4.1), company training raises wages by 11.8%; in the NLS (their Table 4.5), job training raises wages of young workers by 10.8% initially, but the effect declines subsequently.

In sum, estimated effects of an additional year with training appear to range from 4.4% in the PSID for all new hires to 9% for young workers in the PSID, 7% for the new young cohort in the NLS, and 11% for the previous young cohort in the NLS. The 12% "effect" for CPS men is a cross-sectional finding that trainees have higher wages than non-trainees, but it takes no account of the pretraining wage. It is not included in the profitability analysis in Table 2.

Table 2
Rates of Return on Investments in Job Training

Data Set	w (1)	k (2)	r¹ (3)	corrected r (4)	(5)	(6)	Average Tenure (7)
PSID¹, All Males	4.4	.15	29.3	23.5	25.0	6.5	8
EOPP² Young New Hires	4.7	.20	23.5	8.7	8.5	0	3
NLS₁³, New Young Cohort	7.0	.22	31.8	16.0	16.2	5.2	3
NLS₂⁴, Previous Young Cohort	10.8	.25	43.2	26.0	31.0	22.8	4

¹ Based on Mincer (1988a); k from Duncan and Stafford (1980).
² Based on Holzer (1988).
³ Based on Lynch (1989).
⁴ Based on Lillard and Tan (1986); k from Duncan and Stafford.

col (3): $r^1 = w/k$
col (4): $r = r^1 (1 - d) - d$; here $d = .4$ in the PSID, .12 in the other data sets.
col (5): $r = r^1 [1 - (1/1 + r)^T]$; T as shown in col. (7)
col (6): $r = r^1 (1 - d) [1 - (1 - d/1 + r)^T] - d$; Here d as in col. (4)

3. Profitability of Job Training Investments

Table 2 presents the rates of return on investments in job training. Prima facie, these estimates of effects of a year with training on wage growth (column 1) are comparable to effects of an additional year of schooling at the average level of schooling. Yet, viewed as measures of profitability, or as rates of return on the cost of job training (column 3), these numbers appear to be much too large.

The reason is that job training is not a full-time (full-year) activity. If it takes 25% of worktime during an average week of a year with training, the rates of return on worker opportunity costs are four times higher than the estimated rates of wage growth.

Let $k = h/H$, the fraction of work time devoted to job training. Here h is hours of training during the period (week, month, or year) and H average hours of work during the period. Let w_o be the pretraining and w_1 the posttraining wage. Then the (uncorrected) rate of return on training is $r^1 = (w_1 - w_o) \cdot H/w_o \cdot h$. Here the numerator is the annual dollar increase in earnings, the return on the investment, while the denominator is the opportunity cost of training. Let $w = (w_1 - w_o)/w_o$ be the percent increase in wages due to training; then the (uncorrected) rate of return is $r^1 = w/k$. The first three columns of Table 2 show estimates of w, k, and r^1 based on the PSID, the EOPP, and the two young cohorts of the NLS.

The r^1 rates appear to be implausibly high. However, they need to be corrected downward, if skills acquired in training depreciate, and if the payoff period is short. If training is portable, the latter factor may be ignored, as the median age of trainees is about 30, so that, without depreciation, the payoff period may exceed 30 years. Depreciation, however, can be substantial, as suggested by Lillard and Tan (1986). For the previous NLS young cohort, they estimate an initial wage gain of 10.8% due to training and a subsequent decline of 1% per year during years since training. This translates[5] into a 12% exponential rate of decline due to depreciation in returns per year. My attempts to estimate a depreciation rate in the PSID using the Lillard and Tan procedure yielded a depreciation rate close to 4%. This smaller figure in the PSID may be due to the broader coverage of all males, compared to younger males in NLS: If training has substantial elements of specificity, mobility would create wage depreciation. Since mobility of young workers exceeds substantially the mobility of older workers, a smaller depreciation rate in the PSID may be reasonable.

The estimate of corrected rates of return (r) is obtained as follows: Given annual depreciation rates (d), and the payoff period T, equate costs or foregone earnings while training (kw_o) to the present value of the stream of gains (Δw) the first year following training,

$\Delta w \dfrac{1-d}{1+r}$ the next year,

$\Delta w (\dfrac{1-d}{1+r})^2$ the year after, and so on):

$kw_o = \Delta w [\dfrac{1-d}{1+r} + (\dfrac{1-d}{1+r})^2 + \ldots (\dfrac{1-d}{1+r})^T] = \Delta w \dfrac{1-d}{r+d}$, when $T = \infty$

more generally

$\dfrac{kw_o}{\Delta w} = \dfrac{k}{\dot{w}} = \dfrac{1-d}{r+d} [1 - (\dfrac{1-d}{1+r})^T]$

It follows that corrected $r = r^1 (1-d) [1 - (\dfrac{1-d}{1+r})^T] - d$ (1)

---

[5] Half of the gain vanishes in 5.4 years according to the linear estimate. A depreciation rate (d) of 12% produces a half-life of 5.4 years: d is solved from $(1-d)^t = .5$, where $t = 5.4$.

Since the estimates of d were obtained by ignoring labor mobility, they could be an artifact created by negative effects of mobility on gains from (partly) firm specific (nontransferable) training. The polar alternative of complete specificity makes the payoff period T equal to the length of tenure in the firm in which training was received, and d = 0, if there is no obsolescence within the period T. (The observed average values of T are shown in col. 7). In this case, $r = r' [1 - (1/1 + r)^T]$ according to eq. (1); r was solved by iteration, and the results are shown in col. (5). These numbers are rather surprisingly close to those in col. (4). Thus, the estimates do not depend much on whether the observed depreciation is true and training is largely transferable, or it is an artifact due to substantial specificity.

To calculate the profitability rate of employer's investments in training we need to know their returns and costs. In principle, the way to assess returns is to compare increases in productivity resulting from training with increases in wages. The excess is the return on costs borne by the firm. Two recent studies using very different data and approaches suggest that the productivity increase is over twice that of the wage increase caused by training. This is found by Barron et al (1989) in the EOPP data, where a productivity scale is used to gauge the increase. Blakemore and Hoffman (1988) use production and turnover data by industry to estimate effects of tenure on wages and on output per unit of time. They find a doubling of productivity compared to wages, implying that returns to employees are similar to returns to workers. If employer costs are also about the same as those of workers, the uncorrected r' (in col 3 of Table 2) would be the same for employers as for workers. And if depreciation is negligible, the employer rate of return would be again the same as that of workers as listed in col. 5 in which observed tenure is the assumed payoff period. Note that this is always true for the employer who gains only as long as trainees stay in the firm - whether or not training is transferable. However, if depreciation is positive <u>during</u> workers' stay in the training firm, employers rates are lower than those indicated in col. 5 or 4. Assuming a 4% decpreciation rate for the PSID and 12% for the young group results in a lower limit for employer profitability rates, shown in col. 6.

The assumption that employer costs are just about equal to worker costs is more speculative than the proposition of roughly equal returns (r'). It can be defended, if we consider time costs of workers ($\Sigma k w_o$) to be absorbed by workers, while time costs of supervisors, trainers, and of coworkers are absorbed by employers. Except for the time when trainees learn by watching others at work, the time spent on training is the same for trainers and trainees. If so, the EOPP data (Table 1 in Barron et al.) suggest that trainers spend 2/3 of the 150 hours of training reported to be spent by trainees during the 3 months of new hires. Since wages of trainers, supervisors and coworkers are higher than wages of trainees, employer costs are likely to be about as high as employee time costs in the groups covered by the EOPP. Whether this ratio of employer to employee time inputs can be generalized is unknown. Neither is there any evidence that employees absorb precisely the costs of time they spent and employers the rest.[6] In the absence of information on the actual division of costs between employers and workers, we can still consider the profitability of training if we know total costs and total returns. The fragmentary evidence described above suggests a (more than?) doubling of costs ascribed to workers and returns observed for workers. Consequently, the profitability rates in col. 4, 5, an 6 remain conceptually valid, as measures of profitability of training, regardless of who bears the cost.

What does the range of estimates in Table 2 tell us about adequacy of training? As soft as it may be, this is the evidence that could be marshalled. Are the rates too high, suggesting underinvestment? Column 5 in which depreciation is negligible suggests quite ample profitability, even if trainees stay in the firm no longer than non-trainees! In other words, average worker mobility would not deter them or employers from investment in training. However, depreciation is probably not zero, and we need to keep in mind that: (1) The rates in Table 2 are average, not marginal. Bishop (this volume) suggests that marginal rates in the EOPP are about half the size of average rates; (2) Rates of return to schooling of about 10% are not considered exorbitant, and they do not include consumption returns, which are negligible in training.

Consequently, there is no definite evidence of underinvestment, though it clearly cannot be ruled out, given the wide range of estimates.

---

[6] Doubts are sometimes expressed concerning absorption of any costs by trainees on the job in the form of initially lower wages. Three kinds of indirect evidence, however, favor the hypothesis that trainees wages are initially lower than wages they could receive if they did not train, even if they are not lower than wages of non-trainees: (1) Matching and screening selects more promising (productive) workers for training (Barron, et al.); (2) Training affects negatively both quits and layoffs (Mincer, 1988); and (3) Initial wage gains in job changing are (non-spuriously) negatively correlated with wage growth during training in the new firm (Mincer, 1988).

4. Estimating Volumes of Annual Job Training Investments

I proceed to estimate economy-wide annual volumes (flows) of investments in job training, measured in worker opportunity costs. To estimate these costs, we need to know the number of workers engaged in training in the survey period ($n = p \cdot N$, where N is the total workforce and p the proportion of workers engaged in some training or learning on the job), the time (h = hours) they spend in training during the period, and their hourly pre-training wage (w_o). The total worker opportunity costs of training are then the product $C_w = w_o\, h\, p\, N$. Information on such statistics for a sample of the whole U.S. labor force is available only in a PSID survey of Time Use at Work during a week in 1976 (Duncan and Stafford, 1980), a part of which is shown here in Table 3. Information on hours spent in training by new hires during the first three months is available in the EOPP survey and in weeks in the new NLS young cohort. Both cover subgroups of new labor force entrants rather than the whole labor force. The CPS is a large national survey with information on the incidence but not on the hours of training.

Table 3
Time Use in Training
(Survey Week, 1976, PSID, All Workers)

Group	Hourly Wage Rate	Whether Any	On-the-Job Training Mean Weekly Hour		Sample Size
Age:	(1)	(2)	Jointly with Production (3)	Separate from Production (4)	(5)
<25	3.68	.76	9.5	3.2	50
25-34	5.55	.72	7.5	1.8	139
35-44	6.19	.58	6.4	1.7	80
45-54	6.69	.48	2.1	1.3	56
55-64	6.26	.29	2.6	0.4	42
Education (Years):					
0-8	4.08	.39	2.8	0.3	26
9-11	4.47	.56	6.9	1.3	36
12	4.79	.59	8.2	1.4	147
13-15	5.44	.71	6.5	3.2	80
16+	8.33	.58	5.7	1.5	85

Source: Duncan and Stafford (1980), Table 3, Col. (3)--Hours of Training Joint with Production.

Table 4 applies the data from the 1976 Time Use Survey to calculate weekly worker opportunity costs of training on the job, by age groups. The first three columns on wages (w), hours (h), and incidence (p) of training are taken from Duncan and Stafford (1980), here shown in Table 3. Column 4 contains BLS national employment figures (by age) for 1976. Column 5 shows total costs per week; it is a product of columns 1 through 4.

Table 4
Worker Opportunity Costs of Job Training, 1976

Age	Hourly Wage (w_o)	Hours of Training per Week (h)	Percent with Training (p)	Number of Employees (N-millions)	Costs ($mil) per Week ($w_o hpN$)
	(1)	(2)	(3)	(4)	(5)
<25	$3.7	6.4	76	20.0	360
25-34	5.6	4.3	72	22.5	390
35-44	6.2	3.8	58	16.5	225
45-54	6.7	2.2	48	16.1	114
55-64	6.3	1.1	29	10.9	22
				Total Cost	$1,111

Sources: Col. (1), (2), and (3) from Duncan and Stafford, Table 3 here.
Training hours in col. (3) calculated as sum of separate hours in training and one-third of hours spent jointly in training and production.
Col. (4) from Employment and Earnings, BLS, 1976.
Col. (5) is the product of col. (1) through (4).

Statistics on time spent in training by trainees shown in Table 3 overstate and overstate the time cost of training: to the extent that training is joint with production and the marginal product is positive. It is the loss of production during training that represents pure training costs. Thus, if production during training is half of that achieved without training, half the work time with training should be counted as training time. The Time Use Survey lists separately the hours trainees spent in training with and without production (columns 3 and 4 in Table 3).

Weekly hours spent in training by trainees were obtained as a weighted sum of these two components: Only one third of time spent jointly with production was considered as a loss of production, hence as pure training. This is probably a conservative estimate, judging from the work of Bishop (1989). The sum adds up to roughly 4 hours a week per trainee.[7] The average wage in the age group is an approximate estimate of a pretraining or nontraining wage of trainees.[8] The estimates are made separately by age groups, as all components vary systematically with age, then summed to obtain a total of $1.11 billion per week, or $57.7 billion per year in 1976.

Expressing this figure as a fraction of the total wage bill (Total Compensation), which was $1.04 trillion in 1976, yields a 5.6% figure. If the fraction of work time spent in training did not change over time,[9] so that the same ratio held in 1987, it would amount to $148 billion in 1987 dollars.

Worker time costs represent a part of total investment in job training. Time costs of trainers and other resource costs are the other part. If estimates based on the division of time reported in the EOPP can be generalized, total costs would be (over?) double of worker time costs. Total cost would, therefore, amount to $115 billion in 1976 and to $296 billion in 1987.

One check on these orders of magnitude is available from a survey of companies (with 100 or more employees) published in Training Magazine (1988). The survey reported expenditures on formal training programs of about $40 billion in 1987. Based on a Columbia University survey of a national sample of firms, Bartel (1989) reports a larger figure of $55 billion in 1987. These estimates clearly leave out the apparently much larger expenditures on informal training processes. Thus our conservative estimate based on the 1976 Time Use Study suggests that trainees spent an average of 4 hours per week or close to 200

---

[7] This is an average for all workers, including women. For men alone, average hours are closer to 6. The profitability estimates in Table 2 were calculated for men for whom wage gains were estimated in the PSID.

[8] Even if all their opportunity costs were financed by trainees, training costs would be underestimated by no more than 6%; according to the Time Use data. They would be overestimated somewhat if starting wages of trainees and non-trainees are the same.

[9] A preliminary estimate of the average time spent in training in the 1985 PSID sample is quite close to that in 1976.

hours in training per year. This is over six times the number of hours (32) reported for formal training by Training Magazine. If the hourly costs of training were the same for formal and informal training, a global estimate based on formal training costs alone would be $240 billion or $330 billion, depending on which survey in used. Our figure of $296 billion for 1987, estimated in an entirely different manner, is very much within the range of such estimates.

5. Comparing Direct with Indirect Estimates of Training

Extrapolating our estimate of 1976 worker training costs back to 1958 in the same manner as we did in the 1987 extrapolation, that is, assuming that the time spent in training (per worker) did not change, yields a figure of $14.4 billion for 1958. This "direct" estimate for the whole work force compares closely with the indirect estimate of $13.5 billion obtained from wage profiles for the 1958 male labor force (Mincer, 1962, Table 2). Adding another 10 to 15% for costs of women's training would have raised the 1958 indirect estimate for the whole work force to about $16 billion.

Still the $16 billion indirect estimate needs to be revised downward because it should exclude gains from job changes, which according to calculations in PSID data, accounts for about 15% of growth in the wage profile of males (Mincer, 1988). On the other hand, the reduced figure ($13.5 billion) is an underestimate, since it estimates net investments in job training, while the "direct" costs measure the larger gross investments. At the same time the 1958 estimate of direct costs is probably overstated because it assumes that time costs is probably overstated because it assumes that time costs of training amount to the same fraction of the wage bill in 1958 as in 1976. But the fraction must have been lower in 1958, if time spent in training did not change _within_ education groups, since time spent in training increases with schooling, as the PSID data indicate (Mincer, 1988 and Table 3 here). Workers with less than high school spent a little over a half the hours in training that more educated workers did. The size of the two groups in the labor force was about equal in 1958, but the group with less than 12 years shrank to 25% of the labor force by 1976. Hence, average hours of training would have increased by over 15 percent if hours within each education level remained fixed. If so, the "direct" estimate of $14 billion in 1958 should be corrected downward to $12.2 billion. Even the reduced estimate suggests that over 75% of the growth observed in the wage profiles can be attributed to job training, if the biases in the indirect estimates roughly cancel.

However, a positive relation between education and training does not mean that they are related in fixed proportions. To the extent that an (exogenous) expansion of education leads to a substitution of school education for job training, education may grow faster than job training. Indeed, (direct) educational expenditures grew from 4.8% to 7.1% of GNP between 1958 and 1976. If substitution was present, job training grew more slowly than education, suggesting that hours of training declined within school groups. In the aggregate, therefore, time spent in training may not have grown over the period, in which case the initial extrapolation may be valid.

The comparison of direct and indirect estimates is less problematic if carried out for the same year. This requires a calculation of job training costs based on the 1976 wage profile. The use of a parametric wage function (Mincer, 1974) makes such calculation much less laborious than was necessary when the 1958 data were analyzed (Mincer, 1962). The human capital earnings functions contain, among other variables, years of work (experience), variable X, which enters in a nonlinear fashion. Its coefficients are interpretable as postschool human capital investment parameters. On the assumption that time spent in investment declines linearly as working age increases, the expression is:

$$ln w = Z + rk_o X - (rk_o/2T) + ln[1-(k_o/T)X]$$

Here Z is a set of other independent variables, while k_o is the fraction of earnings devoted to human capital investments in the early working age, T the period in the working life at which investments cease, and r the rate of return on the net investments.

In a recent paper, Rosen (1982) estimated these parameters from the 1976 PSID for the male sample. He found $k_o = .32$, $T = 26$, and $r = 12\%$. Assuming that investments of a typical woman worker (in terms of k, or time) are half as large, k_o for all workers is a weighted average of the male and female investment ratio, the weight being total earnings (N · w) of each. Since the female work force was 2/3 the size of the male workforce, and earnings per woman worker 60% of male earnings, the weights are 1 to .4, yielding a k_o of .27. Since $T = 26$, k falls approximately .01, or 1% per year. Thus investments cease at about age 44. Average k in each age group is shown in Table 5.

Table 5

Calculation of 1976 Worker OJT Investments

Derived from Wage Function

Age	Mean Age	k	Nw	Nwk		
<25	22	.23	74	17.0		
25-34	30	.15	126	18.9		
35-44	40	.05	102	5.1		
45+		0	182	0	Ratio	Dollars
	Total		484	41.0	8.5%	$88.4 billion

Sources: k estimated from Rosen (1982); N and w from Table 4.

The ratio of training investments to wage per hour is $\Sigma Nwk/\Sigma Nw = 41/484 = 8.5\%$. This is higher than the direct estimate of 5.6%. Translating the 8.5% ratio to dollar figures by applying it to total compensation of workers in 1976 (it was $1,040 billion) yields a figure of $88.4 billion for the cost of worker training based on wage profiles. This figure is reduced to $75 billion if 15% of the estimate based on wage profiles is attributable to job mobility rather than training. Direct estimates of annual worker investments in training (5.6% of the wage) amounted to $57.7 billion in 1976. The comparison with the $75 billion figure estimated by the wage function suggests that three-quarters (75%) of the growth in the wage profile can be attributed to worker investment in training in 1976. This conclusion is supported by another piece of indirect evidence contributed by Rosen (1982). The PSID sample was divided into two parts: workers who received some training in 1976 and those who did not. Wage functions of the form indicated above were estimated for each group. The estimated k_o for the group without training was less than a third the size of the k_o for the group with training. Indeed, the experience wage profile was very flat in the no-training group.

Since new information on training was provided in the 1978 PSID survey, I replicated the procedure for that year. The linear (B_1) and quadratic (B_2) coefficients on experience (x and x^2) were:

Group	B_1	B_2
With some training in 1978	.0226 (10.2)	-.00027 (5.6)
No training in 1978	.00686 (1.7)	-.000082 (.8)

Note: t-ratios in parentheses.

The growth of wages over a year is ($B_1 - 2B_2 X$). It is over three times as fast for any given working age in the group with training as compared to the group without training.

It is noteworthy that three entirely different methods of estimating volumes of job training yield comparatively similar figures, as shown in Table 6.

It is also interesting to note that by 1976 directly estimated job training costs (see columns marked b) amounted to about half of schooling costs (direct and opportunity costs). In the 1962 study the ratio for 1958 appeared to be higher (first row of Table 6). If a decline in the ratio actually occurred, the substitution of schooling for training may have been dominant. Apparently, increased public expenditures on schools (including especially the growth of 2-year colleges) moved relative prices against training.

The comparison of direct and indirect estimates of job training investments summarized in Table 6 for 1976 (where no extrapolation is involved) suggests that OJT investments account for more than two-thirds of the observed growth in the (cross-sectional) wage profiles. This is consistent with a preponderant human capital interpretation of the wage profile. As suggested in the introduction, an empirically substantial link between wage profiles and training volumes can be used to infer changes in training investments over time. Such changes cannot be observed directly, as training data are reported only sporadically and fragmentarily. Whether and in what way job training was a factor in the pronounced changes in the wage structures over the past two decades in the U.S. is a question left for future research.

Table 6
Estimates of Job Training (OJT) and of Its Ratio to Total Compensation (TC)

	OJT ($billions)			OJT/TC			School/TC
Workers[1]	(a)	(b)	(c)	(a)	(b)	(c)	
1958	16.0	14.4		6.2%	5.6%		8.3%
1976	88.4	57.7		8.5	5.6		11.7
	(75.0)			(7.2)			
1987		148.0			5.6		11.3
Total[2]							
1987		296.0	240.0		11.2%	9.0%	22.6%
1987			330.0			12.4	

[1] Upper Panel: Worker Investments in OJT, School Direct Expenditures
[2] Lower Panel: Worker and Employer Investments in OJT, School Direct and Opportunity Costs

(a) OJT estimates derived from wage profiles. 1976 estimate (in parenthesis) is adjusted for wage growth attributable to job mobility.
(b) OJT estimates based on time spent in training in 1976.
(c) Two OJT estimates based on costs of formal training in 1987, multiplied by ratio of time in all training to time in formal training.
(d) Direct Costs of Education, from OERI, <u>Digest of Education Statistics</u>, 1989. Opportunity Costs assumed equal to Direct Costs.

Summary and Conclusions

With information on time costs of training and gains in wages attributable to training, rates of return for training can be computed. A downward adjustment is required, however, as the acquired skills erode due to obsolescence, or, to the extent that the skills are firm specific, to job mobility. The range of estimates of <u>worker</u> returns to training based on several data sets seems to exceed the magnitude of rates of return usually observed for schooling investments. Given the data on workers' firm tenure, it appears also that training remains profitable to firms, even in the face of average worker mobility.

The rates of return here calculated may be large enough to suggest underinvestment in training relative to that in schooling. However, such conclusions must be qualified in several respects: (1) Marginal rates of return to training are lower than the reported average rates; (2) Schooling investments receive heavy public subsidies, which may lead to overinvestment; and (3) returns to schooling contain leisure during school years and lifetime consumption benefits (skills) not included in the calculation. For both of these reasons observed rates of return are lower on schooling than on job training. Another relevant comparison concerns the trade-off between training and labor mobility: Optimal allocation of human resources in the labor market requires equal marginal rates of return in both activities. The image of the U.S. labor market as one in which mobility is rampant and job training modest (in comparison with Japan and Western Europe) does not necessarily imply that the marginal rates are far out of line: Many American workers may search more intensively for better opportunities afforded by job changing than by attachment to a firm. The picture is suggestive, but better data and deeper studies are needed.

This is not to say that training activities could not or should not be increased. If quality of educational background affects the efficiency of training, the much clamored improvements in education would increase the profitability and the utilization of training.

A further objective of this paper was to estimate total annual costs of job training in the economy. Three entirely different methods were used to estimate these volumes for 1958, 1976, and 1987. (1) The "direct" method used information on time spent in training and on wages. For 1976, investments so calculated amounted to 11.2% of Total Employee Compensation, and about half of the costs of school education.[10] (2) In the "indirect" method, training costs were estimated from wage profiles, using a wage function fitted to 1976 PSID data. The indirect estimate provides an upper limit, since other factors, job mobility among them, also affect the slope of the wage profile. Indeed, the direct estimate for 1976 is about 75 percent of the indirect estimate once gains due to labor mobility are netted out of the wage growth in the profile. (3) A third method uses information on costs of formal training programs and on average time spent in them and inflates the figures to a total training level. Rather remarkably, the three estimates are not far apart. Of course, the estimate based on wage profiles represents an upper limit.

---

[10] These include total, private and public, expenditures and opportunity costs of students.

An important corollary purpose of this work was to evaluate the usefulness of data on job training. Potentially, such data could provide important insights into the wage structure and into a wide range of labor market behavior. Procedures for determining volumes and profitability rates of job training were illustrated here, and these should be instructive. The analysis was performed on the available data which are still incomplete and fragmentary. The conclusions reached are therefore not definitive, even if highly suggestive. Harder estimates will require proper accounting of time and other resources absorbed by training of its distribution across workers and over time, and corresponding histories of wages and of labor mobility.

References

Barron, J., D. Black, and M. Lowenstein, "Job Matching and On-the-Job Training," *Journal of Labor Economics*, January 1989.

Bartel, A., "Formal Employee Training Programs," paper presented at *Symposium on Job Training*, Madison, Wisconsin, May 1989.

Becker, G. S., *Human Capital*, 2nd ed., University of Chicago Press, 1975.

Becker, G., and J. Stigler, "Law Enforcement, Malfeasance, and Compensation of Enforcers," *Journal of Legal Studies*, 1974.

Bishop, J., "On the Job Training of New Hires," paper presented at *Symposium on Job Training*, Madison, Wisconsin, May 1989.

Blakemore, A., and D. Hoffman, "Seniority Rules and Productivity," Discussion Paper, Arizona State University, 1988.

Brown, J., "Why Do Wages Increase With Tenure?" Draft, SUNY-Stony Brook, 1988. Published in *American Economic Review*, December 1989.

Duncan, G., and S. Hoffman, "Training and Earnings," *Five Thousand American Families*, Institute for Social Research, University of Michigan, Vol. 6, 1978.

Duncan, G., and F. Stafford, "The Use of Time and Technology by Households in the United States," *Research in Labor Economics*, Vol. 3, 1980.

Gordon, J., "Who is Being Trained to do What?" *Training Magazine*, October 1988.

Gronau, R., "Sex-Related Wage Differentials," *NBER Working Paper, No. 1002*, 1982.

Holzer, H., "The Determinants of Employee Productivity and Earnings," *NBER Working Paper No. 2782*, 1989.

Jovanovic, B., "Job Matching and the Theory of Turnover," *Journal of Political Economy*, October 1979.

Lazear, E., "Why Is There Mandatory Retirement?" *Journal of Political Economy*, September 1979.

Lillard, G., and H. Tan, *Private Sector Training*, Rand Corporation, R-3331, March 1986.

Lynch, L., "Private Sector Training and Its Impact," Draft, MIT, October 1988.

Mincer, J., "Job Training, Wage Growth, and Labor Turnover," *NBER Working Paper No. 2680*, 1988a.

-------, "Education and Unemployment," *NCEE Working Paper*, 1988b.

-------, "Labor Market Effects of Human Capital," NCEE and NAVE Conference Paper, 1988c.

-------, "On the Job Training: Costs, Returns, and Implications," *Journal of Political Economy*, Part II, October 1962.

-------, *Schooling, Experience and Earnings*, Columbia University Press, 1974.

-------, and B. Jovanovic, "Labor Mobility and Wages," in S. Rosen, ed., *Studies in Labor Markets*, University of Chicago Press, 1981.

-------, and Y. Higuchi, "Wage Structures and Labor Turnover in the U.S. and in Japan," *Journal of Japanese and International Economics*, June 1988.

Parsons, D., "Job Training in the Post-Schooling Period," Discussion Paper, Ohio State University, 1986.

Rosen, H., "Taxation and On-the-Job Training Decisions," *Review of Economics and Statistics*, August 1982.

Salop, J., and S. Salop, "Self-Selection and Turnover in the Labor Market," *Quarterly Journal of Economics*, November 1976.

Sicherman, N., "Human Capital and Occupational Mobility," Ph.D. Thesis, Columbia University, 1987.

Topel, R., *Wages Grow with Tenure*, Draft, University of Chicago, 1987.

Firm Financed Education and Specific Human Capital:
A Test of the Insurance Hypothesis[1]

Michael J. Feuer
Office of Technology Assessment
U.S. Congress[2]

Henry A. Glick
University of Pennsylvania

Anand Desai
Ohio State University

INTRODUCTION

This paper reports results from our continuing research on firm-financed education and training. Our work is motivated by Gary Becker's formulation of general training as a public good that will not be provided by firms unless it is financed entirely by the trainees.[3] So compelling was Becker's model that for many economists the case was closed: if firms are observed to be paying, then either the training is not general or else their investment is being subsidized from trainees' foregone wages or some other source. In place of this tautology we have been investigating whether, indeed, firms pay for training, and if so how those investments affect wages and turnover.

In Glick and Feuer (1984) we argued for the economic viability of firm-financed general training or education, and showed conditions under which investments by firms in this type of training were not vulnerable to risks of poaching by rival firms. We demonstrated that Becker's prediction does not

---

[1] Prepared for the symposium on "An Expanded Public Role in Job Training? The Issue of Market Failure in the Provision of Training", LaFollette Institute, University of Wisconsin-Madison, May 10-12, 1989. We thank Cathy Glen and Abate Mamo for excellent research assistance and programming. Steve Baldwin and Tom Palay gave thoughtful comments on an early draft. Jo Ritzen, Masanori Hashimoto, Lee Hansen and other participants in the symposium also provided helpful suggestions. David Stern offered helpful editorial suggestions. Nonetheless, we remain responsible for any remaining errors.

[2] The views presented in this paper are solely those of the authors, and do not necessarily represent the policies or positions of the Office of Technology Assessment or the United States Congress.

[3] Becker: "Why ... would rational firms in competitive labor markets provide general training if it did not bring any return? The answer is that firms would provide general training only if they did not have to pay any of the costs" (1975, page 20).

necessarily hold if firm-specific training and general training are provided jointly. In addition, we argued that the firm's financing of general training could safeguard shared investments in firm-specific human capital more effectively than wage bonuses or other instruments. The proposition that firm-financed education is a form of insurance is the subject of the present paper as well.

Following Becker, and as in most economic treatments of workplace training, we distinguish between general training and firm-specific training. The former means skills and knowledge that are broad enough to be applicable in other firms, while the latter refers to skills that are primarily useful in the firm where they are taught. In reality the distinction is fuzzy: most forms of specific training involve formation or improvement of skills that are to some extent fungible.[4] On the other hand, course work in a college or university is less ambiguously targeted to the development of basic or general abilities.

Nevertheless, and despite nontrivial empirical barriers, we accept the basic dichotomy between specific and general training, and make it operational by investigating a sample for whom participation in postgraduate course work is defined as a "general training" experience. We call this *education*, which we define as *firm-financed*, when the employee reports that the most important source of support for graduate or professional training is the employer. We distinguish this firm-financed education (FFE) from participation in training at an employer's training facility, in apprenticeships, or in other formal on-the-job training, which we define as *specific training* (ST).

These are relative concepts: while apprenticeship training is often viewed as developing rather basic work skills, it likely imparts more firm-specific information and skills than the education offered in schools away from the workplace.[5] For some authors the demarcation between general and specific training is determined by inspection of wage gains and quit rates: Bishop (in this volume) finds that formal courses result in higher wage gains and quit rates, from which he infers that the formal training must be less firm-specific (and relatively more generic). Our concern, on the other hand, is with the effects of participation in specific and general training on wages and mobility, which requires that the training be defined exogenously.

It is important to distinguish the reasons why firms might *desire* to support their employees' education from the conditions under which that support is economically *viable*. The former issue, i.e., the potential benefits from workplace training, is the concern of human resources planners and industrial psychologists, and less so of economists, who tend to focus on the costs and returns to training and who are therefore drawn to the viability question: under what conditions will training investments generate positive returns that can be recouped?

---

[4] Indeed, the *process* of learning firm-specific skills -- perhaps more than the measureable *outcome* of the process -- may entail team work and may require the development or sharpening of basic cognitive skills that are important in many firms.

[5] Future surveys could be made more useful for the examination of these issues by providing more detailed information on the type of courses taken, and in particular, the level of firm-specificity.

In Feuer et al (1987) we addressed two important aspects of the viability question, and reported two main results:

(1) Workers whose firms pay most of the costs of their postgraduate course work do not necessarily earn less than workers who pay their own way, *ceteris paribus*. We argued that this finding contradicts Becker's claim that general training costs are *necessarily* covered by foregone employee earnings (although we could not test whether the training costs were subsidized by some other source such as through tax deductions); and

(2) Firm financing of education is correlated with lower -- not higher -- separation rates. We found that individuals whose firms pay most of the costs of graduate level courses do not necessarily exercise their enhanced marketability and may, indeed, be more willing to develop a long-term employment relation than those who finance this type of training themselves (or receive support from loans, scholarships, or other sources).[6]

These results suggest not only that FFE is viable, but that it is useful for more than the kinds of reasons typically considered by human resources professionals concerned with the relationship between tangible skills and productivity. However, these findings were derived from an analysis of a sample of workers all of whom had ST, because we were testing the hypothesis that firm financing of education did not create greater poaching risks than self-financed education *if employees were involved in ST*. Thus, one potential benefit of employer-financed education is reduced turnover of individuals who have received ST. We did not explicitly investigate whether employees taking ST were more likely to receive FFE than those not taking ST. Nor did we examine differences in the effects of FFE on separations among individuals involved in ST and those not involved in ST. The empirical analysis in the 1987 paper, therefore, did not provide a direct test of the insurance hypothesis, although its results did suggest that the hypothesis warranted further investigation.

---

[6] The possibility that loyal employees are identified *ex ante* and selected for training could not be ruled out by our analysis reported in the 1987 paper; see below, however, for new empirical results that support our skepticism of this screening hypothesis.

The current effort addresses the insurance hypothesis directly:

• Is the propensity to receive FFE affected by an employee's participation in some form of ST?

• Is there evidence to suggest that individuals who had ST are more likely to remain with the firm if they had FFE than those who did not have ST and had FFE?

The second question is especially important in order to evaluate the insurance hypothesis: if movers with ST are equally likely to have had FFE as movers without ST, and if stayers with ST are equally likely to have had FFE as stayers without ST, then the basis of the insurance hypothesis would be undermined. Conversely, if the relationship between mobility and FFE is found to be a negative function of ST investments, then the insurance hypothesis would gain further credibility.

The paper begins with a discussion of the theory of FFE as insurance. We then describe in section 3 various regression analyses conducted on a portion of the post-1970 census-based survey of scientific and engineering personnel employed in US firms. In the final section we summarize, highlighting the role of transactions costs in understanding human capital investments by firms and workers.

FIRM FINANCED EDUCATION AS INSURANCE

Under what circumstances will *employees* be willing to invest in firm-specific human capital? This question did not preoccupy the early human capital theorists, who were mostly concerned with the *firm's* incentives to invest in specific human capital and with risks to the *firm* in the post-training period.[7] For example, Becker (1975) argued eloquently for bringing the question of turnover into the theory of the firm because "the firm is hurt by the departure of a trained employee because an equally profitable new employee [can] not be obtained" (page 29). He argued that firms could reduce the hazard of turnover by offering trained employees some of the return from training in the form of a wage premium. But because the higher wage would create an excess supply of workers willing to be trained, the "final step would be to shift some training costs as well as returns to employees ..." (page 30). With this explanation Becker established that specific training costs are shared by firms and workers, a fundamental principle that requires an explicit accounting for turnover but which otherwise leaves the microeconomic theory of the firm intact.

Hashimoto (1981) extended Becker's analysis by asking whether the cost-sharing rule would change in the presence of imperfect information. He argued that the *ex ante* cost-sharing agreement could prevent some suboptimal separations that would occur otherwise because of the inability of firms and workers to agree about marginal productivity improvements due to training. Thus, the cost-sharing contract solves an uncertainty problem, although even Hashimoto concluded that *ex ante* contracting cannot entirely

---

[7] For a review, see, e.g., Feuer (1989).

eliminate the risk of suboptimal separations. While Hashimoto's paper added to Becker's model a logic of shared specific training investments as a way to prevent unwanted turnover, it failed to account for other transactions costs in the post-training period.

In addition to uneven information, which limits the *ability* of parties to a contract to evaluate and agree upon the "true" state of nature *ex post*, there are other impediments to efficient resource allocation that arise from opportunistic urges on the part of employers or workers eager to capitalize on perceived bargaining advantages.[8] Even if the *ex ante* cost-sharing contract is optimal given what is known when it is written, there is no guarantee that it will be enforceable after training is over unless one assumes away potentially harmful strategic posturing. Firms face such risks because trained workers who remain with the firm can exploit strategic advantages that accrue from training. If ST is offered to a subset of the total labor pool, then trained workers can hold out for monopoly rents (up to the present discounted value of the firm's training investment) by threatening to quit. Even workers who share in the specific training investment can behave this way if they are willing to gamble the return on their investment.

Some features of "internal labor market" organization partially alleviate these tensions. By assigning wages to jobs rather than individuals and by providing trained workers the expectation of long-term employment, employers motivate workers to restrain their haggling for fear of being labeled 'malcontents', losing favor with their peers as well as with their superiors, and jeopardizing their job security. The advantages of internal labor market organization in mitigating these kinds of risks, which are incurred primarily by employers, were raised by Doeringer and Piore (1971) and again by Williamson (1975).

But what about risks incurred by employees? Assuming that cost-sharing of the specific training investment constitutes an implicit contract, it does not typically guarantee a longterm wage profile. Firms can attempt to keep a portion of the workers' returns to training by bargaining wages down, and firms will usually win in the bargaining contest because of their size advantages. Further, the number of workers with specific training usually exceeds the number of jobs where those skills are needed; this feature of standard workplace organization works against employees, whose bargaining power is inversely related to the number of specifically trained workers in the firm. Unless workers are perfectly omniscient, and know in advance not to join oversized cohorts of trainees, they could find themselves bargaining with a significant handicap. Again, the emergence of a "small numbers" bargaining situation after ST necessarily puts workers at risk.

A second risk faced by workers takes this logic a step further. Consider a two-period model for simplicity. In period 1 the firm offers to pay a share of specific training costs, and attracts a cohort of trainees willing to accept a wage that reflects the added marginal productivity associated with these workers' share of the specific training investment. This training cohort enters into an implicit wage

---

[8]Portions of this discussion are drawn from Glick and Feuer (1984) and Feuer, Glick and Desai (1987). The underlying approach is due to Williamson (1975).

agreement with the expectation of future income tied to their expected marginal product; training is offered at the beginning of the period and workers receive returns throughout the period and in succeeding periods. In period 2, however, the firm can change the terms and offer to pay job applicants a higher proportion of the specific training costs, thereby attracting a second cohort of as-yet untrained employees. The addition of this group lowers the marginal product and thus the wages of all workers, including those in the first cohort (trained in period 1), who originally expected to earn a higher wage. Unless those trained in period-can (1) foresee the firm's ability to behave in this manner and (2) make the necessary adjustments in their contract, employers can theoretically undercut the initial training/employment agreement. This is a type of moral hazard: the employer can alter both the return and the value of the training investment, an option not available to employees.[9] Over time the firm's ability to exploit this advantage will undoubtedly be limited -- to some extent -- by reputation effects. But reputation incentives are imperfect.[10]

Finally, other authors (Cooke, 1981; Thurow, 1970; Gordon, 1974) have emphasized bargaining advantages that stem from firm size and financial resources; and some have pointed to the firm's ability to diversify wealth between physical and human capital, an option not open to workers, whose human capital investments are not as easily sold or rented.

These considerations suggest that the question of investments in workplace training is a special case of a more general problem: parties in an employment relation or other transaction need to find or create a governance structure that will facilitate the monitoring of behavior, make possible the adaptation of agreements to changing circumstances, and provide assurances that *ex ante* commitments will be met even when conditions change. In other words, without special institutional arrangements, it may be difficult for firms and employees to invest in specific training.

The basic hypothesis tested in this paper is that education investments by firms can insure workers against the risks we have described and reduce the transaction costs of shared investments in firm-specific training. In the case of a worker who had not otherwise anticipated a personal investment in general education, the firm's provision of such training raises the worker's market value, lowers the rents firms can extract, and thereby ensures the worker's ST investment. For the worker who had planned to pay for continuing general education anyway, the firm's investment is similar to the offer of a wage premium; but scale economies in the provision of training may make it advantageous.

In our 1984 paper we spoke of the *ex post* small numbers bargaining problem in terms of "hostage risks," by which we meant that following training, firms and workers were beholden to one another in a fashion that ruled out the possibility of efficient bargaining. The solution to this problem, namely the

---

[9] The role of unions in rectifying this imbalance is worthwhile investigating: do unions attempt to ration firm-provided training to their members in order to offset employers' attempts to alter the supply of trained workers to their advantage?

[10] See, e.g., Williamson (1975).

provision of firm-financed education as a form of insurance, can also be viewed as a type of "hostage-taking" situation. To have workers invest in specific capital they need to be assured that they will receive a portion of the returns. To this end, firms offer a "hostage", in the form of general education, which raises the worker's market value and makes the threat of voluntary turnover more credible. Because the worker's investment in specific capital can also be seen as raising the firm's productivity and profit stream, the provision of both types of training -- with the firm paying part of the costs of both -- amounts to an exchange of hostages.[11] Clearly, this governance structure is not the only one that can insure specific training investments, nor do we believe that it is the only governance mechanism at work in firms where specific training is provided (in some firms, as we show below, specific training is provided without education).

MODEL SPECIFICATION AND DATA

We turn now to two empirical questions:

(1) Is there evidence that firms' willingness to invest in education depends in part on the employees' involvement in specific training?

(2) Are the effects of firm financing of education on mobility affected by workers' participation in firm specific training?

Controlling for other determinants of firm-financed training[12] the insurance hypothesis predicts that workers who take part in specific training are more likely to be offered FFE than those with no ST. Our earlier paper (1987) demonstrated that separation rates are lower among individuals whose firm-specific investments have been insured with FFE than among those with no FFE.[13] The current paper goes one step further by hypothesizing that differences in separation rates among persons with and without FFE are affected by their participation in ST.

---

[11] In fact, the employer's offer of general training is an especially economical type of hostage because the firm can retain most of the benefits from the training as long as the worker remains with the firm.

[12] See for example Lilard and Tan (1986).

[13] A complete test of the insurance hypothesis would require comprehensive wage and marginal productivity histories. Until such data become available our inquiry into the differential effects of FFE on movers and stayers with and without ST provides a basis for judging the validity of the model.

Consider a model in which the firm's provision and financing of continuing education depends in part on whether or not an individual employee is involved in some form of ST, as in the following logistic regression model:

$$\text{pr (FFE)} = \beta_0 + \beta_1 (ST) + \sum_{i=2}^{n} \beta_i (CONT)_i + u$$

where

$$FFE = \begin{cases} 1, \text{ if single most important source of graduate or} \\ \text{professional training is the employer, and} \\ 0, \text{ otherwise;} \end{cases}$$

ST denotes participation in apprenticeships, other formal on-the-job training, or courses at employers' training facilities;

CONT is a vector of control variables covering socioeconomic and educational background, scientific or technical field, job tenure and experience, lapsed time since the end of BA-level training, and dummy variables to account for regional differences; and

u is the error term.

To test this model we use data from the first wave of the post-1970 census-based longitudinal survey of natural and social scientists and engineers.[14] The sample consists of US citizens who reported that all of their graduate or professional training occurred while they were working full time in private industry and that their training had already ended. While in our 1987 paper we considered only those individuals who reported involvement in what we defined as firm-specific training, for this paper, which focuses on the possible effects of general training provided with and without specific training, we augmented the sample to include individuals who did not report having participated in specific training. Earnings are linked to a particular training/education and employment episode: we exclude people from the sample whose education might have been financed by more than one firm, as well as those who were no longer employed at the time of the survey, so that the sample contains only those personnel whose education is associated with a single employer. In addition, we restricted the sample to US born American citizens, in order to eliminate possible language or cultural bias in wage determination. Respondents are employed in a wide variety of scientific and technical fields classified by the National Science Foundation.

---

[14] See Feuer et al (1987) for more detailed discussion of the data. For the current paper we augmented the sample to include individuals who did not report having participated in specific training.

Characteristics of the sample are summarized in Table 1.

Education is defined as firm-financed if the respondent reports that the "primary source of funding" was the employer. Because we have already shown that these people experienced no wage loss compared to individuals whose firms were not the primary source of funding, we assume that firm-financing implies a true investment. Note that for respondents for whom FFE = 1, employers paid 80 percent of their graduate or professional education costs, on average. Granted, most tuition bills for full time working students are quite small, which suggests that the firm's sponsorship might actually amount to a negligible investment. Nevertheless, there are still a substantial number of employees in this sample who received *no* firm-sponsored education benefits, so that the comparative question is still relevant.

The first question is whether individuals involved in ST are more or less likely to receive FFE than those not involved in ST, *ceteris paribus*. As shown in Table 2, the probability of receiving FFE appears to increase with participation in ST. But given that the coefficient is not statistically significant ($p = 0.18$), we cannot assert confidently that a positive relationship exists between FFE and ST. However, this result alone can be misleading, and does not necessarily detract from the insurance hypothesis. While it does not appear that individuals were offered FFE principally on the basis of their participation in ST, the more important questions are whether those with ST and FFE (about 21 percent of the sample) exhibit different turnover behavior than those with FFE but without ST (about 24 percent of the sample), and whether those with ST and no FFE behave differently than those with neither ST nor FFE. In other words, are there benefits to firms and workers that accrue when FFE and ST are provided jointly?

To explore this question, i.e., whether firms and workers benefit from FFE provided to workers involved in ST, we divide the sample into movers and stayers. As in the 1987 paper, movers are defined as individuals whose training took place in a previous job and who did not acquire their current job by internal promotion, while stayers are those whose training occurred in their current job or those whose training occurred in their previous job and who acquired their current job via internal promotion.

If the insurance is effective, then we would observe that

$$\Pr\{FFE|ST \cap Move\} < \Pr\{FFE|\overline{ST} \cap Move\} ; \text{ and}$$

$$\Pr\{FFE|ST \cap Stay\} > \Pr\{FFE|\overline{ST} \cap Stay\}$$

These hypotheses follow logically from our earlier finding that individuals with FFE and ST showed lower quit rates than those with self-financed education and ST.

Table 3 shows logit estimates for movers and stayers separately. *The negative coefficient among movers, and the positive coefficient among stayers, on the ST variable, are both significant at the .10 level.* These results appear to support the insurance hypothesis: employees who stayed with the firm after ST were more likely to have had FFE than those who stayed who did not have ST; and people who moved after ST were less likely to have had FFE than those who moved and did not have ST. In other words, we find a strong association between ST and FFE, reflected through predicted differences in mobility. The opposite signs on the ST coefficients for movers and stayers, which strongly support the notion that FFE offers effective insurance, help explain the absence of any statistically significant effect in the model that omits the mobility variable.

Note also several other interesting findings from this analysis. First, job tenure has a negative effect on the likelihood of receiving FFE, which suggests that firms do not necessarily use firm-loyalty as a criterion for human capital investments. As we mentioned in the 1987 paper, the fact that turnover was inversely related to FFE might be due to the firm's ability to single out loyal employees *ex ante* and offer them FFE with relatively low risk of losing the returns to the investment. We were skeptical of this argument, which seemed to assume that managers can detect loyalty traits in advance. The present empirical result raises further doubt about *ex ante* screening on the part of employers. Another possibility is that the longer an individual has been employed without training, the less likely he is to be considered a worthwhile investment, i.e., the firm no longer expects much return from a training investment, nor does the firm expect the employee to leave. A third possibility is that some amount of self-screening goes on, in that individuals who *expect* to be more mobile may pursue advanced degrees at their own expense in order to widen their career possibilities later.

Second, one's probability of receiving FFE is inversely related to the amount of time spent in postsecondary education. This result may indicate that the more knowledge and skills an individual acquires the less interesting it becomes for the firm to pay for additional schooling. Alternatively, it could reflect the firm's preference to pay for continuing education of employees who appear to be "quick learners," i.e., by screening out those who take longer than average to gain their undergraduate degree.

We find also that movers with a masters degree or Ph.D. are significantly less likely to receive FFE than those with no postgraduate degree. If advanced degree holders normally do not require any additional general training, then one would conclude from this finding that the better ones left; those who stayed with the firm perhaps did so to receive additional FFE, which could indicate that their advanced degrees were inadequate to perform in their job (e.g., Ph.Ds in English literature who take general computer courses), and that the FFE they received provided them with the basic tools to do their work.

The principal importance of the results reported in table 3, with respect to the insurance hypothesis, is that the relationship between ST and FFE for movers is different than the relationship for stayers. But these results do not reveal whether movers in general are more or less likely than stayers to receive FFE, nor whether the different results for movers and stayers are statistically significant. It is important to isolate the effects of ST on FFE from the correlation between mobility and FFE.

To explore this issue in the context of the given model we re-combine the mover and stayer groups and define three new dummy variables:

$$\text{ST/Stay} = \begin{cases} 1 \text{ if respondent had specific training and stayed, and} \\ 0 \text{ otherwise;} \end{cases}$$

$$\text{ST/Move} = \begin{cases} 1 \text{ if respondent had specific training and moved, and} \\ 0 \text{ otherwise;} \end{cases}$$

$$\overline{\text{ST}}/\text{Move} = \begin{cases} 1 \text{ if respondent did not have specific training and moved, and} \\ 0 \text{ otherwise.} \end{cases}$$

By including these variables in the regression we can estimate the different effects of ST on FFE for movers and stayers. (Note that the estimated coefficients for the above variables are relative to the excluded variable $\overline{\text{ST}}/\text{Stay}$, i.e., those with no ST who stayed.)

As shown in table 4, there appears to be a marked difference. The coefficient for the group with ST that moved is -0.78, compared to the baseline group of persons with no ST who stayed (i.e., the excluded variable in the regression). The group with ST that stayed has a coefficient of 0.28, which means there is a difference of 1.06 in the coefficients of movers and stayers with ST. This difference is substantially larger than for the group without ST, for whom the difference between movers and stayers is 0.59.[15] Orthodox human capital theorists would anticipate no such difference, because a firm's investments in FFE should be equally susceptible to poaching of workers regardless of their involvement in ST. Similarly, the difference of 0.47 in the coefficients of those with and without ST (i.e., the difference between 1.06, which the relative effect of mobility for the ST group and -0.59, which is the relative effect of mobility on the no-ST group) supports our proposition: workers whose ST is insured by FFE are less likely to become the targets of opportunistic employer haggling -- behavior which induces quitting -- than workers who have no ST requiring insurance.[16] Thus, the finding that FFE is negatively associated with turnover confirms our earlier paper, and extends the result to employees with no ST.

Although the basic model we estimated is specified to explain the marginal effects of ST, mobility, and other variables on FFE, additional insight is gained by considering the reciprocal question and looking at the effects of ST and FFE on worker mobility.

Suppose that firms value ST more highly than FFE. Then it would follow that these firms would be most eager to retain employees with both ST and FFE, followed in order by those with ST and no FFE, those with no ST and FFE, and finally those with neither ST nor FFE. A different ranking would be predicted if firms value FFE more highly than ST.

Table 5, which is simply a reformulation of the results in Table 4, sheds light on this question. Our

---

[15] With this model structure it is not possible to ascertain whether this difference is statistically significant.

[16] Note that this result could also occur if general and specific training were complementary, i.e., if the value of the latter increased with participation in the former.

estimates suggest an ambiguous attitude toward workers with different types of training. First, we find that individuals with ST and FFE are the most likely to stay in the firm, and that those with no ST and with FFE are more likely to stay than those with ST and no FFE. The latter result would be predicted under the assumption that firms value general skills more highly than firm-specific skills (column one in table 5), which is not the typical human capital assumption.[17]

In addition, we find that the probability of having received FFE, given that an employee left the firm, is unaffected by one's participation in ST. In other words, the -.59 and -.78 coefficients in table 4 are not statistically different. This suggests that individuals with ST and no FFE were not necessarily more likely to stay with the firm than those with no ST and no FFE, i.e., that firms are indifferent between individuals with no training and those with specific training only. This last result is particularly counterintuitive for human capital theorists, but follows directly from the insurance hypothesis: excessive haggling and other opportunistic behavior on the part of employers could explain why firms have difficulty retaining workers whose investments in specific human capital are uninsured.[18]

CONCLUDING REMARKS

This paper has addressed the hypothesis that firm financed education can reduce certain risks of shared investments in specific human capital. Our concern is with the state of employer-employee bargaining in the post-training period, and with the inadequacy of cost-sharing as a way to ensure ongoing investments in firm-specific training. Thus, our work differs from Becker -- who concentrated on the shared specific training investment as a way to keep the supply of trainees in check -- and from Hashimoto -- who focused on sharing as a means to reduce unwanted turnover. Accounting explicitly for the firm's tendency to exploit asymmetric bargaining advantages that arise after workers are trained in firm-specific skills, our model suggests that additional governance mechanisms are necessary in order to make it possible for workers to continue investing in those kinds of skills. We argue that firm financing of general training, or education, provides effective insurance of specific training investments, a proposition which is borne out by our empirical analysis. In summary, to the extent that firms value stable and productive employment relations that include ongoing firm-specific training, they are willing to invest in general human capital

---

[17] Becker argued that "firms have less incentive to fire [employees with specific training] than employees with no training or general training ..." (1975, page 32).

[18] It might be argued that the haggling is rational, if the employer can extract enough from the employees with ST and no FFE who stayed to offset the losses from those with ST and no FFE who left because of the bargaining asymmetry. But this is an empirical question beyond the scope of the current paper.

assets of their workers in order to equilibrate subsequent bargaining transactions. There may be some question as to whether we have correctly defined specific and general training with the data set we used. While there is no definitive answer to this question, our results do indicate that firms and employees behave differently as a result of providing and participating in the two types of training that we have identified.

Firm financed education is not the only governance mechanism, but as we discussed in our earlier papers, it can be superior to wage bonuses, the one most often mentioned by those who believe in pecuniary solutions to employment problems. The disadvantage of wage bonuses is that the worker stops receiving the benefit if the adverse event for which he is being insured actually occurs: if the employer attempts to exploit his bargaining advantage and the worker is forced to quit, the worker stops receiving the wage bonus. General training, on the other hand, provides the worker with the benefit even if he leaves (in fact the benefit may be greater if the worker leaves than if he stays), which makes it a more powerful insurance mechanism.

Another commonly cited solution to employer haggling stems from the firm's potential loss of reputation in the labor market. As Williamson (1975) has pointed out, predatory threats against employee training investments can blemish the firm's reputation and disrupt the steady supply of workers willing to invest in specific training. But these so-called reputation effects will be weak where information is costly to obtain, and their usefulness undoubtedly varies by industry. It is not clear that firms will be inclined to promise full disclosure of their predatory bargaining actions -- which would amount to their offering a hostage to deter their own future exploitative behavior -- or that such disclosures would be credible.

In any event, our interest in the insurance effects of firm financed education should not be interpreted as a denial of other governance modes. Rather our aim has been to *broaden* the range of possible ways in which employers and workers can craft mutually beneficial work arrangements. Finding the optimal mode for specific firms and industries under different technological conditions would be a useful exercise for continued research.

REFERENCES

Becker, G., *Human Capital* (New York: National Bureau of Economic Research, 2nd edition, 1975).

Cooke, W. "Human Capital Adjustments to Technological Change in the Computer Industry: The Case of Scientists and Engineers," Report to the National Science Foundation, grant number 79-11318, (Washington, DC, 1981).

Doeringer, P. and M. Piore, *Internal Labor Markets and Manpower Analysis* (Boston: D.C. Heath, 1971).

Feuer, M.J., "Economic Analysis of Workplace Training: Human Capital Theory and Beyond," OTA, draft working paper, Science, Education and Transportation Program, October 1989.

Feuer, M., H. Glick, and A. Desai, "Is Firm Sponsored Education Viable?", *Journal of Economic Behavior and Organization, 8*, 1987.

Glick, H. and M. Feuer, "Employer Sponsored Training and the Governance of Specific Human Capital Investments," *Quarterly Review of Economics and Business, 24*, 2, Summer 1984.

Gordon, D., "A Neoclassical Theory of Keynesian Unemployment," *Economic Inquiry, 12*, 1974.

Hashimoto, M., "Firm Specific Human Capital as a Shared Investment," *American Economic Review, 71*, 3, June 1981.

Lillard, L. and H. Tan, "Private Sector Training: Who Gets It and What are its Effects?", Rand Corporation, March 1986.

Thurow, L., *Investment in Human Capital* (Boston: Wadsworth, 1970).

Williamson, O.E., *Markets and Hierarchies: Analysis and Antitrust Implications,* (New York: Free Press, 1975).

TABLE 1

CHARACTERISTICS OF SAMPLE USED IN REGRESSION ANALYSES

	With Specific Training (n=464)	Without Specific Training (n=641)	Total (n=1105)
Percent with firm-financed education	50%**	41%**	45%
Mean age	36.1*	35.2*	35.5
Years since end of college training	4.8	5.2	5
Years in current job	8.1	7.9	8
Years of postsecondary training	5.7***	6.0***	5.9
Percent with masters degree	46%	45%	45%
Percent with Ph.D.	6.0%***	14.0%***	11.0%
1971 income	$16,734***	$15,883***	$16,240
Management level:			
staff supervisory	42%	41%	42%
team supervisory	47%**	40%**	43%
departmental supervisory	9%	11%	10%
top management	3%	3%	3%

* $p \leq 0.1$
** $p \leq 0.05$
*** $p \leq 0.01$

TABLE 2

LOGIT MAXIMUM LIKELIHOOD ESTIMATES, STANDARD ERRORS, AND P VALUES FOR THE SPECIFIC TRAINING VARIABLE AND FOR OTHER VARIABLES SIGNIFICANT AT THE 0.10 LEVEL OR BETTER [a] (n=1105)

Dependent Variable = Probability of Receiving Firm-Financed Education (FFE)

	ß	SE	PROB
Specific Training	0.18	0.14	0.18
Age	-0.02	0.01	0.03
Years since end of college training	-0.02	0.01	0.01
Years of postsecondary training	-0.16	0.07	0.02
Masters Degree	-0.39	0.16	0.01
Ph.D. Degree	-1.15	0.34	0.01
Management Level			
Departmental Supervisory	-0.59	0.24	0.01
1971 income (in thousands)	0.03	0.02	0.02

---

[a] Coefficients for dummy variables for professional field and residential area omitted from this table.

TABLE 3

LOGISTIC MAXIMUM LIKELIHOOD ESTIMATES (ß) FOR THE SPECIFIC TRAINING VARIABLE AND FOR OTHER VARIABLES, BY MOBILITY, SIGNIFICANT AT THE 0.10 LEVEL OR BETTER [a]
(n=1105)

Dependent Variable = Probability of Receiving Firm-Financed Education (FFE)

	MOVERS (n=287)	STAYERS (n=818)
Specific Training	−0.68*	0.27*
Age	—	−0.02*
Years since end of college training	—	−0.02**
Years of postsecondary training	—	−0.15*
Masters Degree	−1.08***	—
Ph.D. Degree	−2.0**	—
Years in job	−0.18***	−0.01*
Management Level		
Departmental Supervisory		−0.75***
Top management	−2.01*	—
1971 income	—	0.00*

[a] Coefficients for dummy variables for professional field and residential area omitted from this table.

* $p \leq 0.10$
** $p \leq 0.05$
*** $p \leq 0.01$

TABLE 4

LOGIT MAXIMUM LIKELIHOOD ESTIMATES, STANDARD ERRORS, AND P VALUES FOR THE SPECIFIC TRAINING/MOBILITY DUMMY VARIABLES, AND FOR OTHER VARIABLES SIGNIFICANT AT THE .10 LEVEL OR BETTER[a] (N=1105)

Dependent Variable = Probability of Receiving Firm-Financed Education

	ß	SE	PROB
Specific training/ stayed*	0.28	0.15	0.07
Specific training/ moved	−0.78	0.25	0.01
No specific training/ moved	−0.59	0.22	0.01
Years since end of college training	−0.02	0.01	0.03
Years of postsecondary training	−0.18	0.07	0.01
Masters Degree	−0.29	0.16	0.07
Ph.D. Degree	−0.90	0.35	0.01
Years in job	−0.02	0.01	0.04
Management responsibility Departmental supervisory	−0.53	0.24	0.03
1971 income (in thousands)	0.03	0.02	0.07

[a] Coefficients for dummy variables for professional field and residential area omitted from this table.

* Coefficients on dummy variable interaction terms are relative to the excluded variable, no specific training/stayed.

TABLE 5

PREDICTED AND OBSERVED RANKINGS OF EMPLOYEE RETENTION, GIVEN VARYING ASSUMPTIONS OF FIRM'S VALUATION OF SPECIFIC TRAINING AND FIRM-FINANCED EDUCATION

RANK*	Predicted Ranking *Assuming Firms Value FFE More Than ST*	Predicted Ranking *Assuming Firms Value ST More Than FFE*	OBSERVED RANKING
1	ST AND FFE	ST AND FFE	ST AND FFE
2	NO ST; FFE	ST; NO FFE	NO ST; FFE
3	ST; NO FFE	NO ST; FFE	NO ST; NO FFE
4	NO ST; NO FFE	NO ST; NO FFE	ST; NO FFE

* 1 = most likely to remain with firm;
  2 = least likely to remain with firm.

ON-THE-JOB TRAINING OF NEW HIRES

John H. Bishop
Center for Advanced Human Resource Studies
New York State School of Industrial and Labor Relations
Cornell University
Ithaca, New York 14851-0953

If the Germans had any secret weapon in the post-1973 economic difficulties, it is the technical competence of their work force, which is in turn the product of their apprenticeship system.
--Limprecht and Hayes, 1982, p.139.

I think that the Japanese education system is not very good....employer training is much more effective.   --Yutaka Kosai, President, Japan Center for Economic Research, 1989

The heart of this new [flexible] manufacturing landscape is the management of manufacturing projects: selecting them, creating teams to work on them, and managing workers' intellectual development.   --Ramchandran Jaikumar, 1986, p. 75.

A growing number of commentators are pointing to employer sponsored training as a critical ingredient in a nation's competitiveness. American employers appear to devote less time and resources to the training of entry level blue collar, clerical and service employees than employers in Germany and Japan (Limprecht and Hayes 1982, Mincer and Higuchi 1988, Koike 1984, Noll et al 1984, Wiederhold-Fritz 1985). In the 1983 Current Population Survey, only 33 percent of workers with 1 to 5 years of tenure reported having received skill improvement training from their current employer (Hollenbeck and Wilkie 1985). Analyzing 1982 NLS-Youth data, Parsons (1984) reports that only 34 to 40 percent of the young workers in clerical, operative, service and laborer jobs reported that it was "very true" that "the skills [I am] learning would be valuable in getting a better job." The payoffs to getting jobs which offer training appear to be very high, however. In Parson's study, having a high learning job rather than a no learning job in 1979 increased a male youth's 1982 wage rate by 13.7 percent. While the 1980 job had no such effect, the 1981 job raised wages by 7.2 percent when it was a high learning job rather than a no learning job.

If the payoffs to such jobs are so substantial, why aren't such jobs more common? If one were to put this question to an employer, he would point to the high turnover rates of youth as the primary reason why he cannot afford to train new employees more intensely. For American workers with less than one year of tenure, the probability of a separation in the next 12 months is 59 percent. Since comparably defined turnover is only 20 percent in the United Kingdom and 24 percent in Japan, national differences in turnover could be a major reason for the low levels of training investment in the US, if the employer's explanation is right (OECD, 1984, Table 33 and 34).

The theory of on-the-job training says, however, that if training is general, turnover propensities should not matter. The worker pays the full costs of the training and reaps the full benefits whether or not there is subsequent turnover, so the decision to undertake training should be independent of prospective turnover. The problem with the prediction that workers pay all of the costs of general training is that analyses of large representative data sets generally fail to confirm it. In Parson's (1985, table 7.6) study, when a youth reported that it was "very true" that "the skills [I am] learning would be valuable in getting a better job", his job paid on average 2.4 to 14 percent <u>more</u> than when the above statement was "not at all true" even with an extensive set of controls for schooling and academic achievement included in the model. Bishop and Kang (1988) have conducted another test of this hypothesis in the 1984 follow up of the High School and Beyond seniors by regressing the log of the deflated starting wage of the current or most recent job on indicators of the receipt of employer sponsored training. Here again, the jobs offering some training rather than none or which offer greater amounts of training paid <u>higher</u> starting wage rates even when a whole array of human capital characteristics were controlled. For females the positive effect of receiving training on the starting wage was statistically significant. Adding dummies for occupation and industry did not change the results appreciably.

It could be argued, however, that these findings do not constitute a decisive refutation of the proposition that workers pay all of the costs of general training. Hiring decision makers are probably better at assessing the ability of job candidates than econometricians who are limited to the information in the NLS or HSB data file. The positive association between wages and training arises, it could be argued, because workers who are highly able (in ways not observed by the analyst) are both paid more and also recruited for jobs that require large amounts of training.

Unobserved heterogeneity no doubt contributes to the positive association between training and starting wage rates, but to transform a large negative structural relationship into a statistically significant positive relationships just described, sorting of more able job applicants into high training jobs would have to be very powerful indeed. If such a selection process were operating, access to training should depend on ability factors that are visible to the analyst as well as on factors that are not visible to the analyst. Yet models estimated by Parsons and by Bishop and Kang failed to find large effects of ability proxies such as test scores, grades, and being a disciplined student on the probability of receiving training.

One possible explanation of these anomalous findings is that the training is specific and the employer is financing <u>all</u> of its costs. But standard models of the sharing of the costs of specific training do not predict that employers pay all of its costs and some of the new revisionist theories--Salop and Salop's (1976) adverse selection theory--predict that employers pay none of the costs of specific training. A specific training explanation of the these findings is particularly perplexing when to all outward appearances the training is largely general.

Empirical tests of the theory of on-the-job training have been severely hampered by the absence of data on the key theoretical constructs of the theory--general training, specific training and productivity growth. Data on wage growth and turnover have been used to test various propositions of the theory, but definitive results have been elusive because the large number of unobservables result in there being at least two explanations for any given set of phenomena (Garen, 1987). I hope in this paper to overcome some of the limitations of previous research by analyzing the first large-scale data set to contain measures of the time devoted to training activities during the first three months on the job, who does the training, the generality of training and the productivity of the employees both during and after the receipt of training.

The paper is organized as follows. The first section describes how the data has been collected and how the measures of worker productivity and of time devoted to new hire training were constructed. Section 2 presents tabulations of this data by occupation, establishment size, industry, previous relevant work experience, age and education. Section 3 contains a very simple theory of training investment and then offers a multivariate analysis of the determinants of training investment. Section 4 analyzes the effect of training on productivity growth of new hires focusing on how the impacts of training depend on who provides the training, the size of the establishment and the generality of the training. Section 5 examines the effect of training on wage growth during the first 2 years on the job and then compares these wage rate effects with the productivity effects estimated in section 4. Section 6 examines the effect of training on turnover and promotions. The paper concludes with a summary of the major findings and a discussion of how the findings may illuminate the causes of the lower levels of on-the-job training for new hires in the US than in Germany and Japan.

1. DATA ON TRAINING AND PRODUCTIVITY GROWTH

The analysis is based on data from a survey of 3,412 employers sponsored by the National Institute on Education (NIE) and the National Center for Research in Vocational Education (NCRVE) conducted between February and June 1982. The survey was the second wave of a two-wave longitudinal survey of employers from selected geographic areas across the country. The first wave was funded by the U.S. Department of Labor to collect data on area labor market effects of the Employment Opportunity Pilot Projects (EOPP). The survey encompassed 10 EOPP pilot sites and 18 comparison sites selected for their similarity to the pilot sites. The ES-202 lists of companies paying unemployment insurance taxes provided the sample frame for the survey. Because of the interest in low wage labor markets, the sample design specified that establishments in industries with a relatively high proportion of low-wage workers be over sampled. The tax paying units were stratified by the estimated number of low wage employees and the number of establishments selected from each strata was roughly in proportion to the estimated number of low wage workers at the establishments in that strata. Within strata the selection was random. The survey was conducted over the phone and obtained a response rate of 75 percent.

The second wave attempted to interview all of the respondents in the first-wave survey. About 70 percent of the original respondents completed surveys for the second wave. Most of the respondents were the owner/manager of small firms who were quite familiar with the performance of each of the firm's employees. Seventy percent of the establishments had fewer than 50 employees, and only 12 percent had more than 200 employees. In large organizations the primary respondent was the person in charge of hiring, generally the personnel officer. If the primary respondent was unable to answer questions about the training received by newly hired workers in the sampled job, that part of the interview was completed by talking to a supervisor or someone else with line responsibility.

The employers who received the full questionnaire were asked to select "the last new employee your company hired prior to August 1981 regardless of whether that person is still employed by your company." Only 2594 employers had hired someone in the time frame requested and these employers constitute the sample used in the study.

The respondent was asked to report how much time typical new hires for this job spent during the first three months of employment in four different kinds of training activities: (1) watching others do the job rather than doing it themselves, (2) formal training programs, (3) informal individualized training and extra supervision by management and line supervisors, and (4) informal individualized training and extra supervision by co-workers. For the sample of firms and jobs, the means for the typical worker were 47.3 hours watching others do the job (T_w), 10.7 hours for formal training programs (T_F), 51 hours for informal training by management (T_S), 24.2 hours for informal training by co-workers (T_C). A copy of the relevant portions of the questionnaire is available from the author.

A training time index was constructed by first valuing trainer and trainee time relative to that of workers with two years of tenure in that job and then combining the time invested in training activities during the first three months on the job. The employers reported that workers with two years of tenure in the job averaged between 22 and 50 percent (depending on occupation and other worker characteristics) more productive than new hires during their first three months on the job. This ratio was calculated for each job/worker category and used to place a relative value on coworker time devoted to training.[1] The management staff members who provide formal and informal training were assumed to be paid 1.5 times the wage of coworkers. Formal training involves four kinds of costs: development costs, facility costs, trainer time and trainee time. Sometimes, it is one-on-one and sometimes it is done in groups but since most of the establishments in this study are small, class size was probably small as well. Consequently, it was assumed that when all the costs of formal training other than the trainee's time are lumped together--development costs, training materials costs and the value of the trainer's time--they are about 25 percent greater than the time costs of the trainee.[2] When supervisors and coworkers are giving informal training to a new employee, the trainee is almost invariably directly involved in a production activity. Employers report that for informal training, the trainees are typically as productive while being trained as they are when working alone (Hollenbeck and Smith 1984). Consequently, informal training is assumed to involve only the investment of the trainer's time. Thus in units of coworker time the value of trainer time is:

Valued Trainer Time = $T_C + 1.5*T_s + T_F$ (1)

In units of trainee time, the time the trainee spends not producing because of training activities is:

Trainee Time = $T_W + T_F$ (2)

The total investment in training in trainee time units[3] is:

Total Training Investment = $T_W + T_F + (T_C + 1.5*T_s + T_F)/RP$. (3)

where

RP = the productivity of the average new hire during the first 3 months divided by the productivity of typical worker with two years' tenure

The arithmetic mean of this index is 209 hours, implying that the value of the time invested in training a typical new employee in the first three months is about 40 percent of the output that the trainee can produce working full-time during the first three months on the job.

---

[1]. The use of the ratio to estimate the relative productivity implicitly involves an assumption that the productivity reports received from employers are a proportional transformation of true productivity plus a random error. The unknown factor of proportionality can be different for every job, every firm and every respondent but a single respondent is assumed to use the same proportionality factor when answering our questions. If alternatively it were assumed that these reports exaggerate the rate of growth of productivity with tenure by a factor of 2, estimates of training investment would be 7 to 15 percent lower. Comparisons across occupations or of new hires with different qualifications would not change appreciably.

[2]. When many workers can be trained simultaneously, the fixed costs of developing the training package and hiring a trainer are spread over a larger number of trainees. This means that the average hourly cost of formal training is generally smaller at large companies than small companies. For the small companies included in this study was assumed that the cost factor for formal training was roughly 1.8 times the value of an experienced coworker's time. For establishments with more than 200 employees, cost factors for formal training would be much lower, possibly between 1.2 and 1.4.

[3]. The index was constructed under an assumption that the four training activities were mutually exclusive. This implies that if the sum of the hours devoted to individual activities is greater than 520, that a reporting error has occurred which overstates investment in training. In the few cases where the sum of hours devoted to training exceeded 520, the training time index was adjusted downward by the ratio of 520 to the sum of the hours reported for individual activities. This procedure reduces the mean of the index by about 10 percent. The cost of the trainer and amortization of training package development costs was assumed to be two-thirds of the foregone productivity of a supervisor, since formal training often spreads fixed costs over more than one trainee. Thus 1.8 = (2/3)1.5 + .8.

The survey asked the employer (or in larger firms the immediate supervisor) to report on productivity of the typical individual hired in the job after two weeks, during the next 11 weeks and at the end of two years at the firm. The rating was made on a "scale of zero to 100 where 100 equals the maximum productivity rating any of your employees in (NAME'S) position can obtain and zero is absolutely no productivity by your employee." For the full data set at the mean values of these indexes of reported productivity were 49.0 for the first two weeks, 64.6 for the next 11 weeks and 81.4 at the time of the interview. The questions asking for a rating of the productivity of particular workers had a nonresponse rate of only 4.4 percent. Comparably defined nonresponse rates for other questions were 8.2 percent for previous relevant experience, 3.2 percent for age, 6.7 percent for education, 8.6 percent for time spent in informal training by supervisor, and 5.7 percent for a three-question sequence from which starting wage rate is calculated. The low-nonresponse rate implies that our respondents felt that they were capable of making such judgments and augur well for the quality of the data that results.

The interview questions about the productivity of recently hired employees do not measure productivity in any absolute sense and therefore are not comparable across firms or across jobs in a firm. Rather, they are intended as ratio scale indicators of the relative productivity of a typical (or a particular) worker at different points in their tenure at a firm. Under an assumption that these productivity indexes are proportional transformations of true productivity plus a random error, percentage differences in cell means of the productivity index will be unbiased estimators of percentage differences in true productivity. If the variations in the productivity scores assigned by supervisors exaggerate the proportionate variations in the true productivity, our estimates of percentage differences in productivity between two workers will be biased upward. Even though it is possible for a worker's true productivity to be negative, the scale was defined as having a lower limit of zero. Floors and ceilings on a scale typically cause measurement errors to be negatively correlated with the true value. If this is the case, then our estimates of percentage differences in productivity between two workers will be biased downward. This latter type of bias appears to be more likely than the former.

Further evidence that the proportionality assumption results in an understatement of percentage differences in productivity between individual workers doing the same job comes from comparing the coefficients of variation of productivity in this and other data sets. If pairs of workers who are still at the firm are used to construct a coefficient of variation for this data set, it averages .13 for sales clerks, clerical, service and blue collar workers. This estimate of the coefficient of variation is smaller than the estimates of the coefficient of variation for yearly output derived from analysis of objective ratio scale measures of output. These estimates were .35 for sales clerks, .144 for semi-skilled blue collar workers, .28 in craft jobs, .164 for workers in routine clerical jobs and .278 in clerical jobs with decision making responsibilities (Hunter, Schmidt and Judiesch 1988). This means that the estimates of the effect of training on productivity growth reported in this paper are probably conservative. The fact that the employer is reporting on the past productivity of particular employees may also generate biases in data but it is not clear how estimates of productivity growth rates might be influenced by this problem.

Estimates were also prepared of the short run productivity penalty that results when new workers are hired. This productivity penalty has two elements: the opportunity costs of trainer time and the lower output of the trainee resulting from the worker's lack of familiarity with the job and the time devoted to training. When expressed in terms of the opportunity cost of the time of a worker with two years of tenure at the firm, the new hire penalty during the first three months on the job is equal to:

Productivity Penalty = 1 - NP (4)

$$NP = \frac{RPTP}{520} - \frac{T_C + 1.5 \cdot T_S + T_F}{520}$$ (5)

where

NP = productivity net of training cost of typical new hire

TP = time attempting to produce.

There is some uncertainty about the correct way to aggregate training time and productivity growth effects, so three different estimates of the penalty are presented. The preferred "liberal" estimate of the penalty assumes TP = $520 - T_w - T_F$. This estimate assumes there is no double counting of training costs: ie. that when the employers told us that new employees were 26 percent less productive than workers with 2 years of tenure, they were not factoring into that calculation the fact that about 11 percent of the new hires time was spent in a training activity which produced virtually no output (watching others and formal training). The conservative double counting estimate of training costs assumes that TP = 520. In other words, it is assumed that the lower productivity reported for new workers reflects in part that portion of their time devoted to formal training and watching others do the work. The ultra conservative estimate of the penalty uses the conservative double counting assumptions and also substitutes an average of RP and 1 for RP. This estimate assumes that the reports of productivity growth made by respondent employers exaggerates true productivity growth by a factor of 2.

2. ESTIMATES OF THE MAGNITUDE OF ON-THE-JOB TRAINING IN THE FIRST THREE MONTHS OF A JOB

We will begin by examining how the costs and consequences of initial on-the-job training vary by occupation, industry, establishment size, and the previous relevant job experience, age, and schooling of the employee. Multivariate models of the determinants of the length and intensity of training are presented in section 3 of the paper.

Occupation

The impact of occupation on the amount of on-the-job training typically received by a new employee is examined in Table 1. The first four rows of the table describe how the average number of hours devoted to four distinct training activities during the first 3 months after being hired varies by occupation. Even jobs that are thought to require little skill--service jobs--seem to involved a considerable amount of training during the first 3 months: an average of 33 hours of watching others, 5.7 hours of formal training, 35 hours of informal training by management and 17 hours of training by coworkers. Other occupations devoted considerably more time to training. The distribution of training activities was similar across occupations, however. The typical trainee spent most of his training time watching others do the job or being shown the job by a supervisor. Roughly equal amounts of time were spent in each. Informal training by coworkers is next most important and formal training provided by specialized training personnel accounted for an average of only 5 to 10 percent of the time new hires were engaged in a training activities.

The fifth row of the table summarizes this information into an estimate of investment in training during the first 3 months on the job. The index valued the time that managers, coworkers and the trainee devote to training and expressed it in terms of hours of trainee time. Training investment for service jobs was estimated to be 130 hours implying that the time invested in training a typical newly hired service worker in the first 3 months was equal in value to about 25 percent (130/520) of that worker's potential productivity during that period. Investments in training were considerably greater in other occupations. Retail (and service sector) sales and blue collar jobs had a mean index of 185 to 200 hours respectively or 35 to 38 percent of the new employee's potential productivity. Clerical jobs typically required the equivalent of about 235 hours of training or about 45 percent

TABLE 1
TRAINING AND PRODUCTIVITY GROWTH OF TYPICAL NEW EMPLOYEES BY OCCUPATION

	Professional	Managerial	Sales Not Retail	Retail Sales	Clerical	Blue Collar	Service
Hours Spent in Training in First 3 Months							
Watching others do the job	60.0	65.0	82.8	39.2	50.4	48.1	32.7
Formal training programs	9.1	12.1	23.9	8.2	13.5	9.1	5.7
Informal training by management	76.6	80.4	71.8	48.5	54.6	49.3	35.1
Informal training by co-workers	31.8	23.0	33.9	23.9	26.2	26.8	16.7
Investment in Training Time	293	295	350	185	235	200	130
Weeks to become fully trained if no previous experience	11.1	13.4	9.2	6.5	6.7	9.0	3.4
Increase in Reported Productivity (%)							
Betw. first 2 wks. & next 10 wks.	28%	32%	50%	30%	40%	32%	28%
Betw. first 3 mo. & end of year 2	38%	33%	56%	25%	32%	23%	17%
New Hire Productivity Penalty as a % of Productivity of Wkr. with 2 Yrs. Tenure							
Liberal assumptions	69%	69%	74%	51%	60%	50%	39%
Conservative assumptions	58%	56%	59%	44%	50%	43%	33%
Ultraconservative assumptions	43%	43%	43%	32%	37%	30%	23%
Increase in Real Wage in First 2 Yrs. (%)	5.0%	7.7%	22.6%	9.7%	11.5%	11.5%	3.7%
Number of cases	95	112	76	203	429	649	334

NOTE: Sample is limited to jobs for which all the necessary questions on wage rates, training time, and productivity were answered.

of the new worker's potential output. Professional, managerial and non retail sales workers required the equivalent of about 300 hours of on-the-job training or nearly 60 percent of the new worker's potential output.

The sixth row of the table reports the geometric mean of the answers to the question "How many weeks does it take for a new employee hired for this position to become fully trained and qualified if he or she has no previous experience in this job, but has the necessary school-provided training." Service jobs were reported to require an average of only 3 to 4 weeks of training, retail sales and clerical jobs slightly under 7 weeks, and professional and managerial over 10 weeks.[4]

This training seemed to have the hoped-for result of increasing the productivity of the new employees. The reported productivity of new employees increased quite rapidly (by roughly a third) during the first month or so at the firm (see row 7). Despite the much greater time interval, the percentage increases between the first quarter and the end of the second year (see row 8) were smaller than those during the earlier period for blue collar, service, clerical and sales jobs. For these occupations training investments and learning by doing seem to be large in the first few months on the job but to diminish rapidly thereafter. In the higher level, managerial and professional jobs, reported increases in productivity were larger between the third and 24th month than in the first few months. This reflects the more prolonged training period for these occupations. The occupations which devote the least time to training--the service occupations--were the occupations with the smallest increase in productivity with tenure. The reported productivity of service workers improved an average of 28 percent in the first month or so and a further 17 percent in the next 21 months. Occupations for which a lot of time is devoted to training in the first 3 months--professionals, clerical workers, managers and sale representatives outside of retail and service industries--also seemed to have larger than average increases in reported productivity as the worker gains in tenure. Clerical workers, for instance, were reported to be improving their productivity by 40 percent in the first month or so and by a further 32 percent by the end of the second year on the job.

These very rapid rates of productivity growth suggest that the ratio of the productivity increase to the costs of training (combining both worker and employer benefits and costs) may be extremely high during the first months of employment. For clerical workers the total costs of training during the first 3 months was 235 hours or .113 of a year's output by a worker whose skill level is equal to that of a new employee. Since this figure is an upper bound on the investment that contributed to the 40 percent gain during the first months on the job, the average gross rate of return must have been above 354% per year (.40/.113). Since the intensity of training investment falls with tenure at the firm, the cost of training investment during the next 21 months cannot have exceeded .7875 (1.75*235/520) of a year's productivity by a newly hired worker. This implies that the average gross rate of return to training investments during this 21 month period exceeded 40% per year (.32/.7875). However, marginal gross rates of return to training investment are lower and some of the gain in productivity results from learning by doing not training. Multivariate cross section models of productivity growth which yield evidence on the marginal productivity of training are presented in section 4 of the paper.

One of the consequences of the heavy investments in the training of new hires is that new employees make significantly smaller contributions to the firm's current output than other workers who have been with the firm for a couple of years or more. The time specifically devoted to formal and informal training activities is not the only penalty incurred when a new employee is hired. In most jobs, skills are developed and refined through practice. Learning by doing as it is called may not actually involve spending time away from a directly productive activity. It is costly, nevertheless, for the new worker is less productive than experienced workers. Thus the productivity

---

[4]. If the arithmetic mean were being reported these numbers would be considerably larger. Nevertheless these numbers seem low especially for professional and managerial jobs.

penalty when a new worker is hired has two components: training investments and the lower productivity of the new worker and the time others devote to raising the new worker's productivity.

Estimates of the short run productivity penalty when a new worker is hired are presented in row 9-11 of the table. These numbers provide a rough guide to the magnitude of the adjustment costs associated with expansions carried out by hiring additional workers rather than by scheduling extra hours. The other major component of adjustment costs--recruitment and selection costs--tend to amount to only about 1 percent of a year's output by an experienced worker. The new hire productivity penalty is much larger. During just the first 3 months, it was equivalent in value for service workers to an average of about 1 months output by an experienced worker using conservative assumptions about double counting. For professional, managerial and sales representatives outside the retail and service sector, the penalty averaged about 1.65 months of output by experienced occupants of the job. The large magnitude of these costs helps explain why employers tend to hire new employees only when the increase in demand is perceived to be long lasting.

Establishment Size

The relationship between establishment size and training was curvilinear (see Table 2). The very largest and very smallest (10 or fewer employers) establishments invested the greatest amount of time in training. Managers spent 59 hours training the new employee at the smallest establishments and only 44 hours at establishments with 11 to 50 employees. The very smallest establishment invested 43 percent of a new hire's potential productivity (224 hours) during the first 3 months in training while the next largest size category (11-50 employees) invested only 35 percent of the new hire's time. Those with more than 200 employees invested 48 percent of the new hires time in training. The curvilinearity remains when other determinants of training are controlled. Reflecting the pattern of investment in training, wage increases also exhibited a curvilinear pattern being bigger in the very smallest and very largest establishments.

Reported increases in productivity did not, however, have a curvilinear pattern. Rather there was a consistent tendency for the reported increases in productivity to be larger at the larger establishments. The very smallest establishments reported a 29 percent productivity increase in the first few months and a further 26 percent increase by the end of the second year. The largest establishments reported a 49 percent increase in the first few months and a 34 percent increase during the next 21 months. Such a dramatic contrast between the pattern of training investments (input) and training outcomes is unusual. The relationship between training investment measured in time units (line 5 of Tables 1 - 5) and returns to that investment, the increase in productivity (line 7 or line 8) is described by:

$$\frac{P_{2YR} - P_{1Q}}{P_{1Q}} = \%\Delta P = AGROR_j(\Theta_j)(\text{Total Training Investment}) \tag{6}$$

where

$AGROR_j$ is the average gross rate of return on dollars of investment in the training of stayers at the jth establishment

The lower percentage productivity growth to investment ratio of tiny establishments implies that either they have a lower AR_j or a lower Θ_j. It is unlikely that tiny establishments have lower $AGROR_j$ for they have higher turnover and poorer access to capital markets. The probable explanation of their small $\%\Delta P$ is a lower opportunity cost of time devoted to training (Θ_j). The opportunity cost of managerial, coworker and trainee time devoted to informal training are likely to be lower because small establishments are unable to spread the risk of stocastic

TABLE 2

TRAINING AND PRODUCTIVITY GROWTH OF TYPICAL NEW EMPLOYEE BY ESTABLISHMENT SIZE

	Number of Employees			
	0-10	11-50	51-200	201+
Hours Spent in Training in First 3 Months				
Watching others do the job	48.7	45.4	48.3	55.4
Formal training programs	11.8	7.4	9.2	17.0
Informal training by management	59.1	44.4	52.8	48.0
Informal training by coworkers	23.3	24.3	27.5	32.4
Investment in Training Time	224	1835	213	248
Weeks to become fully trained if no previous experience	8.1	6.4	6.1	8.3
Increase in Reported Productivity (%)				
Betw. first 2 wks. & next 10 wks.	29%	33%	37%	49%
Betw. first 3 mos. & end of year 2	26%	24%	26%	34%
New Hire Productivity Penality as a % of Productivity of Wkr with 2 Yrs. Tenure				
Liberal assumptions	55%	50%	55%	61%
Conservative assumptions	46%	42%	46%	51%
Ultraconservative assumptions	34%	30%	34%	37%
Increase in Real Wage in First 2 Yrs. (%)	12.1	7.3	8.7	9.6
Number of cases	792	678	296	123

NOTE: Sample is limited to jobs for which all the necessary questions on wage rates, training time, and productivity were answered.

demand as well as larger establishments and so must typically operate with a higher ratio of capacity (staff on hand) to demand (staff interacting with a customer or engaged in production). Scheduling of training is also probably more flexible so training can be done during periods of slack work when opportunity costs of trainer and trainee time are low.

Relevant Work Experience

The association between training investments that are typically made in new hires and previous relevant experience of the individual actually hired is presented in Table 3. Jobs which were filled by new hires with less than one year of previous relevant experience, typically involve new hire training investment that was 45 percent of the new hire's potential productivity. For jobs filled by new hires with 10 years of previous relevant experience training investment averaged 29 percent of potential productivity. This occured in the face of a strong tendency for the jobs obtained by those with a great deal of relevant experience to be jobs that require a considerably longer training period (see line 5). Clearly when employers filled jobs that require a great deal of training if workers have no previous experience, they tended to give preference to candidates that because of their previous experience were less costly to train. Note also that jobs filled by new hires with greater previous relevant experience received substantially higher wage rates (see line 10).

The pattern of productivity and wage increase follow the pattern of investment. Those with the least experience started out considerably less productive but their productivity grew from this lower base at a faster rate. Their wage rates start lower but rise faster. The new hires with more than 10 years of previous experience, started out more productive and were paid a higher wage. Their productivity rose but at a slower rate and they received no increase in their real wage.

Age

The association between the training normally given to new hires and the age of the new hire is described in Table 4. The relationship was curvilinear. The 25 to 29 year old age group appears to obtain jobs offering the greatest amount of training to typical new hires--235 hours. Teenagers typically entered jobs requiring about 206 hours and those over forty typically entered jobs requiring the least training--156 hours. Productivity growth and wage increases seem to follow an irregular pattern that was roughly curvilinear with a peak in the 20-24 age group. The average wage of a worker with 2 years of tenure in the firm was curvilinearly related to age with the peak in the 30 to 39 age bracket.

Schooling: Type and Amount

The relationship between type and amount of schooling of the new hire and the on-the-job training typically received by the typical occupant of the job is explored in Table 5.
One would expect schooling to be positively related to the rate at which a new hire can learn new skills. This led to a hypothesis that employers would tend to select the better educated job applicants for jobs that require a great deal of training. When the job being filled requires a great deal of training if the new hire has no experience, we would also expect employers to attempt to reduce training costs by giving preference to the graduates of relevant vocational training programs.

Both of these hypotheses were supported by the data. People with more schooling and with relevant vocational training in school took jobs that have longer training periods for inexperienced workers and that offer more intensive training during the first three months on the job. High school drop outs with no vocational training

TABLE 3
TRAINING AND PRODUCTIVITY GROWTH OF TYPICAL NEW EMPLOYEES BY PREVIOUS RELEVANT EXPERIENCE

Typical New Employees	None	Under 1 Year	1-3 Years	3-5 Years	5-10 Years	More Than 10 Years
Hours Spent in Training in First 3 Months						
Watching others do the job	49.8	53.6	47.0	39.3	43.6	35.4
Formal training programs	11.0	11.2	8.2	11.4	11.1	4.9
Informal training by management	51.7	60.9	47.0	43.9	56.7	41.6
Informal training by coworkers	26.9	27.1	24.1	19.5	21.2	18.7
Investment in Training Time						
Weeks to become fully trained if no previous experience	220	242	185	171	203	149
	6.3	7.0	6.7	9.1	8.6	11.1
Increase in Reported Productivity (%)						
Betwn. first 2 wks. & nest 10 wks.	37%	35%	27%	29%	29%	29%
Betw. first 3 mos. & end of year 2	30%	29%	21%	19%	21%	21%
New Hire Productivity Penality as a % of Productivity of Wkr with 2 Yrs. Tenure						
Liberal assumptions	56%	60%	48%	48%	51%	45%
Conservative assumptions	47%	50%	40%	40%	43%	38%
Ultraconservative assumptions	34%	36%	29%	29%	32%	27%
Wage Rate						
Current wage	$ 4.66	5.05	5.62	6.91	6.42	7.90
Increase in real wage	13.9	10.8	8.2	4.7	4.7	0.0
Number of cases	699	382	404	124	193	96

NOTE: Sample is limited to jobs for which all the necessary questions on wage rates, training time, and productivity were answered.

TABLE 4
TRAINING AND PRODUCTIVITY OF TYPICAL NEW EMPLOYEES BY AGE

Typical New Employees	16-19	20-24	25-29	30-39	40+
Hours Spent in Training in First 3 Months					
Watching others do the job	43.7	52.6	52.0	45.5	38.9
Formal training programs	8.9	7.8	17.2	12.1	2.9
Informal training by management	54.7	52.8	58.4	45.9	43.3
Informal training by coworkers	23.8	29.4	23.1	23.3	20.4
Investment in Training Time	206	220	235	192	156
Weeks to become fully trained if no previous experience	5.6	7.4	7.4	8.2	7.0
Increase in Reported Productivity (%)					
Betwn. first 2 wks. & nest 10 wks.	33%	38%	30%	31%	28%
Betw. first 3 mos. & end of year 2	27%	29%	24%	23%	23%
New Hire Productivity Penality as a % of Productivity of Wkr with 2 Yrs. Tenure					
Liberal assumptions	53%	37%	56%	51%	46%
Conservative assumptions	45%	47%	46%	42%	39%
Ultraconservative assumptions	33%	34%	34%	32%	28%
Wage Rate					
Current wage	$4.12	5.25	5.84	6.20	5.80
Increase in real wage	11.8	12.1	9.3	7.5	3.6
Number of cases	346	582	409	332	229

NOTE: Sample is limited to jobs for which all the necessary questions on wage rates, training time, and productivity were answered.

TABLE 5
TRAINING AND PRODUCTIVITY GROWTH OF TYPICAL NEW EMPLOYEES BY SCHOOLING

	LT 12		12		13-15		16+	
Typical New Employees	Voc Ed	No Voc Ed	Voc Ed	No Voc Ed	Voc Ed	No Voc Ed	Voc Ed	No VocEd
Hours Spent In Training In First 3 Months								
Watching others do the job	30.2	25.6	56.4	45.6	61.3	49.0	84	67.1
Formal training programs	4.5	5.4	17.3	7.3	19.3	15.7	10.7	8.3
Informal training by management	40.0	31.6	53.4	54.0	62.4	51.7	68.7	68.9
Informal training by co-workers	23.8	17.3	31.3	23.5	26.4	23.8	27.1	23.9
Investment in Training Time	158	116	246	199	269	226.5	293	279
Weeks to become fully trained if no previous experience	6.5	4.2	9.7	6.3	11.1	7.3	12.4	11.3
Increase in Reported Productivity (%)								
Betw. first 2 wks. & next 10 wks.	33	24	28	35	34	38	35	37
Betw. first 3 mo. & end of year 2	33	17	28	24	28	30	33	41
New Hire Productivity Penality as a % of Productivity of Wkr with 2 Yrs. Tenure								
Liberal assumptions	51	36	58	52	63	58	68	70
Conservative assumptions	45	31	48	44	51	48	54	58
Ultraconservative assumptions	45	31	48	44	51	48	54	58
Wage Rate								
Current wage	$ 4.20	4.26	5.68	5.16	6.19	5.35	7.65	5.37
Increase in real wage	17.1	9.2	11.3	8.7	10.6	13.6	8.9	7.9
Number of cases	46	154	284	823	134	205	47	105

Note: Sample is limited to jobs for which all the necessary questions on wage rates, training time, and productivity were answered.

typically got jobs in which training investments in the first 3 months are only 22 percent of the new hire's potential productivity. Graduating from high school raised the training that was typical for the job to 38 percent of the new hire's potential productivity. Getting vocational training in high school raised training that was tuypical for the job to 47 percent of potential productivity and vocational education at a 2 year college or technical institute raised it further to 52 percent. College graduates with a liberal arts degree got jobs typically requiring only slightly more training during the first 3 months on the job--54 percent of their potential productivity. College graduates who concentrated on vocational subjects such as engineering or business entered jobs offering the greatest amount of on-the-job training to typical new hires--56 percent of a much higher potential productivity.

Productivity growth with tenure seemed to be greatest in jobs normally filled by workers with many years of schooling. While productivity increases for vocational program graduates with 12 or more years of schooling were respectable, graduates of non-vocational programs generally had slightly higher rates of productivity increase despite their somewhat smaller amounts of training investment. The productivity of vocational program graduates probably grew more slowly because they started from a higher base. Evidence for their starting from a higher base is provided by the higher wage rates they were able to command. Graduates of high school vocational programs entered jobs with 10 percent higher wage rates than high school graduates that did not specialize. For those with 13 to 15 years of schooling the wage premium of the jobs which hired vocational graduates was 16 percent. College graduates with degrees in engineering, business or some other vocational subject received a 41 percent higher wage than liberal arts graduates in this data set.

3. THE DETERMINANTS OF TRAINING

The amount of training that is provided to typical new hires (I_j) is influenced by characteristics of the job and the firm which influence the increase in worker productivity resulting from training investments (X_j), the cost of capital to the firm and the worker (r_j), the rate of obsolescence of skills (δ_j), the separation rate (s_j), the share of training that is effectively specific to the firm ($1-g_j$), and the opportunity cost of training time (Θ_j). Let us assume that the impact of training investment on the hourly productivity of a worker can be represented by the following:

$$P_j = f(X_j)I_j^a \qquad \text{where } 0 < a < 1 \qquad (7)$$

$$\frac{\partial P_j}{\partial I_j} = P'(I_j) = af(X_j)I_j^{a-1} \qquad (8)$$

The present discounted value of future productivity gains from training a worker who works H_j hours per month is a perpetuity that is discounted at a rate reflecting the cost of capital, obsolescence, the firm specificity of the skill and turnover. It can be expressed as:

$$PV(I_j) = H_j * P_j \sum_{t=0}^{\infty} e^{-[r_j+\delta_j+(1-g_j)s_j]t} = \frac{H_j P(I_j)}{r_j+\delta_j+(1-g_j)s_j} \qquad (9)$$

$$\frac{\partial PV_j}{\partial I_j} = \frac{H_j P'(I_j)}{r_j+\delta_j+(1-g_j)s_j} \qquad (10)$$

Since the marginal productivity of training declines as training increases, the level of training investment is determined by the point at which the marginal cost of training investment (Θ_j) is equal to the discounted value of its future marginal products ($\partial PV_j/\partial I_j$).

$$\Theta_j = \frac{H_j P'(I_j)}{r_j+\delta_j+(1-g_j)s_j} = \frac{H_j[af(X_j)I_j^{a-1}]}{r_j+\delta_j+(1-g_j)s_j} \qquad (11)$$

Taking logs and solving for the level of investment, we have:

$$\ln(I_j) = \frac{1}{a-1} [\ln[r_j+\delta_j+(1-g_j)s_j] + \ln(\Theta_j) - \ln(H_j) - \ln(f(X_j)) - \ln(a)] \tag{12}$$

Two different indicators of training investment are analyzed in this multivariate framework. The answer to the question, "How many weeks does it take for a new employee hired for the position to become fully trained and qualified if he or she has no previous experience in this job but has the necessary school-provided training?" is the first indicator studied. It is a measure of the length of the training given new employees. The second is a measure of training intensity--the value of the time devoted to training during the first 3 months of a worker's tenure at a firm. Table 6 presents the results of the regressions predicting the logarithm of the two measures of training investment. Multiplying a coefficient by 100 gives a rough estimate of the percentage impact of a right-hand-side variable.

Both of the measures of training analyzed are indicators of the resource cost of training a particular individual and not of the learning that has occurred as a result of the training. Most of the determinants of training that are available in the data set are indicators of demand for and the payoff to training or are variables that influence both the payoff and costs of training. Factors that raise the payoff to training will increase both the cost of training (input) and the learning (output) that results. When one looks across jobs, theory and previous empirical work predict that on-the-job training is complementary with capital, complementary with the skill level of other workers in the firm, and complementary with previous general and occupationally specific training of new hires. All of these hypotheses are supported. Workers who use expensive machinery typically receive a greater amount of training than other workers. The elasticity of response is .066 for training intensity and .081 for weeks to become fully trained and qualified. The skill level of other workers seems to have a positive effect on training. Evidence of this is the large positive effect that the proportion of the work force in skilled occupations (white-collar or craft) has on training.

Jobs for which previous school-provided vocational training is important in selecting new hires tend to involve much more training on-the-job than jobs for which previous school-provided training is not important. Jobs that are considered to require an extensive general educational background also typically involve longer periods of on-the-job training. These results imply that students who take more years of schooling and who obtain vocational training typically find jobs that offer greater on-the-job training as well. When jobs requiring a great deal of training are filled, employers seem to be particularly interested in hiring applicants with a strong educational background and relevant occupational training.

It is generally thought that very large establishments invest more training because the discounted value of future payoffs to training is higher due to lower turnover (s), lower required rates of return (r) (resulting from better access to capital markets) and lower marginal training costs due to economies of scale (one trainer can teach many workers simultaneously). The results presented in Table 2 suggests the following additional, hypotheses, regarding training investments at establishments with fewer than 10 employees. New hires in very small establishments are hypothesized to spend more time in training than new hires at medium sized establishments for two reasons. First, their employees must be taught a broader range of skills because very small establishments have much more limited scope for division of labor. Secondly, the opportunity costs of informal training time are lower because it can be scheduled during slack periods (e.g., when no customers are in the store) and these periods are more frequent in very small establishments. Multivariate analysis supports the hypothesis that the size of an establishment exerts a non-linear effect on the time that is devoted to training. Large establishments devote more time to training new employees than very small establishments, but they in turn devote more time than medium sized establishments. The establishment size which has the minimum level of training is 25 employees for training

Table 6

THE DETERMINANTS OF THE TRAINING OF THE TYPICAL NEW HIRE

Characteristics	Log Weeks to Become Fully Trained		Log Training Intensity In First 3 Months	
Job Characteristics				
Importance of voacational education	.384***	(3.72)	.522***	(5.58)
Specific vocational preparation	-.020	(.67)	-.009	(.31)
General educational requirements	.176**	(2.53)	.067	(1.37)
Clerical	-.257**	(2.06)	.250**	(2.21)
Sales	.046	(.27)	.645***	(4.26)
Retail Sales	.038	(.21)	-.344**	(2.11)
Professional	-.082	(.43)	.121	(.71)
Managerial	.073	(.39)	.066	(.63)
Service	-.332***	(2.83)	.076	(.71)
Craft	.136	(1.19)	.066	(.63)
Log cost of machine	.081***	(3.87)	.066***	(3.49)
Hours per weeks	.0161***	(3.82)	.018***	(4.58)
Temporary job	-.344***	(3.63)	-.295***	(3.54)
Starting wage	.023	(1.55)	-.035***	(2.64)
Wage at or below legal minimum	-.072	(.85)	-.170**	(2.22)
Employer Characteristics				
Log established employment	-.206**	(2.19)	-.317***	(3.72)
Log employment squared	.0273**	(2.17)	.049***	(4.25)
Log ratio firm/establishment employment	-.016	(.60)	.038	(1.60)
Proportion skilled	.452***	(3.76)	.470***	(4.31)
Proportion craft	.302*	(1.92)	-.127	(.89)
Proportion under 25	-.088	(.70)	.237**	(2.07)
Proportion union	-.155	(1.18)	-.114	(.96)
Sales growth last 2 years	-.858***	(2.70)	-.058	(.20)
Sales growth last 2 years if positive	.962***	(2.70)	.065	(.20)
Employment Growth	-.035	(.17)	-.041	(.22)
Past employment growth if positive	-.306	(.99)	-.270	(.97)
Market Characteristics				
Log alter employers using same skills	-.016	(.79)	-.049***	(2.63)
Log labor market size	.017	(.62)	.042*	(1.70)
Standard error of estimate	1.257		1.14	
R squared	.182		.159	
Number of observations	1659		1659	

intensity and 43 for length of training. Being a part of a multi-establishment firm has no significant impact on training time.

High rates of turnover reduce the payoff to training, so we would expect it to be associated with lower levels of training investment per worker and to do so particularly when training is specific to the firm. Endogeneity prevents our using average rates of turnover as a regressor, but variables measuring exogenous determinants of turnover are available. As predicted, temporary jobs offer significantly less training. Models estimated in this data have found that turnover is higher when there are many other local employers which make use of the same skills being taught in the job. As predicted, such jobs offered less training.

Full-time jobs offer more training. If one assumes that hours worked per week are exogenous (ie. hours effects but is not effected by the amount of training), the elasticity of demand for training with respect to changes in its marginal payoff can be calculated from the coefficient on weekly hours of the job. At the mean number of weekly hours in the sample of jobs, the elasticity estimate is -.7 (significantly below 0 and significantly greater than -1), implying that the demand for training with respect to its rental cost is inelastic. This means that a government subsidy equal to 10 percent of the full marginal opportunity costs of training (or a reduction in turnover or required rates of return which had an equivalent impact on rental cost) would increase time devoted to the training of each new hire by 7 percent. An inelastic demand for training also means that holding the job constant, a decrease in learning efficiency (eg. because the workers hired are slow learners or the firm is not very effective in its training) simultaneously increases the time devoted to training and reduces it's value added. The analysis finds support for this prediction because the employers who reported that it was "difficult to find reliable unskilled workers" and who hired many workers under the age of 25 did indeed spend significantly more time training new hires than other firms.

A number of economists have argued that because the minimum wage prevents workers from agreeing to a low wage rate during training, it discourages on-the-job training of inexperienced and unskilled workers (Hashimoto 1982, Leighton and Mincer 1981). Direct measures of OJT have not been available, however, and the indirect tests of the hypothesis using wage growth outcomes as a proxy for training can not be considered conclusive. The hypothesis implies that holding the skill requirements of a job constant, there is a reversal in the sign of the relationship between wage rates and training at the minimum wage. Above the minimum wage where wage rates are unconstrained, lower wage rates are associated with more training. The negative effect of the minimum wage on the intensity of entry level training should be visible in the jobs whose starting wages are at or below the $3.35 minimum that prevailed in 1983.[5] Many of these jobs will have had to be redesigned to minimize the costs of initial training. This might be accomplished by assigning the individual to a very narrow job and teaching only what is absolutely essential to achieve acceptable performance in that job. Training in other tasks might be postponed and spread over a longer period of time. These hypotheses were tested by including continuous measures of the wage rate and a dummy variable for wage at or below the minimum in the training models. As hypothesized, both of these variables had significant negative effects on training intensity and no significant effects on the length of training. Similar models predicting productivity growth were estimated (without including training investment on the right hand side) and the dummy for minimum wage constraint had a significant negative effect (-10 percent) in the linear specification and a small (-4.7 percent) non-significant negative effect in the logarithmic specification (Bishop 1985 Table 6.2).

---

[5]. Many of the new hires who were paid less than $3.35/hr were hired before the increase in the minimum to $3.35/hr.

4. IMPACT OF TRAINING ON WORKER PRODUCTIVITY

New employees experience dramatic increases in productivity in the first 2 years of employment at a firm. A part of this productivity increase is due to learning by doing and would occur even if no training is provided. Formal and informal training is responsible for a major portion of the productivity growth, however. In this section, an effort will be made to determine which training methods are most effective and to measure the rate of return to training investments.

The 1982 Employer Survey distinguished four different types of employer-provided training: (1) formal training (provided by a training professional), (2) time spent watching others do the job, (3) informal on-the-job training by supervisors, and (4) informal on-the-job training by co-workers. The impact of training on productivity growth of typical new employees was estimated by regressing productivity growth during the first 2 years on the hours spent in each training activity, the duration of training and a vector of control variables. Since diminishing returns are to be expected, the square of the total cost of training was included in the model. Productivity growth during the first 2 years was defined in 2 different ways: the log of the productivity growth ratio and the change in productivity ratings on a 0-100 scale.[6]

The measures of time spent in specific training activities in the first 3 months on the job are measures of training intensity rather than of aggregate training investment during the first 2 years on the job. Consequently, the reported required length of training--the log of the weeks before a new employee becomes fully trained and qualified--was also included in the model. A full set of controls for job, occupation, and firm characteristics was included in each model. With the exception of the wage rate and minimum wage variables, the control variables used were identical to the independent variables used in table 7. The specification used was the following:

$$P_{2YR} - P_{2WK} = \underline{AX} + a_1 lnL + a_2 T_F + a_3 T_S + a_4 T_C + a_5 T_W + a_6 T^2 + u \tag{13}$$

where $\underline{X}$ = a vector of control variables listed in Table 3 ($\underline{A}$ is a vector of coefficients on these control variables)

lnL = logarithm of the required length of training

T_F = Hours devoted to formal training during the first 3 months ('00s).

T_S = Hours spent in informal training by supervisors during the first 3 months ('00s).

T_C = Hours spent in informal training by coworkers during the first 3 months ('00s).

T_W = Hours spent training by watching others do the work during the first 3 months('00s).

T = Training Intensity is a weighted sum of the four different types of training where the weight reflect the assumed costliness of this form of training. $T = 1.8*T_F + 1.5*T_S + T_C + .8*T_W$.

P_{2YR} = Productivity of the typical worker at the end of 2 years. In the linear models P_{2YR} is the productivity rating on the 0 to 100 scale divided by 80, the mean productivity rating for workers with two years of tenure. In the logarithmic models, P_{2YR} is the logarithm of the productivity rating plus 5.

P_{2WK} = Productivity of the typical worker during the first 2 weeks. In the linear models P_{2WK} is the productivity rating on the 0 to 100 scale divided by 80, the mean productivity rating for workers with two years of tenure. In the logarithmic models, P_{2WK} is the logarithm of the productivity rating plus 5.

The results are reported in Table 7. The regression with the logged productivity growth as dependent variable is in column 1. Regressions predicting the linear measure of productivity growth are in columns 2 and

---

[6]. Because a number of employers reported that productivity was zero during the first 2 weeks on the job, 5 was added to all productivity index values before the productivity growth ratio was calculated.

Table 7
Impact of Training on Wage and Productivity Growth

	Productivity Growth			Wage Growth (log)	
	Typical Worker (log 2 Yrs.)	Typical Worker (linear 2 Yrs.)	Particular Individual Linear (1.1 Yrs)	Typical (2 Yrs)	Particular Individual (1.1 Yrs)
Ln Length of Training	.068*** (6.43)	.032*** (6.09)	.025*** (4.36)	.010*** (2.84)	.008** (2.49)
Hrs. of Training in first quarter					
Formal Training (100's)	.133*** (3.06)	.046** (2.14)	.048** (2.10)	.043*** (3.13)	.027** (2.05)
Training by Supervisors (100's)	.130*** (3.85)	.067*** (4.01)	.043** (2.44)	.020* (1.83)	.017 (1.61)
Training by Co-workers (100's)	.145*** (4.92)	.077*** (5.30)	.057*** (3.70)	.001 (.15)	-.002 (.25)
Watching Others (100's)	.149*** (7.37)	.053*** (5.30)	.046*** (4.32)	.017** (2.54)	.016** (2.55)
Training Intensity Squared (10,000's)	-.0085** (2.27)	-.0049** (2.61)	-.0050** (2.53)	-.0011 (.92)	-.0011 (.97)
Standard Error of Estimate	.597	.295	.308	.187	.178
R^2	.171	.129	.135	.198	.233
Number of Observations	2116	2116	2002	1986	1963

* Significant at the 10% level (two-sided)
** Significant at the 5% level (two-sided)
*** Significant at the 1% level (two-sided)

3. In both models, the coefficient on the square term is negative and statistically significant indicating that there are diminishing returns to training intensity. When the square of total training intensity is included in the model, all four of the linear terms for a particular form of training have positive and statistically significant effects on productivity growth. The effect of training intensity on productivity is quite large. An increase in any of the training activities from 0 to 100 hours raises the worker's productivity by 13 to 15 percent in the logarithmic models and by 4 to 7.7 percent (calculated at the mean level of productivity at the end of two years) in the linear models. Clearly when training intensity is low, increases in its intensity will produce large increases in worker productivity.

The total effect of training on productivity growth was calculated by multiplying the six estimated coefficients by mean values of the corresponding variables. The calculated increase in productivity was 22 percent (32 percent of the gain over the first two years) in the logarithmic model and 12 percent of final levels of productivity (28 percent of the gain) in the linear model.

An alternative approach to estimating the impacts of training is to examine the productivity growth of particular new hires. Column 3 of Table 7 presents results using productivity data on a particular new hire rather than a typical new hire. Missing data reduces sample sizes by about 100. The variance of productivity growth across firms is larger when actual individuals are the data rather than typical individuals. R squares of the models are slightly higher, however, because characteristics of the worker and the worker's tenure at the time of the interview are included in the structural model of productivity growth. In order to minimize simultaneity problems, the training variables used in these models were for a typical new hire rather than for that particular new hire. Comparisons of the coefficients in column 3 and 2 reveal that substituting data on productivity growth outcomes of particular individuals for data on typical hires and controlling for personal characteristics does not change the estimated effects of training.

The impacts of each type of training are remarkably similar. This was not anticipated because some forms of training (e.g., formal training) have much higher hourly costs than others (e.g., watching others do the work), and this was expected to result in the more expensive forms of training having larger impacts on productivity than the cheaper forms. Measured in the units of productivity of a worker with 2 years of tenure on the job, the hourly cost of learning by watching others is .8. Formal training with a cost factor of 1.8 is the most expensive because it requires the time of both the trainee and the trainer. The cost of informal training by supervisors (a cost factor of 1.5) and by co-workers (cost factor of 1.0) lies between these two extremes because the trainee is engaged in production and only the time of the supervisor and co-worker must be charged off as a cost of training. If one accepts these estimates of the relative costs of different forms of training, the results imply that informal training by co-workers and training yourself by watching others have a higher rate of return than informal training by supervisors.[7]

---

[7]. Measurement error may bias these coefficients in a way that makes these findings stronger. Our respondent (generally a boss, supervisor, or personnel manager) probably had better knowledge of time spent in formal training and informal training by supervisors than of time spent in other forms of training. This should have resulted in the coefficients on these forms of training having a smaller measurement error bias than the coefficients on informal training by co-workers and time spent watching others. Thus, correcting for measurement error might raise the coefficients on these last two forms of training by more than it raises the coefficients on formal training.

Factors Influencing the Marginal Payoff to Training

Equation 11 implies that the impact of an additional hour of training on productivity growth, $P'(I_j)$, will be higher at companies with high required rates of return (r_j), high separation rates (s_j), high skill obsolescence rates (δ_j), high opportunity costs of training time (Θ_j), and low hours per week (H_j). Since workers reap benefits from training even when there is a separation, training investments should, in theory, be carried further (ie. to a point where marginal benefits are lower) when a job requires general skills rather than specific skills (ie. as g → 1). This suggests that an hour of general training will typically have a smaller effect on productivity growth than an hour of specific training. On the other hand, training that is general must be financed by the worker not the firm. Since young entry level workers are generally liquidity constrained, the rates of return required by workers are likely to be considerably higher than the rates of return required by employers. This has the opposite implication. The inability of workers to finance general training may substantially depress such investment and marginal payoffs to such investment may be very high as a result. The relative importance of these two effects can be tested by interacting training intensity with a measure of the proportion of skills that are general (g).

Another job characteristic that is likely to influence the marginal product of an hour of training is the size of the establishment. Large establishments are likely to have higher opportunity costs of training time (Θ) and to be more efficient trainers (because of economies of scale). This suggests that marginal impacts of training may be higher at large establishments than small establishments. Formal training is considerably more common at large establishments and this suggests that the marginal impact of formal training may be particularly high at these establishments. To examine these issues, the models were respecified so as to allow for three-way interactions between training intensity, generality of training, size, and the share of training that was formal, watching others, and informal OJT by a co-worker. The specification used was the following:

$$P_{2YR} - P_{2WK} = BX + b_1 \ln L + b_2 \ln T + b_3 (\ln T)^2 + b_4 E \ln T + b_5 \underline{S} \ln T + b_6 E \underline{S} \ln T + b_7 g \ln T + u \quad (14)$$

where E = logarithm of (Establishment Employment/18.5)

$\underline{S}$ = a vector of shares of training that are formal, watching others, and informal OJT by co-workers. The excluded category is informal OJT by managers and supervisors.

g = the proportion of the skills learned useful at other firms.

The results of estimating various versions of equation 14 are reported in tables 8 and 9. Table 8 reports the results of models predicting the productivity growth of a particular new hire in which coefficients b_3 and $\underline{b_6}$ have been constrained to be zero. These models provide evidence on the effect of the generality of training and establishment size on the marginal product of training. The coefficient on the interaction between the generality of training and training intensity is positive but very close to zero. The two effects discussed above appear to have canceled each other out. It appears that the difficulties that workers face in financing general training are as severe a barrier to investment in general training as high separation rates are to investments in specific training.

The coefficient on size interacted with training is positive and highly significant in both the logarithmic (column 2) and linear (column 5) model of productivity growth. The logarithmic results imply that the elasticity of productivity with respect to training is 0.092 at establishments with 18.5 employees and about 0.1156 for companies with 200 employees.[8] The positive and significant coefficient on interactions between intensity of

---

[8]. Using a single logarithm of training hours variable to predict the productivity growth ratio, Barron, Black and Loewenstein (1989) obtained an elasticity of .11 (using the same metric as that used in the linear model in Table 9). The major differences between the two analyses are: (a) Barron et. al. predict productivity growth from the first 3 months average to the end of 2nd year while this analysis predicts productivity growth from the first 2 weeks to the end of the 2nd year, and (b) length of training was not controlled by Barron et. al. whereas it is controlled in this analysis. It is this second difference that probably accounts for the somewhat larger elasticities

Table 8
Impact of Training on Wage and Productivity Growth of a Particular New Hire

	Productivity Growth (Log)	Wage Growth (Log)	Productivity Growth (Linear)	Wage Growth (Linear)
$\ln$ Training Weeks	.053*** (4.55)	.0073** (2.19)	.0067* (1.93)	.019*** (3.38)	.0046 (.90)
$\ln$ Training Intensity	.115*** (9.35)	.015*** (4.26)	.0089*** (2.92)	.041*** (5.46)	.0064 (.96)
$\ln$ Tr. Intensity x Size	.0099*** (4.11)		-.0001 (.12)	.0064*** (5.48)	.0007 (.68)
$\ln$ Tr. Intensity x Share General	.0043 (.45)		.0029 (1.08)	.0018 (.40)	.0073* (1.76)
$\ln$ Tr. Intensity x Share Formal	.064*** (3.66)		.014*** (2.86)	.011 (1.24)	.022*** (2.86)
$\ln$ Tr. Intensity x Share Co-Worker	.025 (1.51)		-.001 (.23)	.011 (1.37)	-.004 (.52)
$\ln$ Tr. Intensity x Share Watch	.038*** (2.70)		.007* (1.82)	.009 (1.34)	.017*** (2.71)
Tenure	.083*** (2.58)	.104*** (3.20)	.099*** (10.35)	.098*** (10.15)	.091*** (5.78)	.098*** (6.31)
Tenure Sq.	-.0078* (1.73)	-.0094** (2.11)	-.0024* (1.76)	-.0023* (1.71)	-.0088*** (4.07)	-.0045** (2.15)
Standard Error of Estimate	.628	.622	.178	.178	.303	.269
R Square	.164	.181	.233	.238	.162	.126
Number of Observations	2002	2002	1963	1963	2002	1963

* Significant at the 10% level (two-sided)
** Significant at the 5% level (two-sided)
*** Significant at the 1% level (two-sided)

training and the share that is part of a formal training program or that is watching others do the work implies that these forms of training have significantly larger effects on productivity growth than OJT by supervisors, the excluded training category. Clearly, the earlier conclusion that marginal rates of return to watching others and to co-worker OJT are higher than marginal rates of return to supervisor OJT is pretty robust with respect to substantial changes in specification (alternative ways of defining the independent variable, alternative ways of specifying the training variables and the use of productivity growth of particular new hires rather than a typical new hire as the dependent variable). Findings regarding the payoff to formal training, on the other hand, appear to depend upon specification.

Table 9 presents the results of testing the hypothesis that the size of the establishment differentially effects the rate of return to specific types of training. The models presented in this table included interactions of size with (share times log total training). While the coefficients on these interactions are not significant in the particular worker models, interactions between formal training and size are significant in the typical worker specifications. As hypothesized, the payoff to formal training increases more rapidly with establishment size than the payoffs to other forms of training. These results help explain why formal training programs are more common at large companies than at small companies. In the linear typical worker specification, watching others do the work seems to be a less effective learning technique at large companies than at smaller companies. The coefficients on this variable in other specifications are negative but not significantly different from zero.

Past efforts to assess rates of return to OJT have focused on the wage payoff to worker investments in training (Mincer 1989). This effort is fraught with difficulties, however, because it is very difficult (a) to measure what employees [as opposed to employers] invest in training and (b) to distinguish wage increases caused by training from wage increases caused by selective turnover or the need to discourage shirking by back-loading compensation packages.[9] The total returns to employer and employee investments (both general and firm specific) have not been evaluated because data on productivity effects was lacking. This study has generated tentative estimates of both the opportunity costs and the productivity effects of training (general and specific, worker and firm financed combined). It would appear, therefore, feasible to calculate marginal gross rates of return (for general and specific training combined) necessary to cover the cost of capital, losses due to turnover and obsolescence. The data was not collected for this purpose, however, so there are gaps that can only be filled by some judicious assumptions. Consequently, the estimates of marginal gross rates of return for each form of training that are reported in table 11 must be viewed as very tentative results which will hopefully be displaced shortly when better data sets become available. Because the period for which training intensity is measured is

---

in their analysis. The logarithmic model yields elasticities of the productivity level of .148 with respect to training intensity and .06 with respect to length of training.

[9]. Mincer (1989), for example, attempts to calculate a rate of return to the worker's investment in training by dividing the percentage wage increase by estimates of the cost of training (generally running between .2 and .25 of a years productivity) that are based on the fraction of a years time that worker's report they spend in training. This fraction tells us something about the combined employer and employee costs of training not the costs incurred by the trainee. In fact, in the Lillard and Tan (1986 Table 4.3 and 4.5) earnings regression which Mincer uses to estimate the depreciation rate for training, trainees experienced no earnings reduction during the year in which training was received. Similar results have been obtained in other data sets (Parsons 1985, Bishop and Kang 1988, Barron, Black and Loewenstein 1989). While the positive association between current training and current earnings is probably due to the omission of unobserved worker quality, it strains credibility that the true earnings sacrifice is 20-25 percent of a years wages when multivariate models that include schooling, test scores, actual work experience and a host of other variables indicate a positive effect of current training on current wages. The worker's investment in training is probably much smaller so the wage ROR for worker investments in training is probably much higher than the numbers estimated by Mincer.

Table 9
Impact of Training on Wage and Productivity Growth

	Log Productivity		Productivity Growth Linear		Log Wage Growth	
	Typical Worker (2 Yrs.)	Particular Individual (1.2 Years)	Typical Worker (2 Yrs.)	Particular Individual (1.2 Years)	Typical Worker (2 Yrs.)	Particular Individual (1.1 Years)
Ln Length of Training	.060*** (5.59)	.047*** (3.99)	.027*** (5.16)	.019*** (3.40)	.007** (2.05)	.0065* (1.92)
Ln Training Intensity	-.140*** (2.59)	-.097* (1.66)	.003 (.13)	.038 (1.33)	.022 (1.24)	.0056 (.33)
(Ln Training Intensity) sq.	.0313*** (4.72)	.0236*** (3.28)	.0064* (1.96)	.0004 (.13)	-.0025 (.76)	.0007 (.34)
Interaction of Log Training Intensity with						
Share OJT Formal	.028* (1.72)	.051*** (2.82)	.003 (.33)	.009 (1.00)	.018*** (3.27)	.013** (2.54)
Share OJT by Co-worker	.020 (1.24)	.023 (1.36)	.010 (1.30)	.010 (1.24)	.003 (.66)	.0000 (.01)
Share OJT by Watching Others	.044*** (3.34)	.040*** (2.81)	.013** (1.99)	.009 (1.28)	.007* (1.17)	.0075* (1.84)
Size=ln(Estab. Employment/18.5)	.005 (1.21)	.0066 (1.41)	.005** (2.53)	.0058** (2.52)	.0036** (2.54)	.0003 (.24)
Size*(Share OJT Formal)	.024** (2.33)	.012 (1.11)	.0083* (1.67)	.0068 (1.28)	-.0025 (.76)	.0025 (.79)
Size*(Share OJT by Co-worker)	.016 (1.54)	.014 (1.19)	.0067 (1.32)	.0043 (.78)	-.0116*** (3.44)	-.0031 (.93)
Size*(Share OJT Watching Others)	-.009 (.93)	-.000 (.01)	-.0106** (2.27)	-.003 (.63)	-.0045 (1.46)	-.0004 (.15)
Standard error of estimate	.591	.621	.291	.303	.185	.178
R^2	.189	.186	.156	.165	.211	.238
Number of Observations	2116	2002	2116	2002	1986	1963

* Significant at the 10% level (two-sided)
** Significant at the 5% level (two-sided)
*** Significant at the 1% level (two-sided)

much shorter than the period over which productivity growth is measured, an assumption must be made about the strength of the correlation between training intensity during the first 3 months and training hours during the rest of the 2-year period. When the two year productivity gain of the typical new hire is being analyzed, a unit increase in a training activity during the first 3 months was assumed to be associated with a further 2-unit increase in that training activity during the rest of the 2-year period.[10] When the productivity gain during the first fourteen months for a particular new hire is being analyzed, a unit increase in a training activity during the first 3 months was assumed to be associated with a further 1.2 unit increase in that training activity during the remainder of the first year on the job. Marginal GRORs are the ratio of the increment to yearly productivity generated by a small increase training divided by the cost of increased training (A detailed description is in the notes of Table 10).

The estimated marginal rates of return diminish as the intensity of training increases. The mean training intensity for the first 3 months expressed in units of the time of trained workers is 148 hours. As intensity during the first 3 months rises from 100 hours to 300 hours (double the mean), the marginal rate of return (ROR) for informal OJT by co-workers drops from 43-45 percent to 25-32 percent in the two linear models for typical new hires presented in table 8. The linear model's ROR drops from 38-43 percent to 25 percent for watching others and from 17-23 percent to -1 to 10 percent percent for training by supervisors. The ROR of formal OJT is estimated to drop from 11-15 percent at 100 hours to -3 percent at 300 hours. Estimated rates of return for particular workers are generally slightly higher than those calculated for the typical worker. Estimated rates of return calculated from models based on logarithmic specifications are considerably higher than those based on linear specifications of productivity growth. At the training intensities that typically prevail during the first quarter, marginal rates of return seem to be rather high. Since the impacts of training intensity were calculated while holding the length of training fixed, these GRORs should be viewed as placing lower bounds on the true relationship.

It must be remembered, however, that these marginal GRORs include cash flows necessary to compensate for turnover and obsolescence and are, therefore, not directly comparable to the real rates of return to schooling and financial assets that typically lie in the range from 5 to 10 percent. If all training investments are specific to the firm and must, therefore, be written off if workers leave and turnover is high, GRORs of 30 percent or more may be required to induce the firm to invest in specific training. Lillard and Tan (1986) have estimated that training depreciates at 15 to 20 percent per year. This also would imply that equilibrium in the training market would likely yield marginal GRORs of 30 percent or more. With all the uncertainties regarding the best specification of the productivity growth model, measurement error in the training variables, the specificity of the training, turnover rates, and the obsolescence rates, it is my view that robust estimates of net rates of return to on-the-job training are not now feasible and will not be feasible until better data sets become available.

<u>Results Using Instrumental Variables</u>

The discussion so far has assumed that the causation runs from training to productivity growth. It might be argued that when one is examining relationships for a typical worker that firms hiring workers with very low initial productivity will find it profitable to provide more than average amounts of training. Consequently, when

---

[10]. If training intensity in each of the other seven quarters were identical to the first quarter's training intensity, the cost multiplier would be seven rather than two. The correct multiplier is significantly less than seven because training investments in the later period are not perfectly correlated with training investments in the first quarter and because most employers report the training period to be less than 6 months. Given these facts, the two for one ratio is an assumption that magnifies the cost of the reported differences in training intensity quite dramatically and reduces calculated rates of return by a factor of three.

Table 10
Sensitivity of Marginal Gross Rates of Return Estimates to Specification

	Formal Training		Training by Supervisors		Training by Co-Workers		Watching Others	
	100 hrs	300 hrs	100 hrs	300 hrs	100 hrs	300 hrs	100 hrs	300 hrs
Table 7								
Typical Individual								
Linear	11%	- 3%	23%	10%	45%	32%	38%	25%
Logarithmic	38%	15%	46%	24%	85%	63%	113%	90%
Particular Individual								
Linear	15%	- 3%	17%	- 1%	43%	25%	43%	25%
Table 9								
Typical Individual								
Logarithmic	118%	54%	99%	48%	112%	53%	128%	58%
Linear	43%	16%	41%	16%	48%	18%	50%	18%
Particular Individual								
Logarithmic	156%	68%	109%	52%	130%	59%	146%	64%
Linear	46%	16%	38%	13%	47%	16%	46%	16%

Estimates of the marginal gross rates of return to increases in the intensity of training at two different levels of training intensity: a 100 hour investment during the first quarter of the job and a 300 hour investment during the first quarter on the job. Hourly cost factors are assumed to be 1.8 for formal training, 1.5 for training by supervisors, 1.0 for training by coworkers, and 0.8 for watching others. When productivity growth over 2 years for the typical individual is being modeled, duration adjusted cost factor is calculated by multiplying by the hourly cost factor by 3 for the reasons given in the text. When productivity growth of a particular individual during the first 14 months is modeled, the duration adjusted cost factor is calculated by multiplying the hourly cost factor by 2.2. The results presented in the first panel are calculated by taking the derivative of the estimated regression equations reported in tables 4 with respect to hours of the specified kind of training, then multiplying by 2000, the assumed number of hours worked in a year, and then dividing by the duration adjusted cost factor. As an example of the calculation, the formula for formal OJT using the coefficients from the linear model in table 4 for training intensity (T) equal to 300 hours was as follows:
$[(.00046 - .00000049*T*2*1.8)*2000] / [3*1.8] = -.0256$ and the coworker training formula is:
$[(.00077 - .00000049*T*2)*2000]/[3] = .3173$. {Note that the coefficients must be divided by 100 and 10000 in order to scale them in hours of training}. The GROR estimates presented in the second panel assume that the firm has 18.5 employees (this zeros out the 5th and 7th terms of equation 3) and that all of the training received is of the type indicated. For informal training by supervisors, the formula is:
$(b_2 + b_3*lnT*2)*2000/(T*\text{duration factor})$ which is $[(.003 +.0064*4.605*2)*2000] / (100*3) =.4176$ at T=100 for the linear productivity growth model for typical workers. For training by watching others, the formula is $(b_2 + b_{5w} + b_3*lnT*2)*2000/(T*\text{duration factor})$ which is $[(.003 + .013*S_w +.0064*4.605*2)*2000] / (100*3) =.504$.
Obsolescence of skills and turnover mean that these cash flows do not have an infinite duration and should therefore be compared to the sum of the interest rate, the obsolescence rate and the turnover rate times the proportion of skills that are effectively specific to the firm.

initial productivity is not controlled, there may be simultaneity bias in our models. A second econometric problem that is likely to be effecting the results is errors in measuring training. Measurement error is probably biasing down our estimates of the effect of training on productivity growth. To test for these biases, we estimated the model of productivity growth using instrumented values of training rather than the actual training investments.

The X variables used in estimating the models predicting investment in training in Table 6 were divided into two parts: those that theory predicts directly influence productivity growth and those which influence the cost of training without directly affecting rates of productivity growth conditional on training. The variables in this latter category were the number of alternative employers, dummies for industry, the growth rate of employment, the growth rate of sales, the number of employees at the establishment, the size of firm, the wage rate, a dummy for wage at or below the minimum wage, a dummy for temporary job, dummies for no probationary period, the log of length of the probationary period, dummies for not knowing if there is a probationary period, a measure of the difficulty of firing a worker after the probationary period is ended, a measure of the importance of seniority in determining who is laid off, and characteristics of the local labor market. These variables were used as instruments for the training variables. This involves maintaining the hypothesis that these variables influence the cost of training investments, and therefore, the level and composition of training without influencing the rate at which new employees learn. The X variables assumed to have direct impacts on productivity growth were dummies for occupation, the specific vocational preparation (SVP), and the general educational development (GED) that the Dictionary of Occupational Titles (DOT) specified is necessary for the job, percent of work force skilled, percent of work force who are crafts workers, the importance of vocational education in selection, cost of machinery, unionization, hours worked per week, and characteristics of the hires (i.e., percent under age 25), and an employer response that it is hard to find reliable unskilled workers. When outcomes for particular individuals were being modeled, the new hires' education, sex, and work experience were included in the structural model.

The results from a variety of specifications are reported in Table 11. In most cases, estimating by intrumental variables (IV) rather than OLS has the effect of increasing the magnitude of coefficients but reducing their statistical significance. The IV results also reverse the sign of the coefficient on length of training. The fact that the IV estimations increase rather than reduces the estimated effects of training intensity suggests that measurement error biases are more serious than simultaneity bias and lends support to our general conclusion that marginal rates of return to employer-provided training are very high.

5. IMPACT OF TRAINING ON WAGE GROWTH

The costs and benefits of investments in on-the-job training are shared by employer and employee. This implies that jobs with a great deal of training will tend to have lower starting wage rates than would otherwise be predicted and higher wage rates once the training is completed. In other words, jobs with a heavy training component--either because it requires great skill or because the people being hired for it are completely inexperienced--will have higher rates of wage growth than other jobs. The more general the training the greater will be the share of training costs that is paid by the new employee and the greater will be the resulting rate of wage growth. Since some types of training are more effective than others, some are more general than others and some are more visible to other employers than others, one would expect different types of training to have different effects on wage growth. Are the impacts of different types of training on wage growth similar in pattern to their impacts on productivity growth? Or, is the pattern of wage growth responses to different types of training more influenced by the generality and visibility of the specific type of training?

Table 11

Comparison of OLS & Instrumental Variable Estimates of the Impact of Training

	Training Intensity (100's hrs.)	Training Intensity Squared (10,000's)	Log Weeks of Training	R^2
Productivity Growth (Linear)				
OLS Typical Hire	.112*** (9.3)	-.012*** (6.5)	.026*** (4.9)	.142
2SLS	.333*** (3.1)	-.034* (1.8)	-.058* (1.7)	.076
Particular New Hire (1.2 Years) OLS	.107*** (8.)	-.014*** (6.8)	.017*** (3.2)	.152
2SLS	.423*** (3.6)	-.058*** (2.8)	-.064* (1.7)	.115
Wage Growth (Linear)				
OLS Typical Hire	.028*** (3.5)	-.0023* (1.8)	.0082** (2.3)	.197
2SLS	.147* (1.9)	-.025* (1.9)	.010 (4)	.181
Particular New Hire (1.2 Years) OLS	.022*** (2.8)	-.0019 (1.6)	.0072** (2.1)	.232
2SLS	-.009 (.1)	-.0039	.048** (2.1)	.223

* Significant at the 10% level (two-sided)
** Significant at the 5% level (two-sided)
*** Significant at the 1% level (two-sided)

These issues were addressed by estimating wage growth counterparts to the productivity growth models presented in Tables 7, 8 and 9. The first dependent variable studied was the log of the ratio of the firm's current wage for a worker with 2 years of tenure to the actual starting wage of a person who had recently been hired for the position. Models predicting this variable control for the effects of wage inflation by including the date of hire and it's square in the specification. The results are presented in column 4 of Table 7 and column 5 of Table 9.

The second dependent variable is the log of the ratio of the current wage rate (or most recent wage if there has been a separation) and the starting wage rate for a particular new employee who was hired on average 14 months earlier. The models predicting this variable are presented in column 5 of table 8, column 3 and 4 of Table 8 and column 6 of Table 9. The third dependent variable is the difference in dollars and cents between the current (or most recent) wage rate and the starting wage rate of a particular new hire. These models control tenure of the worker on the date for which wages are reported. The results of predicting this measure of wage growth are reported in column 6 of Table 8. All three models contain controls for the characteristics of the new hire, the occupation, SVP, and GED of the job, percent of craft workers and percent of skilled workers at the firm, the cost of machinery used in the job, unionization, importance of vocational training in selection, percentage of the firm's work force under age 25, and reported difficulty in finding reliable unskilled workers.

The first conclusion that can be drawn from an examination of the wage growth results is that training does have the hypothesized positive effect on wage growth. The effect is statistically significant in almost all of the models. Comparisons of these coefficients with the estimates of the impact of training on productivity growth, however, reveal that training has a much smaller impact on wage growth than it has on productivity growth. In table 8, an increase in informal training from 0 to 100 hours raises productivity of typical employees by 13 to 15 percent in the logarithmic model and 5.3 to 7.7 percent in the linear model, but raises wage rates by only .1 to 2.0 percent. A doubling of the length of training raises productivity by 2.2 to 4.8 percent, but wage rates rise only 0.7 percent.[11]

In Table 8's logarithmic models for a particular individual, doubling the length of training increases productivity growth by 3.6 percent and increases wage growth by only .5 percent. Doubling the intensity of training, increases productivity growth by 8 percent but raises wage growth by only 1.1 percent. Productivity growth effects of training are also considerably greater than the wage growth effects in the linear models reported in column 5 and 6.

For findings such as these, the first explanation that comes to mind is that the training is specific and the firm is paying most of its costs and reaping most of its benefits. Since skills are thought to be more specific at large companies, the fact that the gap between the productivity and wage effects of training is largest at big establishments provides further support for the skill specificity explanation. The problem with this explanation, however, is that when employers were asked whether the skills learned on their jobs were specific to the firm, most reported to the contrary that the skills were useful at other firms. Furthermore, the generality of skills taught has only very modest effects on the magnitude of the wage response to training. When training is done by managers and the skills are reported to be entirely general, doubling training intensity raises productivity by 6.7 percent but wages by only .8 percent in the logarithmic model reported in columns 2 and 4 of Table 8. In the linear model in column 5 and 6 of Table 8, doubling training raises productivity by 3 percent while increasing wage growth by only .96 percent. Analysis of data on the typical new hire produces very similar findings. These

---

[11]. As with productivity growth, estimation using instrumental variables increases the size of coefficients (probably because of the correction for measurement error in training) but decreases their statistical significance. In the IV models wage effects of training are much larger than the productivity effects.

results appear to contradict an important prediction of Becker's theory--when training is general, its impact on wage growth should equal or exceed its impact on productivity growth. Even though employers claim the skills they are teaching are general, the labor market is not treating these skills as if they were general. How can these puzzling results be explained?

One explanation of the phenomenon is that different firms require different mixes of general skills. The firm that does the training concentrates on those skills it needs the most, some of which may not be as highly valued by alternative employers. Skills that would be highly valued by an alternative employer may not be taught because others on the staff already fulfill that function. As a result, the package of general skills that workers develop are always more valuable at the training firm than at other firms even when each individual skill is correctly perceived to be useful elsewhere.

A second reason why the market behaves as if general skills are effectively specific to the firm is that other employers will generally be ignorant of the exact character of a new hire's general skills and, consequently, will often not assign the worker to a job that puts the skills to work. Even when a worker's next job makes use of the general skills learned, there is no guarantee that new hires with better than average skills will be offered comparably higher entry wages. These phenomena have the effect of transforming some skills which are technically general into skills which are effectively specific to the firm. To the extent training is effectively specific, wages will rise more slowly than productivity net of training cost (Bishop and Kang 1984, 1988).

Support for this signaling/visibility explanation of the gap between productivity and wage rate effects of training comes from comparing the gaps for specific types of training. In table 8, all forms of training had roughly equal effects on productivity growth. For wage growth, however, formal training has much larger effects than other forms of training and OJT by co-workers has no effect. Apparently, formal training is less specific to the job and more visible to the employee and other employers, and thus workers are more willing to contribute to its costs. The importance of OJT provided by co-workers is apparently underestimated by all concerned, the employee, the supervisor, and other employers.

The third reason why general training masquerades as specific training is the inability/unwillingness of most young workers (the ones who have the greatest need for general training) to finance large amounts of general on-the-job training. Most of these workers are liquidity constrained--that is they are unable to shift as much consumption from the future into the present as they would like because they have neither assets which can be depleted nor access to credit at reasonable terms.[12] Half of households headed by someone under the age of 25 have less than $746 in financial assets and 19 percent have no financial assets at all. Half of households headed by someone between 25 and 34 have less than $1514 in financial assets and 13 percent have none (Survey of Consumer Finances 1984). Subsidized or guaranteed student loans are not available to finance on-the-job training and banks will not lend money for this purpose without collateral. Borrowing against the equity in one's home is a possibility for some but only 34 percent of households with heads under the age of 35 own a home and many of the houses have been owned for only a short while, so the equity that can be borrowed against is small. Even with collateral, the loans available to individuals usually carry higher interest rates than those charged businesses. Studies of the willingness of consumers to substitute consumption over time have all concluded that the intertemporal elasticity of substitution is no higher than one and most studies conclude it is .5 or below (Friend

---

[12]. Becker clearly recognized the existence of liquidity constraints in his 1962 paper. "Since employer specific skills are part of the intangible assets or good will of firms and can be offered as collateral along with tangible assets, capital would be more readily available for specific than for general investments (p.42)." He did not, however, explicitly analyze how such constraints might effect the predictions of his model.

and Blume 1975; Hall 1988; Hubbard and Judd 1986). A substitution elasticity of .5 implies that reducing a liquidity constrained worker's wage by one half (in order to pay for general training) roughly quadruples the worker's marginal utility of consumption. Such a worker would be willing to give up four dollars of future income in return for one dollar of current income. The liquidity constraint phenomenon has little effect on the wage profile of jobs requiring no general training and which, therefore, have a flat productivity profile. Where significant general training is occurring, however, it comes into play and may result in an employment contract in which the employer shares the costs of general training (Glick and Feuer 1984; Feuer, Glick and Desai 1987).

6. IMPACT OF TRAINING ON TURNOVER

One would expect more productive workers to be more likely to be promoted and less likely to be separated involuntarily. Consequently, the amount and nature of training that is typical at a firm should influence turnover. To test this hypothesis, models were estimated predicting the actual tenure, probability of a dismissal, probability of a quit and probability of a promotion of particular new hires. Controls were included for the log of potential tenure and its square, background characteristics of the individual worker, and characteristics of the job, the firm and the local labor market.

The training variables were specified so as to allow a test of three hypotheses. The first hypothesis was that a policy of providing greater amounts of training lowers turnover and increases the propensity to promote new hires. The second hypotheses was that this effect would be strongest at the larger firms where training has larger effects on productivity. The third hypotheses is that because formal training is more visible to the firm providing the training, the employee, and other employers, it tends to raise the quit rate, reduce the dismissal rate, and raise the promotion rate more than other forms of training.

The results are presented in Table 12. Establishment size was scaled as a ratio to its geometric mean of 18.5 before being logged and interacted with training intensity. Consequently, the coefficient on training intensity estimates the magnitude of the training intensity's impact on turnover for establishments with about 19 workers. Surprisingly, there is no statistically significant effects of either the length or intensity of training on expected tenure or rates of dismissal or quitting at the small establishments that predominate in the sample. There is a statistically significant interaction between establishment size and training intensity, however. At larger companies, a higher training intensity for typical workers is associated with longer tenure. At small companies, the reverse association exists. Effects are very small, however. A doubling of training investment raises expected tenure by only 1.3 percent at a company with 200 employees and lowers expected tenure by only 1.7 percent at a company with 2 employees. In these results, we have still another reason why large companies typically make greater investments in training than small companies.

The hypotheses that formal training would have larger effects on turnover than other forms of training is supported by the data. For quit rates, there is a statistically significant difference between the impact of formal and informal types of training. Point estimates imply that informal training reduces the quit rate and that formal training increases the quit rate. This lends support to our hypotheses that formal training is both more useful at other firms and more visible to other employers and that informal training is either in skills specific to the firm or invisible to other employers.

The training provided to typical new hires has a much more significant impact on promotions than it has on turnover. At a company with 19 employees doubling the amount of training raises promotion propensities by 3 percentage points. There is a significant interaction with establishment size. If the establishment has 200 employees, doubling training intensity raises promotion propensities by 4.6 percentage points.

Table 12

IMPACT OF TRAINING ON TURNOVER AND PROMOTIONS

Training	Log Tenure	Involuntary Separation	Quit	Promotion
Log Length of Training	.011 (1.1)	.004 (.6)	-.007 (1.0)	.004 (.4)
Log Intensity of Training	-.002 (.1)	.004 (.6)	-.006 (.7)	.040*** (3.8)
Interaction of Training Intensity With:				
Establishment size	.009* (1.8)	-.004 (1.3)	-.005 (1.2)	.010** (2.1)
Share formal training	.014 (1.1)	-.011 (1.3)	.017* (1.8)	-.001 (.1)
Share OJT by co-worker	.004 (.3)	-.006 (.8)	.004 (.4)	-.015 (1.2)
Share watching others	-.007 (.6)	.009 (1.3)	-.005 (.6)	-.010 (.9)
R Squared	.658	.050	.049	.108

* Significant at the 10% level (two-sided)
** Significant at the 5% level (two-sided)
*** Significant at the 1% level (two-sided)

7. IMPLICATIONS OF EMPIRICAL FINDINGS FOR THE HYPOTHESIS THAT AMERICANS UNDER-INVEST IN ON-THE-JOB TRAINING

The major findings derived from the analysis of the data on new hire training may be summarized as follows:

* Training investments in new hires are substantial even for jobs that are generally considered unskilled.

* Formal training provided by specialized training personnel accounts for only a small portion of the training received by new hires.

* Productivity rises substantially during the first year on the job.

* To fill jobs requiring a great deal of on-the-job training, employers prefer applicants who have previous relevant work experience, who are well educated and who have vocational training in a relevant field.

* Large establishments invest more in the training of their new hires than small and medium sized establishments because (1) they have lower turnover, (2) they have better access to capital markets, (3) the marginal product of an hour of training time is higher at large establishments and (4) training lowers turnover more substantially at large establishments.
* The elasticity of demand for training is below unity.

* When it is a binding constraint, the minimum wage lowers training investment by roughly 17 percent during the first 3 months on the job and productivity growth by 5 to 10 percent.

* Informal training by coworkers and training by watching others do the job appear to have a higher benefit cost ratio than informal training by management.

* Estimates of rates of return to training derived from this data should be treated with a great deal of caution. Nevertheless, *marginal rates of return to training appear to be quite high.*

* The estimated benefit cost ratio for formal training depends on how the model is specified. The productivity growth effects of formal training are bigger at large establishments. Formal training has significantly larger effects on wage growth than informal training. Formal rather than informal training significantly increases the worker's propensity to quit. *Formal training's tendency to have larger effects on wage growth and quit rates than informal training probably results from the fact that formal training is better signaled to the labor market.*

* The reported generality of training has no significant effects on its marginal productivity or on the effects of training on turnover.

* When training is reported to be highly general, training has a larger effect on wage growth than when training is reported to be specific. Nevertheless, *training that is reported to be entirely general has much larger effects on productivity growth than wage growth implying that the labor market treats this training as if it were at least partly specific to the firm.*

These results provide support for the view that workers do not pay the full costs of general training and do not receive wage increases equal to the full productivity effects of general training. They also lend support to our hypothesis that the outcomes of training, particularly informal training, are poorly signaled to the labor market. Because other employers are unaware of its exact character and unable to assess its quality prior to making hiring decisions, training that is technically general often becomes effectively specific to the firm and employers choose to share the costs and benefits of investments in general training [see Bishop and Kang (1984, 1988) for a formal proof of this statement]. The second hypothesized reason why shared financing of general training may be in the joint interest of employees and employers is the fact that young workers are typically liquidity constrained while employers are not.

If these conclusions are true, turnover becomes a more important determinant of training investments than previously thought. In the standard model, turnover propensities influence the amount of specific training supplied but not the amount of general training undertaken. However, if employers finance some of the costs of general training (or general and specific training are joint products of the same training activity), worker's with high turnover propensities are likely to find it hard to obtain jobs that offer general as well as specific training. For those with less than one year of tenure, the probability of staying at the firm for at least 12 additional months is over 80 percent in the United Kingdom, 76 percent in Japan but only 41 percent in the US (OECD, 1984, Table 33 and 34). The high rates of turnover in America, then, help explain why investments in both specific and general on-the-job training of new hires are lower in this country than in Japan and Germany.

One important reason why turnover is so high in the US youth labor market is job shopping and tryout hiring. When the match is first arranged, both the employer and the job seeker are poorly informed about each other, so they spend the first months learning about each other and, if they do not like what they discover, they terminate the relationship. If they knew more about each other going into the match, there would be fewer surprises, fewer quits and fewer dismissals. There are good reasons why try out hiring is so prevalent in the US. There are major institutional barriers to the free flow of information about job applicants--such as EEO testing guidelines, the failure of high schools to send out transcripts and the threat of law suits if bad recommendations are given--that do not exist in other countries. German and Japanese employers are much more careful in their selection of blue collar and clerical employees than American employers (Rosenbaum and Kariya 1987; Koenig 1987).

A second reason why turnover is higher in the US is that there are fewer legal and contractual obstacles to layoffs in the US (Sengenberger 1985; Flanagan 1986).[13] Thirdly, turnover appears to be less costly for young American workers than for young German and young Japanese workers. It has already been noted that specific training is more extensive in Japan, and the loss of these investments is a disincentive to turnover. Transition costs also discourage turnover (Bishop and Kang 1988) and there is reason to believe that there may be differences across countries in the magnitude of these transition costs. In some countries, quitting or being laid off does serious damage to the worker's reputation and the likelihood of finding another good job. The best Japanese employers hire straight out of high school and are said to discriminate against those with work experience. The reverse prevails in the US. Quitting appears to be much less stigmatizing in the US than in Japan particularly for young workers.

In Germany, the apprenticeships have a three month probationary period during which either party may opt out of the contract without serious consequences. Nevertheless, only 5 percent of apprentices change employers during this period. An apprentice who quits his apprenticeship after the probationary period will find it very difficult to get another one. As a result, about 95 percent of those who finish the first 3 months of their apprenticeship stick with it for the full three years and pass the performance exam that comes at the end. While, apprentices are not subject to layoff when there is slack work, journeymen are. Who is laid off is often based on job performance not seniority, so being laid off is more stigmatizing than it is in the US. To protect themselves from this stigma, German workers bargain for employment contracts which reduce the probability of layoffs by front loading compensation and mandating severance pay.

---

[13]. Flanagan argues that the increasing number of wrongful discharge cases being won by plaintiffs with large jury awards has significantly raised the risks and costs of dismissing workers in the US. This may be the case for senior employees but such cases are seldom brought when the dismissal comes in the first two years of employment. Rates of turnover of workers with more than 5 years of tenure do not appear to be appreciably higher in the US than in Europe (OECD 1984)

The result is lower turnover, a higher payoff to employer investments in specific and general training, greater training investment and, as a result, strong productivity growth. Mincer and Higuchi (1988) correctly point out that causation also runs in the opposite direction--high rates of investment and technological progress increase the returns to training and raise the disincentives for turnover.

An examination of equations 11 and 12 suggest a number of additional reasons for the relatively low level of on-the-job training investment in the United States. The most obvious explanation of the heavier investment in training by Japanese corporations is the very low costs of capital they face. The fact that Japanese companies operating in the US spend more on training than American companies in the same industry provides further support for this hypothesis (Mincer and Higuchi 1988). A second possible explanation is that Japanese and German workers are better educated and consequently faster learners (ie. P'(I) is higher in Japan). A third explanation is the minimum wage which prevents unskilled American workers from offering to pay for general training by accepting a sub-minimum wage during the training period.

A fourth reason for the contrast is the lack of a strong apprenticeship system in the US. The standardized curriculums and the proficiency exam at the end of the apprenticeship mean that the quality and nature of the training is well signaled to employers in Germany, Switzerland and Austria. The result is that the worker can count on benefiting from doing a good job in their apprenticeship even if the training employer does not keep them on. Since the future payoff is certain, German apprentices are willing to start out at a wage that is only about one-quarter of the wage they will be able to command at the end of the apprenticeship. If the apprentices were adults, they could not afford to accept so low a wage. They are, however, teenagers who because they live at home are heavily subsidized by their parents. Consequently, the liquidity constraint that is such a barrier to heavy investments in general training in the US is much less of a problem in Germany.

BIBLIOGRAPHY

Becker, Gary. "Investment in Human Capital: A Theoretical Analysis." Journal of Political Economy, Vol. 70, No. 5 pt.2, October 1962, 9-50.

Bishop, John. "Job Performance, Turnover and Wage Growth." Journal of Labor Economics, Vol. 8, No. 3, September 1990, pp. 363-386.

Bishop, John and Kang, Suk. "On-the-Job Training/ Sorting: Theory and Evidence" National Center for Research in Vocational Education, Ohio State University, 1984.

Bishop, John and Kang, Suk. "A Signaling/Bonding Model of Employer Finance of General Training." Center for Advanced Human Resource Studies, Cornell University, Ithaca, New York, 1988.

Bishop, John; Hollenbeck, Kevin; Kang, Suk and Willke, Richard. Training and Human Capital Formation. Columbus: The National Center for Research in Vocational Education, The Ohio State University, 1985.

Feuer, M., Glick, H., and Desai, A. "Is Firm-Sponsored Education Viable?" Journal of Economic Behavior and Organization, March 1987, Vol. 8, No. 1.

Flanagan, Robert. "Labor Market Behavior and European Economic Growth." paper prepared for conference on Impediments to European Economic Growth, The Brookings Institution, 1986

Friend, Irwin and Blume, Marshal. "The Demand for Risky Assets." American Economic Review, Vol 65, December 1975, pp. 900-922.

Garen, John. "Empirical Studies of the Job Matching Hypothesis," in Ron Ehrenberg ed., Research in Labor Economics, Vol. 9, Greenwich, Conn.: JAI Press, 1988.

Glick, Henry A. and Feuer, Michael J. "Employer-Sponsored Training and the Governance of Specific Human Capital Investments." Quarterly Review of Economics and Business, Vol. 24, No. 2, Summer 1984.

Hall, Robert. "Intertemporal Substitution in Consumption." Journal of Political Economy, Vol. 96, No. 2, April 1988, pp. 339-357.

Hashimoto, M. "Firm-Specific Human Capital as a Shared-Investment." American Economic Review, 71, no. 3, March 1981, pp. 475-482.

Hashimoto, M. "Minimum Wage Effects on Training on the Job." American Economic Review, Vol 72, No. 5, December 1982, pp. 1070-1087.

Hollenbeck, K., and Smith B. The Influence of Applicants' Education and Skills on Employability Assessments by Employers. Columbus: The National Center for Research in Vocational Education, The Ohio State University, 1984.

Hollenbeck, Kevin and Wilkie, Richard. "The Nature and Impact of Training: Evidence From The Current Population Survey." In Training and Human Capital Formation, edited by John Bishop et al., The National Center for Research in Vocational Education, The Ohio State University, July 1985.

Hubbard, R. Glenn and Judd, Kenneth L. "Liquidity Constraints, Fiscal Policy and Consumption." Brookings Papers on Economic Activity, 1986, # 1, pp. 1-60.

Hunter, John E.; Schmidt, Frank L. and Judiesch, Michael K. Individual Differences in Output as a Function of Job Complexity, Michigan State University and Department of Industrial Relations and Human Resources University of Iowa, June, 1988.

Jaikumar, Ramchandran. "Postindustrial Manufacturing." Harvard Business Review, November-December, 1986, pp. 69-76.

Koenig, Richard. "Toyota takes Pains and Time, Filling Jobs at its Kentucky Plant." Wall Street Journal, December 1 1987, p. 1.

Koike, Kazuo. "Skill Formation Systems in the U.S. and Japan: A Comparative Study." The Economic Analysis of the Japanese Firm, edited by M. Aoki, New York: Elsevier Science Publishers B. V., 1984, pp. 47-75.

Kosai, Yutaka. "Japan's Economic System--Will It Change?" seminar presentation, Department of East Asian Studies, Cornell University, April 26, 1989.

Krafcik, John F. Training and the Automobile Industry: International Comparisons. Contractor Report prepared for the Office of Technology Assessment under contract N3-1910, Feb. 1990.

Leighton, Linda and Mincer, Jacob. "Effects of Minimum Wages on Human Capital Formation." in The Economics of Legal Minimum Wages, edited by Simon Rottenberg, Washington DC: American Enterprise Insitiute, 1981.

Limbrecht, Joseph H. and Hayes, Robert H. "Germany's World- Class Manufacturers." Harvard Business Review, November-December, 1982, pp. 137-145.

Mincer, Jacob and Higuchi, Yoshio. "Wage Structures and Labor Turnover in the U.S. and Japan." The Journal of the International and Japanese Economy, Kyoto and Stanford, 1988.

Noll I., Beicht U., Boll G., Malcher W. and Wiederhold-Fritz S. Nettakosten der Betrieblichen Ber Ufsbildung Schriften Berufsbildungsforschung, Band 63. Beuth Verlag GMBH, Berlin, 1984.

Organization of Economic Cooperation and Development. Employment Outlook. Paris: OECD, September, 1984, Chapter 4.

Parsons, Donald. "Wage Determination in the Post Training Period." Pathways to the Future, Vol. 7, Chapter 7, Center for Human Resource Research, Ohio State University, 1985.

Salop, Joanne and Salop, Steven. "Self Selection and Turnover in the Labor Market." Quarterly Journal of Economics, Vol. 91, November 1976, p. 619-627.

Sengenberger, Werner. "Job Security--Germany." unpublished paper, OECD, 1985.

"Survey of Consumer Finances, 1983." Federal Reserve Bulletin. Vol 70, September 1984, p. 686 and December 1984, p. 863.

Weiderhold-Fritz, Susanne. "Is There a Relationship between Cost of In Company Vocational Training and the Offer of Training Places in the Federal Republic of Germany." Social Forces: Supplement on Youth Pay and Employers' Recruitment Practices for Young People in the Community, Commission of the European Communities, Directorate-Generale for Employment, Social Affairs and Education, 1985.

EMPLOYEE TRAINING PROGRAMS IN U.S. BUSINESSES

Ann P. Bartel
Columbia University Graduate School of Business
New York, NY 10027

I. Introduction

According to a recent issue of Training Magazine, U.S. organizations with fifty or more employees spent $32 billion on formal programs for employee training and development. Although human resource managers argue that training is critical for developing a productive workforce, very little is known about how companies make decisions about budgets for formal training and whether such training increases measured labor productivity. Previous research by labor economists on employee training has focused on the impact of training on the individual's success in the labor market, i.e. how training raises the individual's wage and reduces the probability of a layoff. Economists have also studied why employers are more likely to train certain individuals than others, and, in particular, have shown that individuals who are expected to stay with the firm are more likely to be the recipients of training. Hence, economic research on training has been concerned with the impact of investments in training on the distribution of earnings. Likewise, research on training by industrial and organizational psychologists has been conducted at the individual level, focusing on the impact of training on the employee's cognitive skills, work effort, and morale.

This article is unusual in that it focuses on the organization as the unit of observation. Although economic models of training decisions are framed in terms of a company's calculation of the costs and benefits of such training, empirical work has seldom been able to test this model directly on company behavior. With a few exceptions (Bishop, 1991; and Stern and Benson, 1991), researchers have been forced to make inferences about company behavior based on data on the careers of individuals. By utilizing a new data base on human resource practices in U.S. businesses, I am able to describe the variation in the training effort across companies. A simple economic model is then used to derive several testable hypotheses about the determinants of the variation in employee training across businesses. The role of firm characteristics, such as technological change and firm size, as well as characteristics of the company's industry, such as the extent of competition in the product market, are studied. The impact of formal training programs on labor productivity is also analyzed.

In the next section of the paper, the literature on employee training is summarized in order to show the types of data that have been available to researchers who have previously studied the topic of employee training. In Part III, I describe the survey I am using and discuss its strengths and weaknesses relative to other databases that have been used for the study of employee training. A description of the amount of training undertaken by the businesses in the survey is included in this part. Part IV specifies a simple model that is tested with the survey data. In Part V, the impact of training on labor productivity is measured. Conclusions are provided in Part VI.

II. Literature Review

In this section of the paper, I summarize the literature that exists on the subject of employee training and development. In preparing this summary, I have reviewed work by economists and industrial psychologists as well as the results of previous surveys of corporate training programs.

A. Economists

Economists who study on-the-job training have primarily been interested in modelling who receives training and how it affects the individual's growth in earnings over his working life. Examples of this literature are the studies by Mincer (1983, 1987), Brown (1983), Lillard and Tan (1986), Pergamit and Shack-Marquez (1986), Barron et al. (1987, 1988) and Lynch (1988). These studies use data from national surveys such as the Panel Study of Income Dynamics, the National Longitudinal Surveys, the Current Population Survey and the Employment Opportunities Pilot Project. Information on training from the first three data sets is obtained directly from the individuals who are surveyed. For example, in the Panel Study of Income Dynamics, which was used by Mincer and Brown, individuals are asked "On a job like yours, how long would it take the average person to become fully qualified?" and "Are you learning skills on the current job which could lead to a better job or promotion?" The National Longitudinal Surveys, which were used by Mincer, Lillard and Tan, and Lynch, contain a variety of training questions depending on the particular cohort that was surveyed. For example, in the older NLS cohorts, the training questions are "Do you receive or use additional training (other than schooling training) on your job?" and "What was the longest type of training you have had since the last interview?" The NLS youth cohort, however, contains information on all training spells in the respondents' working life and it is possible to separate company training from apprenticeship training. The individuals in this survey were first interviewed in 1978 when they were between the ages of 14 and 21 and have been resurveyed every year or two since that time. The January 1983 Current Population Survey, used by Lillard and Tan and Pergamit and Shack-Marquez, contains the following questions on training: "What training was needed to get the current or last job?" and "What training is needed to improve skills on the current job?" Finally, the 1980 Employment Opportunities Pilot Project Dataset, used by Barron et al., is unusual in that it surveys employers. The employers were asked to provide information on the amount of on-the-job training provided their most recently hired worker, as measured by the number of hours typically spent by various personnel in training such an individual.

The main findings of this research can be summarized briefly. Individuals who receive training are likely to be young, white males. Most studies also find that the more educated individuals receive more training than the less educated. Private sector training is found to play a significant role in the wage determination and career patterns of young workers; individuals with more training have significantly larger wage growth and longer job tenure. The data from the EOPP Survey also show that individuals who received more training in their first three months of employment have significantly faster productivity growth during their first two years with the employer.

B. Industrial Psychologists

Industrial psychologists have studied the effects of employee training utilizing experimental methods and case studies. They have measured the effectiveness of training in one of four ways: (1) subjective learning (judgments of course participants or trainers); (2) objective learning (results on standardized tests); (3) subjective behavior (changes in on-the-job behavior, as perceived by course participants, peers or supervisors); and, least commonly of all, (4) objective results (tangible indicators such as reduced costs, improved quality or quantity of output). An excellent survey of studies conducted by industrial psychologists on the subject of managerial training is provided in Burke and Day (1986). They review seventy articles that evaluated the effectiveness of training programs for managerial or supervisory personnel in various companies. In all of these studies, the individual is the unit of observation and individuals who received training are compared to those who were not in the training program. The comparisons are made on the basis of scores on skill or knowledge tests, performance rankings, ratings during role play, and survey ratings by subordinates. Only a handful of these studies evaluated training programs in terms of objective <u>results</u>. The best example of the latter type of study is the one conducted by James S. Russell et al (1985) in which 62 retail stores belonging to the same international merchandising organization were the units of observation. Russell *et al* found that sales volume per employee was positively and significantly correlated with the percentage of sales personnel who received training in basic sales procedures and with the sales personnel's perceptions of the emphasis given training in the store.

The main problem with these studies is that each one is limited to a relatively small group of individuals (normally between 50 and 100) in one company so that it is difficult to generalize the findings beyond the company under study. Although the Russell article examines 62 companies, they are in the same industry and belong to the same organization. In her critique of the psychological research, Ingols (1987) accuses the researchers of minimal crossreferencing; "they do not look for common themes across companies, but focus on the specific case at hand." She concludes that this line of research has left us with a limited and fragmented knowledge about the role of training in corporations.

C. Surveys of Corporate Training Programs

Information on investments in employee training can also be obtained from surveys that are conducted by various organizations. For example, each year, Lakewood Research, a division of Lakewood Publications, the publisher of

Training Magazine, conducts a survey of U.S. organizations with 50 or more employees. Respondents are asked for information on the amount their organization budgets for formal training, the number of individuals who receive training during the year, and the number of hours of training they receive. The information from approximately 2400 respondents is extrapolated by Lakewood Research to a universe of 230,000 organizations and reported in aggregate figures only. For example, the results of the 1987 survey, published in May 1988, indicate that $32 billion was budgeted for formal training that year with 38.8 million workers scheduled to receive 1.2 billion hours of training. The survey also described the types of training (e.g. management skills, technical skills, clerical skills, sales skills, etc.) provided by the respondent companies and showed how these differ across industries and size of firm.

A second example of a corporate survey is the study prepared by The Conference Board in 1975 (Lusterman, 1977). They surveyed 2800 companies that had at least 500 employees and received usable responses form 610 firms. These data were then extrapolated to the universe of 7600 firms. Information on per employee expenditures for formal in-house training, tuition aid and other outside training was obtained. The main findings of this study were that the companies spent an average of $60 per employee on the three types of training, $48 of which was spent on formal in-house training; large companies spent more per employee than small companies; and the share of the training budget attributed to formal in-house training rose from 47% for the firms in the smallest size category to 87% for the firms in the largest size category. Converting the 1975 expenditures to 1987 dollars would produce an expenditure of $93 per employee on formal in-house training.

In 1985, The Conference Board surveyed 218 companies to obtain information on changes in corporate education and training that had occurred in the previous five years (Lusterman, 1985). While this new report did not contain any cost information, it discussed how the training function had increased in importance at the surveyed companies. A larger proportion of employees in all major job categories were involved each year in formal training as compared to five years earlier. The companies reported that they were strengthening and widening the role of corporate training departments and were using more sophisticated methods to evaluate the need for and to assess the impact of employee training.

A third example of a corporate survey is the one conducted by the Battelle Human Affairs Research Center in 1987 (see Saari et al., 1988). This group sent a mailed questionnaire to 100 U.S. companies randomly selected from all private-for-profit companies having at least 1000 employees. While the response rate was excellent (61%), the survey only collected data on management training. The information is in the form of categorical variables such as the company's use of formal on-the-job training, mentoring, job-rotation, training needs assessment and training evaluation systems. The survey also collected information on the reasons companies give for selecting various training program approaches (e.g. external vs. internal), and the process used to select participants for these programs. The major finding from this survey is that 89% of the companies reported using formal training/education programs with use of this training being positively correlated with company size. In spite of the prevalence of formal training, there was limited evidence of systematic evaluations of management training by the companies in this sample.

D. Summary

As this literature review has revealed, what we know about employee training is that it has positive career impacts on the individuals who receive it, that U.S. companies spend a fair amount on formal training, and that many case studies conclude that employee training is effective in improving job performance. What is lacking, however, is a clear understanding of why some companies invest heavily in employee training and others do not. To date, almost no one has been able to study the variation in formal training across businesses, to describe the factors that determine that variation, and to analyze the impact of formal training on the organization's labor productivity; with the exception of the Stern/Benson studies and the EOPP survey, the focus has always been on variation in training across individuals. It is the purpose of the current research to shift the focus of analysis to the company that is making the training decision.

III. The Columbia Business School Human Resources Survey

In 1987, the Industrial Relations Research Center of the Columbia Business School conducted a survey of human resources policies and practices in American businesses. A questionnaire was sent to the executives responsible for 7,765 business units during the time period covering the fall of 1986 through the spring of 1987. A business unit is defined as any portion of a corporation responsible for generating ten percent or more of sales. In light of the wide diversification among United States corporations today, financial and economic information reported by business unit, rather than by company, gives a clearer picture of the level of economic activity within industries. The name and address of the executive in charge of each unit was obtained from the Compustat data files. Responses were received from 854 business units (11 percent response rate), though useable data were received from only 493 business units (6.4 percent overall response rate). Although this response rate is low, it is not substantially different from the response rates obtained by analysts who conducted much less comprehensive surveys of organizations' HRM policies (for example, see Hitt and Ireland, 1986). The businesses in the Columbia survey are smaller than those used in the Battelle survey. Fifty-percent of our businesses have fewer than 900 employees; twenty-five percent have fewer than 240 employees. Recall that the Battelle survey only included businesses with at least 1000 employees and this may, in part, explain why their response rate was so high. The Columbia survey did indeed have a better response rate from larger business units. Responding business units tended to be larger than nonrespondents and reported significantly higher sales, operating income, capital expenditures, assets, and equity than nonrespondents. Since human resource management policy innovations are initiated in large businesses, the respondent firms are likely to be pattern-setters, thereby providing an appropriate baseline for studying American organizations' HRM policies. The industrial distributions of the two groups were, however, very similar.

The survey instrument sent to COMPUSTAT business units elicited detailed data pertaining to 1986 on organizations' HRM policies and practices covering various occupational groups: (1) managers; (2) unionized and (3) nonunion professional and technical workers; (4) unionized and (5) nonunion clerical workers; and (6) unionized and (7) nonunion manufacturing and production workers. Information on training and development, selection, evaluation and compensation policies, and communication and employee involvement policies was obtained for each of these groups. In addition, the business units provided information about their overall human resource planning.

The data from the human resources survey have been merged with the data on the COMPUSTAT files. Hence, for each of the business units in the survey, we have information on capital expenditures, value of assets, operating income, research and development expenditures, and net sales. Demographic characteristics of the business's employees are proxied by the characteristics of the employees in the organization's industry and geographic labor market, as reported in the Current Population Survey data. In addition, for the business units in the manufacturing sector, we have information on the following attributes of the business unit's four-digit SIC category: concentration ratio, value of exports, value of imports, value of the capital stock, value of inventories, value of shipments, total factor productivity, energy expenditures, and number of employees. Data on these variables are available for the time period 1958-1984 inclusive.

On the subject of employee training and development, the survey asks several questions as they pertain to _each_ of the seven occupational groups. The questions for each of these groups are:

(1) Does your business have a formal employee training and development program?

(2) If yes, when was the program instituted?

(3) If yes, who participates in decisions about the types of training and development program undertaken by your business?

(4) What was the approximate cost of formal training and development programs per employee in your business last year?

(5) What indicators are used to assess employee training and development (e.g. employee opinions, productivity on the job, cost-benefit analysis)?

As this list indicates, the only measure of amount of training is the cost figure. Unlike the EOPP Survey, information on time spent by supervisors or others in training individuals or the amount of time it takes for a newly hired individual to become "trained", was not solicited. A follow-up questionnaire was sent to the 495 respondents at the end of 1989 requesting information for each of the occupation groups on the following items:

(6) The percentage of employees receiving formal training in the last fiscal year.

(7) The percentage of total work hours spent by a newly hired employee with no prior experience in formal training during the first three months on the job.

(8) The percentage of employees receiving informal training in the last fiscal year.

(9) The percentage of total work hours spent by a newly hired employee with no prior experience in informal training during the first three months on the job.

The response rate for the follow-up questionnaire was 26 percent, producing a sample of 130 respondents.

Although the response rate in the Columbia survey is low relative to those of the surveys of corporate training programs discussed in the previous section, the Columbia survey clearly surpasses the others in terms of the wealth of detail that is available on the company's human resource policies and its economic characteristics. As I show in the next section of the paper, these data are critical elements of a model of corporate investments in employee training. The earlier studies that utilized corporate surveys were not concerned with hypothesis testing regarding variation in the training effort across businesses and, hence, could conduct a less intensive data collection effort while concentrating on maximizing sample size. The Columbia Business School Survey took an alternative approach, namely, the need to collect a large amount of information from each respondent in order to be able to systematically study how and why human resource policies and practices differ across American businesses.

Table 1 reports mean values for training questions (1) and (4) from the original survey and (6), (7), (8) and (9) from the follow-up questionnaire. In 1986, formal employee training programs were used in one-third to one-half of the businesses in the sample, depending on the occupational group under study. Unfortunately, data on the cost of formal training per employee were reported by a small percentage of the businesses in the sample. However, these data can be utilized to make a rough estimate of the total amount that the average business spent on training. Assuming that it had the average number of employees in each employee category, the average business would have spent about $5.5 million on training in 1986. Multiplying this figure by the number of businesses in the COMPUSTAT files (including those without useable names and addresses for executives) would result in a total expenditure of $55 billion for 1986. The follow-up questionnaire, although answered by only 25% of the original respondents, provides information on the amount of time that new employees typically spend in formal and informal training. Comparing rows (4) and (6) in Table 1, shows that informal training is more common than formal training, especially among clerical and manufacturing employees. This finding confirms the analysis conducted by the American Society for Training and Development in the mid-1980's (see Carnevale, 1986). Rows (5) and (7) demonstrate the importance of informal training during the first three months of the employee's tenure on the job; indeed, among all occupation groups, new employees spend one-third of their time in informal training.

Table 2 provides information on the variability of the training effort across industries. Column (1) shows the percentage of occupations in each business for which a formal training program existed. The mean of this variable ranges from a low of 8.3% in the entertainment services industry to a high of 63.5% in the transportation industry. Columns (2) and (3) report the mean values of the percent of time spent by new employees in formal and informal training during the first three months on the job. Here too there is wide variation across industry groups. In the case of formal (informal) training, the industry mean ranges from a low of 2.12% (15.62%) in wholesale trade to a high of 24.17% (54.17%) in professional services.

As the data in Table 1 indicated, many companies with formal training programs did not respond to the question regarding the cost of formal training per employee. Since this variable is particularly important for measuring variation in training intensity across businesses, we need to explore why some businesses answered this question and others did not. In particular, the existence of selectivity bias must be considered. Table 3 provides more detail on this issue by showing how the response rate varied across occupation groups and across size categories where the businesses are divided into four quartiles based on number of employees. Each entry in Table 3 shows, for each occupation, the percentage of businesses with a formal training program that reported cost of training for that program. The entries in parentheses show the percentage of businesses with formal training programs for that occupation. The data show no clear pattern. While the response rate initially rises with size, it falls off for the very large businesses. Although these large organizations are most likely to have formal training programs, they either do not have or choose not to report information on cost of training. The entries in Table 3 are highly correlated _across_ occupations. In other words, if a company reports training costs for one occupation, it reports it for the others as well. Indeed, the correlations across occupations are all above .75, and, in many cases, exceed .9. This suggests that firm characteristics aside from size may be important in explaining the response rate.

To test this hypothesis, I estimated a binary logit model on the subset of firms that reported having a formal training program for the particular occupation under study; the dependent variable equals one if the business reported cost of training information, and equals zero if it did not. Three categories of variables are used. The first describes the economic characteristics of the business unit and includes SIZE - the number of employees, ROA - return on assets, calculated as the ratio of net income to identifiable assets and CAPLAB - the capital-labor ratio, calculated as the ratio of the value of the capital stock to the number of employees. The second category describes the business's human resource policies and includes YRPGM - the year in which the training program was instituted, and POLICY - an index measuring the degree of sophistication of the business unit's human resource policies. The index is defined as follows. The organization receives one point for each yes answer to the following questions: (1) Does the organization have a formal written HRM plan? Does the organization formally evaluate policies developed in the following HRM areas: (2) Work organization and job design? (3) Employee selection and staffing? (4) Employee training and development? (5) Communication and participation programs? (6) Performance appraisal? (7) Compensation? (8) Union-management relations? (9) Employee relations? The third category is a set of industry dummies where the excluded category is finance, insurance and real estate. The binary logit results are shown in Table 4 for managers and the three nonunion occupations; sample sizes were too small for the unionized occupational categories. There is no evidence in Table 4 of any systematic relationship between the business's economic characteristics and the probability of reporting training cost information; neither SIZE nor ROA have significant effects and CAPLAB is significant in only one equation. Businesses with more sophisticated human resource policies are not more likely to report cost information, and in one case, are even less likely to report it. The year the training program was instituted is significant in only one case. In sum, there is no obvious explanation as to why some companies reported training costs and others did not. My guess is that many respondents were not sure what costs should be included in our definition and/or they were unable to readily locate a cost measure for their organization.

IV. Determinants of Company Training Programs

    A. A Basic Framework

Using the assumption that the businesses are profit-maximizers, several hypotheses about the determinants of company training expenditures can be derived. The company's profits are defined as gross sales minus the wage bill, training expenditures, and all other expenditures on inputs:

(1) $$\Pi = P_x X - wL - tL - rK$$

where P = the price of the the product X, X = the quantity of output produced, w = the wage rate, L = the quantity of labor utilized, t = training expenditures per unit of labor, K = a composite index of all other factors of production, and r = the per unit cost of this composite index.

Maximizing Π with respect to t, training expenditures per unit of labor, results in the following condition:

(2) $$\frac{\partial}{\partial t}(\frac{X}{L}) P_x = 1$$

which simply states that the business will choose that level of t where the marginal return from an additional dollar spent per worker on training just equals its marginal cost. According to the left-hand side of equation (2), the marginal return from an additional dollar spent per worker will be higher in those businesses where the average product of labor is more sensitive to investments in training. Equation (1) can be modified to describe the company's maximization problem as one of maximizing the discounted flow of future profits. In this case, the marginal return on a current expenditure on training will equal the discounted sum of increases in the average product of labor over the expected working life (T) of the company's employees:

$$(3) \quad \sum_{i=1}^{T} \frac{\partial}{\partial t}(\frac{X}{L})_i \cdot P_{x_i} = 1$$

We can derive several hypotheses about the variation in per worker training expenditures across businesses by considering what factors are likely to lead to a greater sensitivity of the average product of labor to training expenditures. First is the degree of technological change in the firm. Companies that are introducing new technology have a greater need to train their employees in order to implement the technology and reap its benefits. The productivity of labor in this type of company will be more sensitive to training because the potential for learning is greater. A second variable to study is the average tenure of the workers in the company. As equation (3) indicates, the payoff from training is higher in those companies where employees are likely to stay longer. Third, the role of company size needs to be considered. As the literature review indicated, previous surveys have shown that large companies spend more per employee on formal training than small companies. If tenure is longer, on average, in large companies than small ones, this could explain the role of size. If this is not the case, then, according to equation (2), the only way to explain the role of size is to argue that labor productivity is more sensitive to training in large firms than in small ones. There are two possible explanations. The first is based on the argument that it is more difficult to monitor worker productivity in large firms. According to this view, training is more critical in large firms than small firms, ceteris paribus, because workers are more likely to shirk there. A second explanation relies on the notion of public goods. Instead of expressing training expenditures as the product of per worker expenditures and the number of workers, we could simply write total training expenditures, T. Then the marginal return from an additional dollar spent on T will be greater in large firms because a one dollar increase in T will increase the productivity of all workers. While this is a somewhat extreme case, it is consistent with a perhaps more realistic notion that there are "economies of scale" in the provision of training; one supervisor can teach a class of trainees and each trainee could learn as much as he would have in a private training session. Finally, product competition should play a role in the firm's calculation of the returns to training. For example, a company that is facing tough competition from domestic competitors or from foreign companies may increase its investments in employee training as a way of improving product quality and lowering production cost.

B. Empirical Specification

Since the response rate for the question on cost of training was so low, it is unwise to utilize this variable for an analysis of why the extent of training varies across the business units in the sample. Similarly, the follow-up questionnaire was only answered by 25% of the original respondents, producing a sample of only 125 businesses. Ruling out the variable from the follow-up questionnaire as well as the cost question from the original questionnaire leaves only one candidate for the dependent variable in a multivariate analysis, i.e. the question regarding the presence of a formal employee training program in the business. Admittedly, this variable is imperfect because it does not measure how much formal training employees actually receive nor does it take into account the amount of informal training that may occur as a substitute for the establishment of a formal training program. Hence the results presented here should only be interpreted as answers to the question of why some firms have formal training programs and others do not; they can not safely be interpreted as explaining why some firms train more than others. And, admittedly, the predictions regarding the effects of the independent variables on per worker training expenditures derived in the previous section have not been shown to necessarily hold when the dependent variable is the presence of a formal training program.

The data are stacked so that the number of observations equals the number of companies multiplied by the number of occupation groups in the company. The equation that is estimated is:

(4) $$TR_{ij} = \alpha_0 + \alpha_1 \, FIRM_j + \alpha_2 \, OCCV_{ij} + \alpha_3 \, OCCDUM_i$$

where TR_{ij} equals one if business j has a formal training program for occupation i, and zero otherwise; $FIRM_j$ is a vector of characteristics describing the firm such as size, technological change, industry dummies, industry characteristics, and the extent of human resource planning in the company; $OCCV_{ij}$ is a vector of variables describing the business's human resource practices that are specific to the occupation; and $OCCDUM_i$ is a vector of occupation dummies. As equation (4) is specified, the coefficients on the variables in $OCCV_{ij}$ are constrained to be the same across all occupations but the equation will also be estimated without this restriction.

The variables in the vector $FIRM_j$ are measured as follows. First, the degree of technological change in the business is measured in several ways. I use the ratio of R&D expenditures to sales (RDRATIO) and the logarithm of the ratio of capital expenditures to the number of employees in the business (LKEXP). These two variables are calculated from the COMPUSTAT files. The extent of technological change in the business's industry is also proxied by the average education level of workers in that industry. As Bartel and Lichtenberg (1987) have shown, industries undergoing technological change increase their demand for educated workers because education increases an individual's ability to learn new things and to adapt to environmental changes. Hence, we would expect that businesses in industries with highly educated workers are more likely to be introducing new technology, and, as the model showed, will therefore be more likely to invest in employee training and development. Education can also have a direct effect on formal training, rather than simply working indirectly through technological change. Since more educated individuals are better learners, the marginal return on a dollar spent on training will be higher for these people. The average education of workers in the company's three-digit SIC industry (EDUC) is calculated from the 1983 Current Population Survey. The size of the business is obtained directly from the survey and the logarithm of this value is used in the equation (LSIZE). When this was unavailable, information on the number of employees was obtained from the COMPUSTAT files. In order to control for variation in the importance of human resource policies to business strategy, a variable measuring the extent of human resource planning in areas other than employee training in the organization was calculated from the survey. This variable, called HRPOLICY, is similar to POLICY defined in Part III; the only exception is the deletion of the response to the question on training. Information on product competition in the business's industry is only available for the businesses in the manufacturing sector and refers to the four-digit SIC category of which the business is a member. Two variables are used to measure product competition. The first, the concentration ratio in the industry (CRATIO), is a measure of the extent of domestic competition. There are two problems with this variable. First, the latest date for which it is available is 1982, and, second, it can be argued that even in industries with high concentration ratios, the degree of competition among the leaders in the industry can be very intense. In the absence of these problems, CRATIO should have a negative coefficient. The second variable, the ratio of the sum of imports plus exports divided by the industry's total value of shipments (TRADE), is used to measure the degree of foreign competition that the domestic firms face both in the U.S. and abroad. The coefficient on TRADE should be positive if employee training is used as a device to improve productivity and competitiveness relative to foreign producers.

Two variables are included in $OCCV_{ij}$. The average tenure of employees in each occupation was not available on the survey, but was proxied by the response to the following question: "To the best of your knowledge, about what percentage of your nonentry level jobs have been filled from internal sources in recent years?" This variable (INTPROM) should be highly correlated with average tenure, since businesses that rely on internal promotions will have long tenure employees compared to businesses that hire from the outside. The variation in the extent to which the businesses screen job candidates for different occupations may also play a role in the decision to train. Presumably, organizations that benefit from trained workers will screen applicants more carefully in order to reduce training costs. A variable measuring whether or not job candidates are required to take a written or other formal test of skill (SCREEN) is used and is expected to be positively correlated with training; this positive correlation was found by Barron et al (1987) for the EOPP data.

The occupation dummies are defined as UPROF -- unionized professional and technical, NUPROF -- nonunion professional and technical, UCLER -- unionized clerical, NUCLER -- nonunion clerical, UMFG -- unionized manufacturing and production workers, and NUMFG -- nonunion manufacturing and production. The excluded category is managers.

C. Results

Table 5 contains the results of estimating a binary logit model where the dependent variable equals one if the business reported that it had a formal training and development program for the particular occupational group, and zero otherwise. In Column (1), businesses in all industries are included, while Columns (2) and (3) include only those in manufacturing. The predictions of the model are generally confirmed. Two of the three indicators of technological change, LKEXP and RDRATIO, are positive and significant in all three columns. EDUC is positive but close to significance in Column (1) only. The weak effect of this variable may be due to the fact that it is measured for the industry group as a whole and is not specific to the business itself. The size of the business, LSIZE, is always positive and significant. Whether this is due to the "shirking" problem or to economies of scale in the provision of training unfortunately cannot be determined. Since the dependent variable refers to formal training only, the impact of firm size on informal training can not be ascertained, but evidence in Haber (1989) shows that individuals who work in small firms are more likely to receive informal training than individuals in large firms. The other firm characteristics, CRATIO and TRADE, also have the expected signs in the manufacturing sector; formal training programs are more likely to be used as product market competition increases, as measured by either a decrease in CRATIO or an increase in TRADE.

The occupation related variables, INTPROM and SCREEN, also have the predicted signs. Training programs are more likely to be used as average tenure, as proxied by INTPROM, increases, and as screening intensity increases. The occupation dummy variables themselves are also significant, indicating greater reliance on formal training for managers as compared to the other groups. Table 6 shows the interactions of INTPROM and SCREEN with the occupation dummies. The effect of tenure on the probability of a formal training program is strongest for managers. According to the model, this implies that a business's calculation of the returns on formal training is more closely related to tenure when training managers as compared to the other occupation groups. Screening and training are also more highly correlated for managers as compared to all other groups except unionized professionals. It is possible to estimate a fixed effects model by including a set of business dummy variables in equation (4). The fixed effects model only includes the variables in $OCCV_{ij}$ and the occupation dummies since the variables in $FIRM_j$ are perfectly correlated with the business dummies. When this model was estimated, the coefficients on INTPROM and SCREEN decreased in magnitude but remained significant, and the pattern of the coefficients on the occupation dummies followed the one shown in Table 5.

V. The Effect of Training on Labor Productivity

A. Empirical Specification

In order to measure the impact of formal employee training on labor productivity, I assume that the production functions for the businesses in the survey can be represented by a Cobb-Douglas function and that there are two inputs in the production process, capital, K, and "effective labor", EL. Effective labor is the amount of labor services that are actually supplied by the workers that the company employs. Let the number of workers employed be represented by the variable, R, or reported labor. Then the effective labor input is given by:

(5) $$EL = R(1+\lambda t)$$

where t is an index of the amount of training that each worker receives and λ is less than one. According to equation (5), workers that receive more training provide more "effective labor" input to the firm. The production function can be written as:

(6) $$Q = AK^\beta EL^\gamma$$

or substituting equation (5) into (6), results in:

(6a) $$Q = AK^\beta (R(1+\lambda t))^\gamma$$

In the data I observe output per worker, or Q/R, which is written in equation (7) as:

(7) $$Q/R = AK^\beta R^{\gamma-1}(1+\lambda t)^\gamma$$

Taking logarithms of both sides of equation (7) gives the equation that will be estimated:

(8) $$\ln(Q/R) = \ln A + \beta \ln K + (\gamma-1)\ln R + \gamma\lambda t$$

assuming that λt is a small number.

Equation (8) is estimated across all of the businesses in the survey and each business is treated as an observation. The dependent variable is calculated as sales per worker, K is the value of the capital stock (LCAP) and R is the number of employees (LSIZE). In order to measure the extent of training in the organization, the variable PCTTRAIN, the percentage of occupations in the business for which formal training is conducted, is calculated. If training programs exist for all of the occupations in the business, this variable equals one; if there are no formal training programs, the variable equals zero; if there are training programs for some occupations and not others, the variable takes on a value between zero and one. An alternative variable is the percentage of employees for whom the business provides a formal training program. Unfortunately, about one-quarter of the businesses did not provide complete data on the number of employees in each occupation category (even when they provided data on the human resource policies applicable to each occupation) so utilizing this variable would have substantially reduced the sample size. The other variables that are included in the labor productivity equation are a set of industry dummies, the percentage of employees in the business that are unionized, (PCUNION), the average job tenure of all employees, calculated as an average of the proxy for tenure used in the previous analysis, (INTPROM), and the percentage of occupations for which job candidates are required to take a formal test based on the occupation responses to the variable SCREEN.

B. Results

The results of estimating equation (8) are shown in Table 7. In columns (1) and (3), the effect of formal training on labor productivity is estimated without controlling for the other human resource policy variables INTPROM and SCREEN. In columns (2) and (4), INTPROM and SCREEN are included in the equation. Formal training has a positive and significant effect on labor productivity only when the other human resource policy variables are deleted along with the business's capital stock (column 3). In other words, the high correlation between formal training programs and capital intensity prevents finding an independent effect of formal training on labor productivity. Moving from column (3) to column (4) shows that the cross-business correlation between training and skill testing and tenure reduces the partial effect of training on productivity. An important finding is that businesses that skill test their applicants have significantly higher labor productivity even when the capital stock variable is included in the equation (see column (2)).

VI. Conclusions

This paper has utilized corporate survey data to study employee training and development. The review of previous research showed that most studies of training rely on data provided by individuals and therefore focus on the variation in training across individuals and its impacts on their career advancement. Although economic models of training decisions are framed in terms of a company's calculation of the costs and benefits of such training, empirical work has never been able to test this model directly on company behavior.

The results from the survey demonstrated the difficulty firms have in calculating training costs. While most firms could provide information on the existence of formal training programs for various occupation groups, a much smaller group provided data on costs. This made it impossible to directly test the predictions of the model on per-worker training costs and the empirical work focused instead on the determinants of the presence of formal training programs. It was found that large businesses, those introducing new technology, and those with a high proportion of internal promotions were more likely to have formal training programs. In addition, the extent of product competition in the business's industry had the expected sign. The analysis also considered the impact of formal training programs on labor productivity and found that the observed positive effect of formal training on labor productivity disappeared when the analysis controlled for the capital intensity of the business.

How does this analysis contribute to the debate on the market's ability to provide "enough" formal training for employed adults? On the one hand, we can argue that the companies in this sample are providing the right amount of formal training because we observe their behavior to be consistent with the predictions of the profit-maximization model. These companies provide formal training when it is in their best interests to do so. Alternatively, we saw that only one-third to one-half of the businesses have formal training programs for various occupation groups. If the goal is to insure that virtually all American workers have the opportunity to participate in <u>formal training programs at the work site</u>, this statistic suggests that there is not enough training. In order to induce American businesses to provide more formal training, public policy makers would need to create the right incentives; policy changes that increase the perceived marginal return or reduce the marginal cost (e.g. training vouchers) of providing such training would be required. But it seems more reasonable to argue that employers themselves have better information regarding labor market conditions, the market for their goods and services, and the potential benefits of new technology, all of which are used to judge the potential benefits from additional investments in training.

Bibliography

Barron, J., Black, D. and Lowenstein, M., "Employer Size: The Implications for Search, Training, Capital Investments, Starting Wages and Wage Growth," *Journal of Labor Economics*, January 1987.

_____, "Job Matching and On-the-Job Training," February 1988.

Bartel, Ann P. and Frank R. Lichtenberg, "The Comparative Advantage of Educated Workers in Implementing New Technology," *Review of Economics and Statistics*. February 1987.

Brown, James, "Are Those Paid More Really No More Productive? Measuring the Relative Importance of Tenure as On-the-Job Training in Explaining Wage Growth," Princeton Industrial Relations Papers, 1983.

Burke, Michael J. and Russell R. Day, "A Cumulative Study of the Effectiveness of Managerial Training," *Journal of Applied Psychology*, 1986, Vol. 71, No. 2.

Carnevale, Anthony, "The Learning Enterprise: A Report on the Size and Scope of Training," *Training and Development Journal*, January 1986.

Haber, Sheldon, "Returns to Workers from On-the-Job Training and Its Relationship to Firm Size," mimeo, 1989.

Hitt, Michael A. and R. Duane Ireland, "Relationships Among Corporate Level Distinctive Competencies, Diversification Strategy, Corporate Structure and Performance," *Journal of Management Studies*, July 1986.

Ingols, Cynthia A., "Management Education: Articulating the Unspoken, Riding the Herd, Wasting Money, or Preparing for Tomorrow?" in Leslie S. May, Carol Ann Moore and Stephen J. Zammit, eds., *Evaluating Business and Industry Training*, Kluwer Academic Publishers, Boston, 1987.

Lillard, Lee and Hong Tan, "Private Sector Training: Who Gets It and What Are Its Effects?", Rand Monograph R-3331-DOL/RC, 1986.

Lusterman, Seymour, *Education in Industry*, The Conference Board, 1977.

_____, *Trends in Corporate Education and Training*, The Conference Board, 1985.

Lynch, Lisa, "Private Sector Training and Its Impact on the Career Patterns of Young Workers," mimeo, Massachusetts Institute of Technology, October 1988.

Mincer, Jacob, "Union Effects: Wages, Turnover, and Job Training," in *Research in Labor Economics*, 1983.

_____, "Job Training, Wage Growth and Labor Turnover," mimeo, Columbia University, November 1987.

Pergamit, M. and J. Shack-Marquez, "Earnings and Different Types of Training," mimeo, BLS and Board of Governors of the Federal Reserver, 1986.

Russell, James, S., James R. Terborg and Mary L. Powers, "Organizational Performance and Organizational Level Training and Support," Personnel Psychology, 1985.

Saari, Lise M., Terry R. Johnson, Steven D. McLaughlin and Denise M. Zimmerle, "A Survey of Management Training and Education Practices in U.S. Companies," Personnel Psychology, Winter 1988.

Table 1

Training Programs and Training Expenditures[a]

Variable	Managers	Professional/ Technical Employees		Manufacturing/ Clerical Employees		Production Employees	
		Union	Nonunion	Union	Nonunion	Union	Nonunion
Original Survey (1986)							
1. Percent With a Formal Training Program	49.2% (488)	47.3% (55)	45.1% (468)	37.7% (85)	32.9% (474)	47.5% (162)	40.6% (323)
2. Mean Cost of Training Per Employee	$1,343 (101)	$1,037 (3)	$1,408 (84)	$873 (6)	$368 (70)	$470 (26)	$359 (49)
3. Total Cost of Training Per Business[b]	$1,164,821 (89)	N.A.	$2,108,745 (74)	N.A.	$229,513 (62)	$706,526 (23)	$1,299,167 (42)
Follow-Up Survey (1989)							
4. Percent of Employees Receiving Formal Training	36.7% (125)	27.4% (34)	31.8% (112)	20.4% (42)	27.0% (116)	21.7% (47)	21.1% (62)
5. Percent of Time in Formal Training During First Three Months on the Job	13.7% (106)	9.4% (35)	13.0% (106)	9.6% (41)	11.1% (114)	13.4% (43)	14.0% (62)
6. Percent of Employees Receiving Informal Training	44.3% (114)	43.5% (29)	47.7% (107)	45.7% (36)	47.7% (111)	49.0% (39)	51.9% (64)
7. Percent of Time in Informal Training During First Three Months on the Job	32.9% (206)	31.8% (30)	32.7% (106)	32.8% (38)	32.6% (108)	32.3% (41)	38.2% (65)

[a] The sample size is in parentheses.

[b] Calculated by multiplying the training cost per employee by the number of employees in the occupational category.

Table 2
Industry Means for Selected Training Variables

		Percent of Occupations With Formal Training Programs	Percent of Time Spent By New Employees In Formal Training	Percent of Time Spent By New Employees In Informal Training
1.	Mining (N=28)	20.0%	6.9%	25.3%
2.	Construction (N=3)	16.7	N.A.	N.A.
3.	Nondurable Mfg. (N=70)	46.3	15.3	35.7
4.	Durable Mfg. (N=154)	25.4	11.9	37.5
5.	Transportation (N=83)	63.5	13.3	33.6
6.	Wholesale Trade (N=10)	24.2	2.1	15.6
7.	Retail Trade (N=27)	53.6	16.3	23.6
8.	Finance, Insurance & Real Estate (N=59)	53.1	16.3	23.6
9.	Business and Repair Services (N=34)	48.0	5.3	30.9
10.	Personal Services (N=8)	21.7	6.0	21.0
11.	Entertainment Services (N=5)	8.3	9.4	32.2
12.	Professional Services (N=10)	46.7	24.2	54.2

Table 3

Proportion of Businesses With Formal Training
Programs That Reported Cost of Training, By Size Quartile*

		SIZE 1 (2-241)	SIZE 2 (242-898)	SIZE 3 (899-3900)	SIZE 4 (3901-316900)
1.	Managers	.386 (.358)	.386 (.396)	.413 (.563)	.337 (.769)
2.	Unionized Professional/ Technical	0.0 (.286)	0.0 (.273)	.333 (.500)	.063 (.666)
3.	Nonunionized Professional/ Technical	.328 (.382)	.368 (.355)	.400 (.519)	.343 (.638)
4.	Unionized Clerical	0.0 (.167)	0.0 (0.0)	.375 (.381)	.091 (.611)
5.	Nonunionized Clerical	.395 (.247)	.371 (.321)	.413 (.422)	.291 (.519)
6.	Unionized Manufacturing/ Production	.111 (.581)	.333 (.462)	.400 (.392)	.270 (.627)
7.	Nonunionized Manufacturing/ Production	.378 (.336)	.357 (.373)	.313 (.421)	.244 (.594)

*Numbers in parentheses show the proportion of businesses with formal training programs.

Table 4

Probability of Reporting Cost of Training Given that Formal Training Program Exists

	Managers	Nonunion Prof/Tech	Nonunion Clerical	Nonunion Mfg/Prod
SIZE	-.128 (-1.45)	-.038 (-.41)	-.025 (-.26)	-.298 (-1.27)
ROA	.604 (1.24)	1.07 (1.41)	.55 (.75)	1.95 (1.02)
CAPLAB	-4.82 (-.98)	-5.52 (-.83)	-3.56 (-.72)	40.48 (1.86)
YRPGM	-.01 (-.32)	.002 (.13)	-.01 (-.68)	-.05 (-2.05)
POLICY	-.014 (-.32)	-.03 (-.64)	-.01 (-.15)	-.15 (-2.19)
NONDUR	.198 (.34)	-.40 (-.65)	-.80 (-.96)	1.58 (.82)
DUR	.785 (1.49)	-.01 (-.11)	--- ---	2.19 (1.18)
TRANSP	1.30 (2.49)	.53 (.94)	.73 (1.41)	.89 (.47)
WHTRADE	.93 (.63)	--- ---	--- ---	--- ---
RETAIL	1.54 (2.38)	1.15 (1.32)	1.36 (1.78)	3.73 (1.87)
BUSSERV	1.05 (1.67)	1.11 (1.63)	1.99 (2.57)	.45 (.21)
PERSERV	2.19 (1.57)	--- ---	--- ---	--- ---
Constant	-.55 (-.44)	-.70 (-.55)	-.136 (-.09)	1.08 (.57)
N	186	155	121	102

Table 5

Binary Logit Models of Presence of Formal Training Program
(Stacked Data)

Independent Variable	(1) All Industries* (N = 1694)	(2) Manufacturing Only (N = 868)	(3) Manufacturing Only (N = 849)
LSIZE	.26 (7.40)	.19 (3.61)	.21 (3.69)
LKEXP	.12 (3.03)	.20 (2.90)	.19 (2.56)
RDRATIO	3.25 (2.67)	4.68 (2.33)	4.31 (2.10)
HRPLCY	.13 (7.22)	.17 (6.14)	.17 (6.29)
SCREEN	1.04 (7.23)	1.32 (6.28)	1.23 (5.79)
INTPROM	.01 (4.70)	.02 (5.16)	.02 (5.24)
EDUC	.13 (1.55)	.02 (.19)	.13 (1.03)
UPROF	-1.10 (-2.94)	-1.55 (-1.87)	-1.74 (-1.96)
NUPROF	-.28 (-1.69)	-.11 (-.46)	-.08 (-.34)
UCLER	-2.28 (-6.77)	-2.44 (-4.09)	-2.46 (-4.06)
NUCLER	-1.49 (-7.69)	-1.75 (-5.99)	-1.67 (-5.66)
UMFG	-.62 (-2.62)	-.93 (-2.70)	-.86 (-2.46)
NUMFG	-.44 (-2.34)	-.69 (-2.69)	-.66 (-2.52)
TRADE			1.16 (3.73)
CRATIO			-.01 (-1.47)

*The excluded industry category is finance, insurance, and real estate. The coefficients and t-values on the industry dummies are MIN, -2.80 (-6.39), CONS, -1.89 (-1.94), NONDUR, -1.34 (-4.48), DUR, -1.90 (-6,80), TRANSP, -.74 (-2.49), WHTRADE, -2.05 (-4.52), RETAIL, -.75 (-2.05), BUSREP, -.34 (-1.82), PERSS, -2.12 (-2.42), ENTERT, -2.87 (-3.52), and PROFSER, -1.62 (-2.45).

Table 6

Interactions of SCREEN and INTPROM with Occupation Dummies*

Independent Variable	(1) SCREEN	(2) INTPROM
No Interaction	1.01 (2.94)	.01 (4.00)
UPROF Interaction	1.33 (1.59)	-.003 (-.27)
NUPROF Interaction	.05 (.45)	-.005 (-1.04)
UCLER Interaction	-.17 (-.23)	-.03 (-2.50)
NUCLER Interaction	-.41 (-.95)	-.02 (-3.02)
UMFG Interaction	.46 (.80)	-.003 (-.40)
NUMFG Interaction	.26 (.57)	-.01 (-1.23)

*All other variables shown in Table 5 were included in these regressions.

Table 7

Dependent Variable: Log (Output per Worker)*

Independent Variable	(1)	(2)	(3)	(4)
LSIZE	-.79 (-35.29)	-.80 (-34.72)	-.20 (-5.84)	-.22 (-6.26)
LCAP	.78 (38.34)	.78 (36.98)		
PCTTRAIN	-.03 (-.43)	-.10 (-1.30)	.26 (1.70)	.21 (1.27)
PCUNION	.13 (.98)	.09 (.65)	-.16 (-.58)	-.31 (-1.07)
INTPROM		.17 (1.46)	-- --	.69 (2.87)
SCREEN		.30 (2.77)	-- --	.15 (.67)
CONSTANT	-1.28 (-10.24)	-1.43 (-10.52)	-.53 (-2.07)	-.83 (-2.95)
R^2	.82	.82	.20	.22
N	455	428	455	428

*All equations include a vector of industry dummies.

FIRMS' PROPENSITY TO TRAIN

David Stern and Charles S. Benson
School of Education
University of California, Berkeley

This chapter considers why some firms spend a great deal of time and money to encourage continual learning by employees. The question is relevant to public policy, given the widespread belief that demands for continual learning by the workforce at large are increasing and will continue to increase. It is also relevant to ongoing research by economists seeking to understand the process of skill formation and the possible existence of market failure.

The chapter begins with a review of empirical research by economists on inter-firm variation in propensity to provide learning opportunities (usually called on-the-job training, or OJT) for employees. It then reviews basic economic theory, which clearly specifies conditions necessary for OJT to produce net benefits, but is not clear about whether or how these benefits will be shared by employers and employees. Given prevailing views about the increasing importance of OJT, it would be useful to have a better understanding of how some firms manage to do it, and to develop insight into possible reasons for market failure.

In the absence of sufficiently detailed quantitative data on any large sample of firms, research in this area must rely heavily on case studies. One phenomenon described in several recent case studies is the emergence of a learning-intensive mode of production, in which the opportunity cost of OJT is greatly reduced by integrating it as closely as possible into the work process itself. One of the conditions that appears necessary to sustain learning-intensive production is a high degree of employment security. However, market failure may occur because of positive externalities associated with the assurance of stable employment, since it is, in theory, less costly for any one firm to give such an assurance if a larger number of other firms are doing the same thing. The last part of this chapter summarizes the argument that under-provision of OJT may be linked to under-provision of employment security, and briefly examines alternative remedial policies.

This paper draws in part on research conducted by David Stern in collaboration with Clair Brown and Michael Reich, supported by the U.S. Department of Education through a grant to the National Center for Research in Vocational Education at the University of California, Berkeley. Conclusions do not necessarily represent official U.S. Department of Education positions or policy. Any errors in this chapter are the responsibility of the authors alone.

The Empirical Literature on Human Capital Theory Applied to Firms

Traditionally in the study of human capital, the unit of analysis is the individual person (or household). People are seen to make investments in human capital on their own account. Government enters the process by providing subsidies to individuals and to institutions of learning. Yields are measured as social and private rates of return to types and quantities of education held by different classes of individuals. Alternatively, we can view the firm as the unit of analysis and we could seek to describe the choices that firms make with regard to the accumulation of human capital, meaning the decision as to how skill-intensive the firms seek to become; the bases for the choices about skill-intensity; and the returns that can be attributed to a firm's making use of defined types and quantities of human capital. In acquiring human capital, firms may simply hire people with certain skills, produce skills in the firm's own training programs, or make contracts with outside agencies for training. These are not exclusive choices, but it should be useful to understand these choices among alternative sources of human capital, as well as the total amount desired.

Unfortunately, the literature dealing with these questions is relatively sparse, in large part because there is so little comparable data on training by firms. Benson and Lohnes (1959) conducted a survey of durable goods manufacturers in New England to describe intensity of formal training efforts and to try to explain differences among plants in commitment to human capital development. The intensity of training efforts in the plants appeared to vary to an extraordinary degree. Two variables were statistically significant in accounting for the differences: type of market and main process. Firms that served mainly government (in those days in New England, these firms supplied equipment for defense and aerospace) did the most training, firms that served the producers' goods market were in a middle position, and firms that made goods for households did the least training. Firms whose manufacturing was based on "scientific processes" did a great deal of training, on the average; firms in which machining of metal was an important aspect of production were in the middle of the training scale, and firms that used non-machined fabrication were low on training effort.

Barron, Black, and Loewenstein (1987) used the 1982 EOPP employer survey on wages, hiring activities, training and capital equipment, to investigate the relationship between employer size, on the one hand, and search processes, training activities, capital investment, starting wages, and wage growth, on the other. It was found that larger employers devote more effort to search, are more likely to engage in training activities, have a higher capital/labor ratio, and offer higher starting wages. These results are seen to be related to the difficulties that large employers face in monitoring on-the-job performance of workers. Another result indicates that wage growth is less in large firms. This finding is consistent with the authors' view that the difference in proficiency between a new worker in a large firm and a probationary worker in a small firm is likely to be greater than the difference in proficiency between experienced workers in the two types of establishments.

In a 1989 paper, Barron, Black, and Loewenstein, using the same data base, analyzed the processes by which a heterogeneous body of workers is matched to jobs with different training requirements. They indicate that employers do seek to match workers of greater ability to jobs that require more intensive types of training and that higher ability workers do seek to place themselves in those kinds of jobs. That these two processes are simultaneouly at work makes it difficult to separate the effects of training costs and worker ability on starting wage. A subsidiary finding is that on-the-job training is a primary factor affecting wage and productivity growth.

Bartel (1988) used a new survey of firms to investigate the question of why some companies maintain formal training programs and some do not. Results indicate that the ratio of capital expenditures to the number of employees and the ratio of R&D expenditure to total sales are both positively related to the presence of formal training programs. These and other results are included in Bartel's chapter in this volume.

Bartel's findings are broadly consistent with results of previous studies which have found that more highly educated labor is complementary with plant and equipment (Hamermesh and Grant, 1979), in particular new plant and equipment (Bartel and Lichtenberg, 1987). Mincer (1989) and Tan (1988) also have found higher average levels of education among employees in industries where productivity growth is high. These findings, as well as research on farmers (Jamison and Lau, 1982; Wozniak, 1987) support the view (Schultz, 1975; Welch, 1970) that human capital enhances individuals' ability to improvise solutions for problems arising from use of new equipment, materials, or other forms of new technology.

The connection between technology and skill demands has been the subject of much study outside economics. Despite evidence from some case studies showing that introduction of new technology has led to "de-skilling" of certain jobs, the majority of evidence appears to indicate that new technology works best if operators have the skills to understand it and use it properly (Hirschhorn, 1984; Thompson and Scalpone, 1985; Jaikumar, 1986; National Academy of Sciences, 1986, 1987; Zuboff, 1988; Helfgott, 1988; Adler, forthcoming).

In addition to demanding higher skills, technology may also promote training in other ways. Companies that make their living from computer-based technologies, in particular, can use those same technologies to reduce the cost of training. IBM, for example, carried out a thoroughgoing rationalization of its training activities during the 1980s, moving away from classroom instruction to more decentralized, computer-based "self study", which is considerably cheaper (Galagan, 1989). Digital Equipment Corporation also makes use of its extensive computerized telecommunications network to support learning by employees (Eurich, 1990, p. 63).

Maintaining a significant degree of technological independence may also be part of a company's motivation to acquire or produce human capital. Technological assistance can be bought in the market, in the same way that other business services can, but purchased assistance for design of new products and processes may not assure that the firm keeps a competitive edge in technology to the degree that "owning" one's own bank of highly competent workers does. The desire for technological independence may transcend the search for profits, because it is a source of managerial satisfaction to have one's firm recognized as a leader in technology.

As mentioned, research in this field suffers from lack of comparable data across firms. Much training is informal, but companies ordinarily keep no record of it, and we are aware of only two surveys that have tried to measure informal training in a sample of firms: the EOPP in the U.S., and one done for the U.K. Training Commission (Sloman, 1989). Even measuring formal training is not easy, since reported training budgets may or may not include trainees' time, payment to outside contractors, and tuition reimbursements. Until more definitive numbers become available, it will not be possible to calculate precise rates of return or test many other quantitative hypotheses about firm-based training.

Fortunately, there are some good descriptive accounts of training in various firms (Casner-Lotto, 1988; U.S. Congress, Office of Technology Assessment, 1990; Eurich, 1990; Carnevale, Gainer, and Villet 1990). Such information provides at least a qualitative picture of what companies are doing. While it does not permit testing quantitative hypotheses from economic theory, case study information may serve the more useful purpose of reframing the questions.

What Economic Theory Does and Does Not Clearly Imply about Provision of OJT

A necessary and sufficient condition for training to increase both trainee's and employer's income, <u>ex ante</u>, is that the present value of additional output due to training exceed the present value of resources invested. The main expense of OJT for employed people is the value of what they would have produced during the time taken up in training. The additional output from OJT depends on whether the trainee remains with the same employer after training, as Becker (1964) explained. Since some of the content of OJT may apply only, or most directly, to the current employer, some of the potential output from OJT is lost if people move to different employers after they have received OJT. Variables that influence the expected net gain in trainee's or employer's income produced by OJT therefore include (1) the productivity of employees during OJT; (2) their expected productivity after OJT if they stay with the same employer; (3) expected productivity if they go to work elsewhere; (4) the expected probability that they will remain with the same employer; and (5) the discount rate(s) implicitly or explicitly applied to this decision (Stern, 1982a). Firms themselves have a considerable degree of control over variables 1, 2 and 4, as will be described below.

The theory becomes less straightforward when trying to determine whether and how the costs and benefits of OJT are shared between employer and employee. Becker's conclusion that employees must finance their own general OJT because they receive all the benefit, while employees and employers share both the cost and benefit of firm-specific training, leaves unanswered both the question why some firms may decide to sell general training to their employees while others may not, and the question how the bilateral monopoly problem created by firm-specific training is resolved.

Theoretical progress in determining an efficient division of costs and benefits from specific OJT has been made by Hashimoto (1981, this volume; also Hashimoto and Yu, 1980). The major problem is how employers and employees can deal with ex post deviations in productivity. That is, after a worker has received specific training, his or her productivity with that employer or with other employers may be different from what was expected. Differences can arise either because the worker's true ability to benefit from training was unknown ex ante, or because of changes in technology or market conditions. If recontracting were possible and costless, these ex post variations would not be a problem. In fact, however, the possibility of such recontracting is limited because of asymmetric information: employers have more accurate information about current employees' productivity, and employees know more about their potential earnings elsewhere. Therefore, ex ante contracts, which maximize the joint gains from specific OJT, can achieve only a second-best optimum. Inefficiency still occurs because ex post deviations in productivity may result in one party terminating the employment relationship even though the employee is less productive with another employer. Hashimoto (in this volume) argues that Japanese firms are able to reduce this inefficiency in part by investing in communication, thereby reducing the transaction costs of ex post recontracting.

Ex post variation in the return from training has also been identified by Ritzen (in this volume) as a source of inefficiency in provision of general training. Ritzen demonstrates that some kind of training insurance can produce a Pareto superior allocation.

Recently, Becker's conclusion that employees must finance their own general OJT has been questioned by Feuer, Glick, and Desai (1986) and, for different reasons, by Barron, Black, and Loewenstein (1989). Feuer et al. argue on theoretical grounds that, to protect their employees' investment in firm-specific training, companies may also share some of the cost (and benefit) of general training. Barron et al. propose a different theoretical rationale: that OJT is complementary with ability, so that more able employees, who must receive higher wages, also receive more training, both specific and general. Feuer et al. and Barron et al. both tested their predictions with data sets that include direct measures of how much OJT individuals received. Both tests failed to confirm Becker's prediction that employees receiving more OJT (some of which is assumed to be general) had to accept lower wages.

Furthermore, the basic distinction between specific and general training, which Becker described as a continuum, has not been amenable to direct empirical measurement. The main empirical support for the existence of firm-specific human capital is the virtually ubiquitous finding that an additional year of working for the current employer is associated with a larger increment in earnings than an additional year of working for other employers before the current one. However, alternative explanations of this finding are possible. One is Lazear's (1981) theory of lifetime wage-effort bargains, which implies that individuals who have been with the same employer for a long time are finally collecting payments they deferred earlier for incentive purposes. Another is that individuals are more likely to stay employed in firms that are growing and offering opportunities for promotion. Still another is that bigger annual pay raises with the current employer are the reason why this employer is the current one: individuals tend to stay where they are while they are personally experiencing bigger pay raises, whether the company is growing or not. Given the difficulty of directly measuring the degree of specificity in training, we may never know which of these or other possible theories account for the observed greater payoff to continued experience with the same employer.

Workers as Researchers: Learning-Intensive Production

Recently there have been examples of firms making investments in training that seem anomalous from the viewpoint of standard human capital theory. One is Corning Inc., which in 1991 increased the proportion of employees' time spent in training from four to five percent. Much of that time will be given to remedial instruction in reading and math (Business Week, December 17, 1990, p. 74). Improvement in their reading and math skills will benefit these employees beyond their work at Corning, yet, contrary to standard human capital theory, Corning is not requiring them to pay through reduced wages. Similarly, Motorola Inc. has launched a well-publicized campaign to raise its manufacturing employees' basic reading and math skills (Wiggenhorn, 1990; National Comission for Employment Policy, 1990). Most of this will take place on company time, at a reported cost of $35 million over a period of three to five years. But Motorola is not reducing wages or charging employees in any other way for the cost of this general training.

Corning and Motorola are not alone. Various surveys indicate that approximately 10 to 20 percent of large firms provide remedial education in reading, writing, and math for their employees (U.S. Congress, Office of Technology Assessment 1990, p. 168).

The explanation for these anomalies is that Corning, Motorola and other firms have changed their method of operating. Instead of expecting hourly employees simply to do what they are told and not ask questions, these companies are now enlisting production workers in a ceaseless search for better quality and higher productivity. One Corning production worker expressed the new attitude: "Everybody that works here is competitive.... We want to be multi-skilled and learn how we can make the product better so we can be the best in quality and service to the customer. And if we do all that, this plant will be around a long time." (Business Week, December 17, 1990, p. 72) Similarly, Motorola's Wiggenhorn declares, "At Motorola we require three things of our manufacturing employees. They must have communication and computation skills at the seventh grade level, soon going up to eighth and ninth. They must be able to do basic problem solving -- not only as individuals but also as members of a team. And they must accept our definition of work and the work-week: the time it takes to ship perfect product to the customer who's ordered it. That can mean a workweek of 50 or even 60 hours, but we need people willing to work against quality and output instead of a time clock. These requirements are relatively new. Ten years ago, we hired people to perform set tasks and didn't ask them to do a lot of thinking." (p. 71)

An assembler in an automobile plant that has undergone similar change described the new expectations: "This is the kind of involvement they want of people: not just the hands, it's the mind." His tongue-in-cheek reaction was, "Uh oh, this is tough -- they're going to ask me to work and think at the same time."

Now that employees are being paid to think, they need the basic skills to process the information they are expected to think about. Rather than dismiss all their existing employees who lacked these skills, Corning and Motorola are investing the money to upgrade them. In defense of standard human capital theory, such investment might be seen as a transitory phenomenon. It would not occur in equilibrium, where every firm already had the kind of workforce that was suited to its method of production.

Whether or not one concludes that such investments violate stardard human capital theory, it is important to recognize that numerous firms are currently moving toward a method of operation that engages production workers in constant learning. Some of this learning is training in the conventional sense of transferring skills and information from one group of people to another. But much of the learning is more like research: the discovery of information, principles, or techniques that no one knew before.

For example, the fabrication of certain printed circuit boards requires repeated baking of the boards as successive layers of conductors and resistors are applied. Sometimes this changes the conductivity of the materials enough to cause defects. Redesigning the board to avoid the problem would require costly engineering and start-up time. One manufacturer has found that these costs can sometimes be avoided by production workers tweaking the fabrication process so that the original design can be produced without defects. The knowledge acquired through such experimentation does not exist in any manuals.

Similar examples can also be found in the service sector. In one small mutual life insurance company, the rate of introduction of new insurance products has increased from approximately one new product every three years in the 1970s to three new products a year in the 1980s. New options include conversion from different term insurance policies to whole life or universal life policies, and premium schedules that buy additional coverage over time or use dividends to offset premium payments. Non-salaried customer service representatives test the computer routines for handling these new options. They also test new software for implementing changes in tax laws. Through their involvement in updating procedures, these clerical workers are helping to write the new manuals. Furthermore, since universal life policies allow a whole range of individual options, customer service representatives must learn to deal with unique customized configurations that have never been seen before.

Some companies encourage employees' inventiveness by soliciting formal suggestions and paying them a portion of the value. For example, in the restructured automobile assembly plant mentioned above, a conveyor chain broke down four times during a nine-month period, resulting in costly downtime and destruction of materials. Rather than buy a new chain, employees suggested purchasing additional trolley wheels and standardizing the distance between the wheels, which previously had been inconsistent, resulting in undue stress on the chain. The resulting net saving, after deducting the cost of implementing the suggestion, was approximately $100,000 per year.

Another suggestion in the same auto plant was a better method for removing sludge deposits from overspray basins in a paint shop. Instead of shutting down operations and contracting with outside companies for cleaning out the sludge, non-salaried employees suggested using a submersible pump attached to a small portable frame that can be manually maneuvered into the sludge basins. This suggestion saved an estimated $17,000 per year.

Formal suggestion systems are used extensively by large firms in Japan. It is not uncommon for these firms to receive an average of 50 to 100 suggestions per year from their employees. Workers are strongly encouraged to fill out suggestion forms: failure to do so can result in negative evaluations from supervisors. Small payments, e.g. 500 yen, are awarded for each suggestion, and larger payments may be given for more significant ideas. Most of the suggestions are for very small improvements, but they may add up to substantial productivity gains for the company, and they signify that workers are thinking about what they do.

Womack, Jones, and Roos (1990) give an account of how the practice of kaizen, or continuous improvement, was developed at Toyota in the 1950s. In assembly-line production as invented by Ford, "workers wouldn't volunteer any information on operating conditions -- for example, that a tool was malfunctioning --

much less suggest ways to improve the process. These functions fell respectively to the foreman and the industrial engineer, who reported their findings and suggestions to higher levels of management for action." The foreman and the industrial engineer were in addition to "the battalions of narrowly skilled indirect workers," including repairmen, quality inspectors, housekeepers, and rework specialists, who "became ever more prominent in Fordist, mass-production factories as the introduction of automation over the years gradually reduced the need for assemblers." (p. 32) In contrast, the new style of "lean production" pioneered at Toyota gave responsibility for many of these functions back to teams of assemblers, who were able to achieve standards of quality and efficiency that soon surpassed what Fordist factories could do.

"Lean production" is the term used by Womack et al. to describe a whole management system that integrates product design, production, marketing, and finance. Similarly, the U.S. Congress Office of Technology Assessment describes a new model of "flexible decentralization" that is displacing the old model of mass production. The same kind of image also appears in Dertouzos, Lester, and Solow (1989) and in the America's Choice report issued by the National Center on Education and the Economy (1990) -- though this latter report finds that a disappointingly small fraction (only five percent) of U.S. employers have yet made a clear commitment to what is called a "high performance work system".

An essential feature of all these descriptions is the role of production workers as learners: trouble-shooting equipment malfunctions, monitoring quality and hunting down the causes of defects, discovering how to produce or deliver new products most efficiently, obsessively refining existing methods of operation to improve quality and reduce cost. As the union chairman in one restructured plant expressed the new attitude, "If you don't have a problem, that's a problem." Workers are expected to be continually seeking problems to solve -- rather than hiding problems or blaming someone else. To elicit this kind of initiative, managers must encourage workers by actively soliciting ideas and responding to them constructively. Instead of managers always having the answers and telling subordinates what to do, managers are expected to learn from subordinates as well as teach them. This feature of continuous learning at all levels of the organization is what we denote here by the term learning-intensive production.

Just-in-Time Training

As learning becomes part of the job for more people, more attention is being given to how the structure of work itself can facilitate learning. For instance, the Office of Work-Based Learning in the U.S. Department of Labor has recently sponsored efforts to develop better techniques of work-based learning. The National Alliance of Business (NAB) received one of these development contracts. The first principle of "Job Performance Learning", as defined by NAB, is that "Learning is treated as an integrated whole. Learning in different settings and using various media is integrated to support the overall skill and knowledge needs of workers. Whether in the classroom, on the job, or at a computer work station; or delivered through demonstration, relevant practice, interactive video, print, or human coaching, all learning is treated as part of a single learning process." (Komatsu, 1990, p.2)

It is increasingly recognized that trying to stockpile knowledge in people's heads just in case they might need it is less efficient than providing quick access to knowledge at the time and place when people actually do need it. Similar to the way in which just-in-time delivery saves money on inventories of parts and finished products, what we might call just-in-time training economizes on people's time and mental effort. There are several reasons why just-in-time training should be more efficient. First, people are more motivated to learn when they see an immediate purpose for it. Second, people are more likely to forget what they do not use. Third, recent research in cognitive science has demonstrated that people are better able to use new knowledge if learning is "situated" in the actual setting where the new knowledge is to be applied (Resnick, 1987a,b; Lave, 1988; Scribner and Stevens, 1989; Brown, Collins, and Duguid, 1989; Raizen, 1989). The situation in which a learner encounters a problem is an inextricable part of the learner's mental representation of that problem. A problem that is to be solved in the context of work is therefore best understood when it is encountered in the work process, rather than in a classroom. Sticht (1979, 1987) has demonstrated that functional context instruction can be effective even in teaching basic literacy skills.

The increased attention being given to on-the-job learning is resulting in greater awareness of the different forms such learning can take. One useful taxonomy has recently been developed by De Jong (1991). He distinguishes between on-site practice, on-site instruction, and on-site study. On-site practice is learning by doing. This is the predominant form of training in traditional apprenticeships, where trainees are given a sequence of tasks to learn by trial and error. On-site instruction is formal instruction and demonstration of task performance by a supervisor or instructor, followed by the trainee performing the task alone. Over the years, various routines have been formulated for delivering such instruction most effectively. Komatsu (1990) describes several of these as variations on a basic four-step method: prepare the learner, present the task, let the learner try, then follow up.

What De Jong calls on-site study is active exploration of problems by employees. It differs from on-site practice because it involves cognitive rather than motor skills. It differs from on-site instruction because it entails more initiative by learners. In one example, employees at a paper mill were assigned to study a new machine as it was being installed. One assignment was to crawl inside the machine and make a drawing of the ventilation system. This resulted in the discovery that one of the contractors had mistakenly connected a water hose where an air hose should have been.

This example illustrates what Stern (forthcoming) has called "doing by learning": an instructional exercise produces new information that is directly useful in the work process. Stern has described how learning-intensive firms apply this principle to formal off-site instruction. They use classroom time as an opportunity for employees to analyze problems from the worksite, using new concepts presented by the instructor. Trainees thus produce suggestions that can be immediately applied to their work. Whether on-site or off-site, doing by learning makes training part of the productive process itself.

Just-in-time training is also facilitated by various kinds of "job aids" (Komatsu, 1990; U.S. Congress, Office of Technology Assessment, 1990). Conventional job aids include concise checklists and decision tables that are posted where people work. Keyboard templates showing the location of function keys on a computer are another example. "Help" menus are another familiar form of just-in-time instruction.

With the computer's ability to "informate" (Zuboff, 1988), computerized job aids have evolved into "embedded training" (U.S. Congress, Office of Technology Assessment, 1990). Computers and microprocessor-controlled machines come equipped with self-diagnostic sequences to help operators correct malfunctions. Application of artificial intelligence to guide a user's questions promises to increase the scope and depth of learning possible from this kind of medium.

In economic terms, all of these mechanisms to integrate learning into the work process have the effect of reducing the opportunity cost of OJT. As stated earlier, this increases the amount of OJT that is economically feasible.

In addition to making it easier for employees to learn on the job, some firms are also providing more explicit financial incentives. Pay for knowledge is a compensation scheme that has spread rapidly since its invention only two decades ago (Jenkins and Gupta, 1985; Lawler and Ledford, 1985; U.S. Department of Labor, 1988; Casner-Lotto, 1988). Conventionally, employees' pay is determined by their job assignment. Pay for knowledge, in contrast, compensates employees according to demonstrated mastery of certain skills and knowledge, regardless of the job they happen to be performing during the pay period. This creates a clear and direct incentive for employees to learn while they work.

From the employer's viewpoint pay for knowledge has several advantages. First, workers may spend their slack time acquiring knowledge and skill instead of gossiping or relaxing. This reduces the opportunity cost of OJT practically to zero. Second, a multi-skilled workforce is more flexible. When someone is absent, a new product is introduced, or a new staffing pattern is instituted, employees who are cross-trained are better able to adapt. Third, employees who understand more aspects of the production process are in a better position to make suggestions for improving it.

A fourth advantage of pay for knowledge is that it gives employees an incentive to develop their ability to learn on the job. From the employer's point of view, this is the most durable kind of expertise. Hardware and software become obsolete, products and processes come and go. Constant change means it is impossible to maintain a workforce who are all experts in the current technology and product mix. The best an employer can hope for is that workers are willing and able to keep learning.

The ability to keep learning is also highly transferable to other firms. Therefore, while the knowledge rewarded by a pay-for-knowledge plan may be highly specific to the particular firm, the employees involved are also developing a very general kind of skill. For instance, in one manufacturing plant that has had pay for knowledge since it started in the early 1970s, the plan was being revised in the late 1980s. The individual responsible for coordinating the revision -- gathering views, coordinating committee meetings, drafting a report -- was a woman with no formal education beyond high school, who was still classified as a machine operator. Under the existing pay for knowledge system, she was qualifying for a higher wage by doing this administrative work. Although the content of what she was doing was specific to that plant, she was acquiring a great deal of competence that would be tranferable to other firms. Yet, again in apparent contradiction to standard human capital theory, her wage was being increased rather than reduced during this experience.

Policy Options to Promote Learning at Work

Stern (forthcoming) has described significant changes firms must make in order to become learning-intensive. Some of these changes are difficult, e.g. getting managers to encourage more ideas from subordinates. Another problematic change is the promise of greater employment security. This is an important condition for learning-intensive production because employees are reluctant to suggest ideas for improving efficiency if they fear their jobs might be eliminated as a result. More generally, both employers and employees have a greater incentive to invest in training if they expect the employment relationship to last.

For example, at Motorola all employees with ten years seniority become members of the Service Club, which means they cannot be dismissed except for poor performance or dishonesty (Wiggenhorn, 1990). Similarly, two of the Japanese automobile plants in the U.S. that are unionized, New United Motors Manufacturing Inc. and Mazda Motor Manufacturing (USA) Corporation, both have provisions in their contract that forbid layoffs unless the company has first taken such measures as reducing the salaries of managers. The connection between longevity of employment and OJT in Japan has been substantiated by Mincer and Higuchi (1988). References to other evidence are given in Stern (forthcoming).

However, employment security has been highly problematic in the U.S., where periods of high unemployment rates have been a fact of life and layoffs are a standard operating procedure. Stern (forthcoming) reviews the argument that there are positive externalities from a company's decision to minimize layoffs and increase employment security. Given positive externalities, it follows that firms in the aggregate provide too little employment security. Given that employment security is a condition for learning-intensive production, it follows also that firms in the aggregate provide less than the optimal amount of learning on the job.

More generally, if OJT is linked not just to employment security but also to employee participation, then OJT is under-provided if participation is under-provided. Levine and Tyson (1990) argue that this is the case. Other organizational practices that support employee participation include compression of wage and salary differentials within a firm to promote group cohesion, and long-term relationships with providers of capital who can appreciate the value of intangible investments in trust and cooperation with employees. As with employment security policies, firms or lending institutions that adopt these practices incur costs, which decrease as others follow suit. Levine and Tyson's analysis implies that collective mechanisms to encourage employee involvement as well as employment security will have a more powerful stimulating effect on OJT. Hashimoto's analysis in this volume implies a similar conclusion.

If markets fail to provide the socially efficient level of education and training for adult employees, some kind of collective action is warranted. One simple form of collective action would be government subsidies paid to firms for provision of education and training. However, the government would want to ensure that such subsidies support only activities that would not have taken place without them. This entails a certain amount of monitoring, which could be cumbersome. Monitoring is also necessary if, instead of a subisidy, the government levies a tax on firms that fail to invest a certain percentage of their payroll in training, as is done in France.

Both subsidies and tax levies can be attached much more easily to formal training than to informal training -- but informal training probably accounts for a larger share of total training activity, and probably contributes more to employees' continued learning, than formal education and training do. As discussed above, learning at work is not just a matter of going to classes. Simply paying all firms to provide more formal education and training, or taxing them for not providing enough, may not be the most efficient or effective means to promote learning by adult employees.

Promoting employment stability. The powerful connection between firm-based learning and employment security suggests that one set of policies might seek to increase investment in adult employees by enhancing employment stability. Macroeconomic policy is important here. Maintaining a low aggregate unemployment rate directly improves employment security. The resulting increase in firm-based training investments should be counted as one of the benefits of such policy. The longer a low unemployment rate can be sustained, the more employers must adapt to it by learning how to cultivate the knowledge and skill of their existing workforce, rather than relying on a hire-and-fire policy to upgrade workers' skill and knowledge (Stern, 1982b). Soskice (1989), among others, has argued that a low-unemployment macroeconomic policy goes hand in hand with firm-based human resource investments that have made some countries relatively successful in international competition. Japan is a pre-eminent example.

Macroeconomic policy is limited, however. It cannot prevent all recessions. Nor can it prevent slowdowns in particular industries and firms from time to time. Here is where some targeted subsidies to firms can be useful. Funds can be provided for training current employees who would otherwise become unemployed. In case of a general recession, such subsidies can help keep employees on the payroll until economic conditions improve. If the problem is limited to an individual industry or firm, training subsidies can be used to help change over to new products, services, or methods of production. In the U.S., the state of California's Employment Training Panel since 1983 has provided subsidies for training employees whose employers identify them as likely to become unemployed if they are not retrained (Schneider, 1988; Creticos and Sheets, 1989). These subsidies are financed by a 0.1 percent addition to the Unemployment Insurance Tax. The rationale is that providing training subsidies to prevent unemployment reduces claims on the Unemployment Insurance fund. In the Netherlands, similar subsidies are provided by the Kaderregeling Scholing. By helping to keep employees on the payroll, such countercyclical training subsidies provide some protection for employment stability, and preserve incentives for both workers and firms to invest in continued learning.

A similar form of targeted training subsidy awards training funds to companies that are upgrading their productive technology. An example in the U.S. is the Michigan Modernization Service (U.S. Congress, Office of Technology Assessment, 1990, p. 61). The state of Michigan established this service in 1985 to help companies adopt programmable automation. Training specialists work alongside engineers, advising firms on how to deploy new technology and how employees can learn to use it. Training grants can be used for current employees. This protects employment security in the face of technological change. Other states sponsor similar programs (Creticos and Sheets, 1989).

Enhancing employees' mobility. Although employment stability is conducive to firm-based investment in employees' knowledge and skill, it is unrealistic to expect that most companies will give workers lifetime employment contracts, even if government policies try to help. In fact, it seems that increasing volatility in world markets is making it harder for firms to maintain such commitments (Osterman, 1988). Philips is a notable case in point: faced with a sudden drop in profits, the company is abandoning its traditional job security policy and cutting its worldwide workforce by approximately one-sixth (Business Week, November 12, 1990, pp. 58-59).

Since worker mobility is unavoidable, and to some degree desirable, another set of public policies can be designed to improve employees' prospects in case they lose their jobs. One such policy would subsidize firms for helping current employees acquire knowledge and skill that are demonstrably general, i.e., useful in other firms. An example is the current set of federal and state programs in the U.S. to support workplace-based literacy programs (U.S. Congress, Office of Technology Assessment, 1990, pp. 57, 171; see also Carnevale, Gainer, and Meltzer, 1990). Federal funds to develop such programs were made available in 1988 by amendments to the Adult Basic Education act. The immediate purpose is to upgrade workers' skill in reading, writing, and mathematics. Many of these programs are designed for experienced workers whose employers want them to operate new technologies or carry out new responsibilities such as statistical process control. In such cases, literacy training helps workers keep their current jobs. But, in addition, reading, writing and mathematics are general skills, used in many jobs. Literacy upgrading therefore enhances these employees' prospects in the labor market even if they do not retain their current jobs.

A second kind of training-support policy that is consistent with worker mobility would focus on strengthening ties among groups of firms. Earlier in this chapter, studies were cited which indicate that employees do not, in fact, pay for general training by accepting lower wages while they are being trained. Bishop, in this volume, suggests that one reason why workers will not accept lower wages during training is that they correctly perceive that other employers will not give them credit for the general skill and knowledge they are acquiring in their present job. A direct solution to this market failure is to create certification systems that will indicate clearly what a worker has learned. Where formal apprenticeship systems have been successful, they have created explicit standards of proficiency in an occupation. The National Center on Education and the Economy (1990) has argued for creation of such standards for major occupations in the U.S. Public agencies could stimulate efforts along these lines by existing trade associations or by ad hoc groups of firms in an industry. Creating an institutional mechanism to certify, for example, that a secretary has become competent with a particular word-processing program, or that a machinist has learned to operate a particular automated milling machine, would provide greater incentive for workers and firms to invest in general training. Creating proficiency standards may also be a first step toward inter-firm collaboration in the actual delivery of training.

A third kind of mobility-enhancing policy would provide financial incentives directly to individuals for further education and training. Like subsidies to firms, financial incentives for individuals are most easily attached to formal, rather than informal, training. Section 127 of the U.S. Internal Revenue Act has permitted employees not to pay taxes on tuition reimbursements received from their employers. There have also been proposals to allow individuals to set aside funds for "individual training accounts", modeled on existing individual retirement accounts, where interest on investments would accrue tax-free, and which could be withdrawn for educational purposes. Schutze and Istance (1987) describe four other proposed mechanisms. One would be an individual entitlement to money for further education. Another is a more general drawing right to income that would finance time away from work, whether for educational purposes or not. A third proposal would use non-governmental agencies as financial intermediaries, and a fourth would establish guarantees for educational loans. All of these encourage individuals to undertake the kind of formal education that would enhance their prospects for job mobility.

<u>Other policies to promote firm-based training</u>. In addition to programs that would actively intervene in the market for adult education and training, public policy could also play a useful role by providing additional information. Simply accounting for the amount of formal training that currently exists is difficult. It would be useful to conduct descriptive surveys, with consistent definitions to describe the prevalence of training activities.

It would also be useful to conduct further research on informal training. Surprisingly, despite the extent of the literature about training and skill formation in workplaces, the process itself remains a black box. Scribner (e.g., see Scribner and Stevens, 1989), Komatsu (1990), De Jong (1991) and others have begun to peer inside the box, but most of the mechanisms are still unknown. Descriptive accounts have identified ways in which some companies are trying to promote learning on the job, but quantitative evaluations have yet to be done. It would be worthwhile to try to understand better how learning occurs at work, and what conditions support it.

Conclusion

There is good reason to believe that the demand for continued learning by adult workers will continue to grow. Learning-intensive production is likely to be increasingly important in both manufacturing and services. There is also reason to believe that free markets do not provide enough opportunity for employees' continued learning. Government can intervene in various ways to promote further education and training of adults. Formal training and education are relatively simple to support, but informal learning in the context of work itself is both more important and more difficult to stimulate through public policy. Designing effective policies to promote informal learning on the job will require a more thorough understanding of how such learning actually happens.

References

Adler, P. (ed.), forthcoming. Technology and the future of work. Oxford: Oxford University Press.

Barron, J. M., Black, D. A., and Loewenstein, M.A. "Employer Size: The Implications for Search, Training, Capital Investment, Starting Wages, and Wage Growth," Journal of Labor Economics, Vol. 5, No. 1 1987, pp. 76-89.

Barron, J.M., Black, D.A., and Loewenstein, M.A. 1989 Job matching and on-the-job training. Journal of Labor Economics 7(1): 1-19.

Bartel, A. P. & Lichtenberg, F.R.. 1987. The comparative advantage of educated workers in implementing new technology. The Review of Economics and Statistics 69(1): 1-11.

Bartel, A. P. "An Analysis of Company Investments in Employee Training and Development," A Paper Prepared for the Conference on Employer-Sponsored Training, Washington, D.C., December 1, 1988.

Becker G.S. 1964, second edition 1975 Human capital. Chicago, IL: University of Chicago Press.

Benson, C. S. and Lohnes, P. R. "Skill Requirements and Industrial Training in Durable Goods Manufacturing," Industrial and Labor Relations Review, Vol. 12, No. 4, July 1959, pp. 540-553.

Brown, J. S., Collins, A. & Duguid, P.. 1989. Situated cognition and the culture of learning. Educational Researcher 18(1): 32-41.

Carnevale, A. P., Gainer L.J. and Meltzer, A.S.1990. Workplace basics. San Francisco: Jossey-Bass Publishers.

Carnevale, A. P., Gainer, L.J. and Villet, J. 1990. Training in America. San Francisco: Jossey-Bass Publishers.

Casner-Lotto, J. 1988. Successful training stategies. San Francisco: Jossey-Bass Publishers.

Creticos, P. A., and Sheets, R.G.. 1989. State-financed, workplace-based retraining programs. The National Commission for Employment Policy and the National Governors' Association. Washington, D.C.: National Commission for Employment Policy.

De Jong, J.A. 1991. The multiformity of on-site training. Utrecht (Netherlands): Utrecht University, Department of Education.

Dertouzos, M.L., Lester, R.K. and Solow, R.M., 1989. Made in America: Regaining the productive edge. Cambridge, MA: MIT Press.

Eurich, N.P., 1990. The learning industry. Princeton, N.J.: Carnegie Foundation for the Advancement of Teaching.

Feuer, M., Glick, H., and Desai, A. 1986 Is firm-sponsored education viable? Journal of Economic Behavior and Organization, December.

Galagan, P.A. 1989. IBM gets its arms around education. Training & Development Journal 43(1): 35-41.

Hamermesh, D. S. & Grant, J.. 1979. Econometric studies of labor-labor substitution and their implications for policy. The Journal of Human Resources 14(4): 518-42.

Hashimoto, M. 1981. Firm-specific human capital as a shared investment. American Economic Review 71(3): 475-482.

Hashimoto, M. 1989. The role of transaction costs in training on the job: the Japanese experience. Paper presented at conference on Market Failure in Training, University of Wisconsin, Madison, May 11-12.

Hashimoto, M. and Yu, B. T. 1980. Specific capital, employment contracts, and wage rigidity. Bell Journal of Economics 11(2): 536-549.

Helfgott, R. B. 1988. Computerized manufacturing and human resources. Lexington, MA: Lexington Books.

Hirschhorn, L. 1984. Beyond mechanization. Cambridge, MA: MIT Press.

Jaikumar, R. 1986. Postindustrial manufacturing. Harvard Business Review November-December: 69-76.

Jamison, D. T., and Lau, L.J.. 1982. Farmer education and farm efficiency. Baltimore, MD: Johns Hopkins University Press.

Jenkins, D. G., Jr. & Gupta, N.. 1985. The payoffs of paying for knowledge. National Productivity Review 3: 121-30.

Komatsu, N.B. 1990. Expert performance: designing on-the-job learning. Washington, D.C.: National Alliance of Business.

Lave, J. 1988. Cognition in practice: Mind, mathematics and culture in everyday life. Cambridge, England: Cambridge University Press.

Lawler, E.E., & Ledford, G.E. 1985. "Skill-based pay: a concept that's catching on." Personnel, 62(9): 30-37.

Lazear, E.P. 1981 Agency, earnings profiles, productivity, and hours restrictions. American Economic Review 71(4): 606-620.

Levin, H.M. 1987. Improving productivity through education and technology. In Burke, G. and Rumberger, R.M. (eds.): The future impact of technology on work and education. Philadelphia, PA: Falmer Press.

Levine, D. and Tyson, L.D. 1990. Participation, productivity, and the firm's environment. In Blinder, A.S. (ed.): Paying for productivity, a look at the evidence. Washington, D.C.: Brookings Institution.

Mincer, J. & Higuchi, Y.. 1988. Wage structures and labor turnover in the U.S. and in Japan. Occasional Paper No. 6. New York: National Center on Education and Employment Teachers College, Columbia University.

Mincer, J. 1989. Labor market effects of human capital and of its adjustments to technological change. New York: Institute on Education and the Economy, Teachers College, Columbia University.

National Academy of Sciences, Committee on the Effective Implementation of Advanced Manufacturing Technology 1986. Human resource practices for implementing advanced manufacturing technology. Washington, D.C.: National Academy Press.

National Academy of Sciences, Panel on Technology and Employment 1987. Technology and employment. Washington, D.C.: National Academy Press.

National Center on Education and the Economy 1990. America's choice: high skills or low wages. Rochester, N.Y.: National Center on Education and the Economy.

National Commission for Employment Policy 1990. Employer strategies for a changing labor force: A primer on innovative programs and policies. Washington, D.C.: National Commission for Employment Policy, Research Report 90-01.

Osterman, P. 1988. Employment futures. New York: Oxford University Press.

Raizen, S. A. 1989. Reforming education for work: A cognitive science perspective. National Center for Research on Vocational Education, Institute for Education and the Economy, Teachers College Columbia University.

Resnick, L. B. 1987a. Learning in school and out. Educational Researcher 16: 13-20.

Resnick, L. B. 1987b. Education and learning to think. Washington, D.C.: National Academy Press.

Schneider, J. 1988. Training and employment security: the role of California's Employment Training Panel. San Francisco, CA: Coro Foundation.

Schultz, T. W. 1975. The value of the ability to deal with disequilibria. Journal of Economic Literature 13: 827-46.

Scribner, S. & Stevens, J.. 1989. Experimental studies on the relationship of school math and work math: Technical paper number 3. New York: National Center on Education and Employment, Teachers College, Columbia University.

Sloman, M. 1989. On-the-job training: A costly poor relation. Personnel Management, February, pp. 38-41.

Soskice, D. 1989. Reinterpreting corporatism and explaining unemployment: Coordinated and non-coordinated market economies. Forthcoming in R. Brunetta and C. della Ringa (Eds.), Markets, institutions and cooperation: Labour relations and economic performance. London: Macmillan.

Stern, D. 1982a Economic feasibility of on-the-job training. Economics of Education Review 2(2): 157-173.

Stern, D. 1982b Managing human resources: the art of full employment. Dover, MA: Auburn House.

Stern, D., forthcoming. Institutions and incentives for developing work-related knowledge and skill. In Adler, P. (ed.): Technology and the future of work. Oxford: Oxford University Press.

Sticht, T.G. 1979. Developing literacy and learning strategies in organizational settings. In H. F. O'Neil Jr. and C. D. Spielberger (Eds.): Cognitive and affective learning strategies. New York: Academic Press.

Sticht, T.G. 1987. Functional context education. Workshop resource noteboook. San Diego, CA: The Applied Behavioral & Cognitive Sciences, Inc.

Tan, H.W. 1988 Private sector training in the United States: who gets it and why. Santa Monica, CA: RAND Corp.

Thompson, H. and Scalpone, R. 1985. Managing the human resource in the factory of the future. Human Systems Management 5: 221-230.

U.S. Congress, Office of Technology Assessment 1990. Worker training. OTA-ITE-457. Washington, D.C.: U.S. Government Printing Office.

U.S. Department of Labor, Bureau of Labor-Management Relations. 1988. Exploratory investigations of pay-for-knowledge systems. BMLR 108. Washington, D.C.: author.

Welch, F. 1970. Education in production. Journal of Political Economy 78: 35-59.

Wiggenhorn, W. 1990. Motorola U: When training becomes an education. Harvard Business Review, July-August, pp. 71-83.

Womack, J.P., Jones, D.T. and Roos, D. 1990. The machine that changed the world. New York: Rawson Associates.

Wozniak, G. D. 1987. Human capital, information, and the early adoption of new technology. Journal of Human Resources 22(1): 101-12.

Zuboff, S. 1988. In the age of the smart machine. New York: Basic Books.

TRAINING AND EMPLOYMENT RELATIONS IN JAPANESE FIRMS

Masanori Hashimoto
Department of Economics
The Ohio State University
410 Arps Hall
1945 N. High Street
Columbus, Ohio 43210-1172

1. Introduction

Japan's recent emergence as a global economic power has attracted international attention to the Japanese management system.[1] An important question is why and how management and labor seem to have cooperated so effectively in helping Japan achieve such a status. To shed light on this

---

1. This paper is an outgrowth of my project on a comparative study of labor markets in Japan and the United States supported by the Upjohn Institute for Employment Research as well as a current research project on Japanese automobile manufacturers in the United States. A related paper on productivity growth was supported by the Brookings Institution. For additional discussions, see Hashimoto (1990a, b). I thank my discussants at the conference, Michael Feuer and Richard Murnane, and the editor of this volume, David Stern, for offering useful comments on this paper. I incorporated into this article some information I gathered in my current research into the training and employment practices at the Japanese automobile transplants in the U.S. Midwest. The information was gathered during interviews of key personnel at Subaru-Isuzu Automotive Inc. (SIA), Diamond-Star Motors, Mazda Motor Manufacturing (USA), Toyota Motor Manufacturing, USA, and Honda of America Manufacturing. I wish to thank these companies for agreeing to participate in my study.

question, this paper discusses certain key features of the Japanese industrial relations and training practices and sketches a theory to help understand them.

In an industrialized economy, a firm's production activities inevitably entail interdependence among the workers. Interdependence is the essence of team work, and it runs across workers of different ranks in the hierarchy as well as workers of the same rank. The firm's performance, therefore, depends critically on its employment relations system, which defines the environment for team work. The quality of the employment relations system, in turn, is determined by the investments made to maintain and improve it. Such investments are made by all the workers involved, and in this paper, the term training refers to these investments rather than to the usual, narrower, definition of technical training. The postwar Japanese experience suggests that such training helps foster a strong sense of identification with and commitment to the company on the part of both the management and the worker (Cole 1979, p. 253).

To be sure, investments in machinery and other non-human resources undoubtedly played an important role in the high growth of Japan's postwar economy. Jorgenson *et. al.* (1987), for example, argue that the high rates of growth in capital and intermediate inputs were largely responsible for the rapid growth in Japan's output after 1960. This paper directs attention, however, to the importance of investments in the employment relationship in making the machines run efficiently. As Hayes (1981) observed, Japanese machinery and equipment are not always that much newer than those in America, but they tend to run like new because, I argue, workers tending them are well trained.

2. Key Features of the Japanese Industrial Relations System

Space does not allow detailed discussions here on such celebrated Japanese features as the seniority wage system, the lifetime employment system, and enterprise unionism (see Hashimoto 1990b for discussions on these features). Instead, I focus here on some Japanese industrial relations practices, which bear on the issue of private sector training.

Flexibility of Work Organization and Contracts

The first point to note is that work organization and industrial relations in Japan exhibit greater flexibility than in most other developed countries (cf. Tachibanaki 1986, and Koshiro 1986). Flexible work organization is supported by the job rotation system whereby a typical worker is rotated among different tasks during his tenure in the firm. It should be stressed that job rotation refers to a long-term process involving a worker's entire career in the firm rather than to the commonly understood practice of a process whereby a worker performs different tasks on a regular basis, say within a week.[2] Job rotation enables a worker to acquire a wide range of skills (Koike 1984 and Aoki 1988, Chapter 2). As a result, workers become functional in a variety of tasks, a characteristic which facilitates

---

2. I have detected the practice of Japanese type job rotation at Honda of America Manufacturing, where an associate--a term referring to Honda employees--has experienced several different tasks, painting, welding, assembling, purchasing, etc., during a period lasting ten years or so. Other Japanese transplants are newer than Honda, and it is too early to tell if job rotation in the true sense occurs in them.

a quick and flexible response to changes in work requirement as well as enables them to understand and correct the conditions which give rise to defective products (Aoki 1988, pp. 35-37). This way, the job rotation system helps promote the zero, or low, defect production process. Not to be overlooked is the fact that most of those in the management ranks were once ordinary employees *within the same firm*, have gone through the job rotation process, and were members of enterprise unions. It is reasonable to expect these management to be more closely attuned to the idiosyncrasies of the firm's operations and therefore to incur lower transaction costs with the employees than U.S. type managers, many of whom may have been at the firm for only a short period of time.

The job rotation system makes the workers' skills *intra-firm general* so that a decline in demand in one locality within the firm does not necessarily lead to layoffs or dismissals of affected workers. Thus, this system is an integral part of the long-term employment relationship and is an important factor behind the typically low unemployment rates in Japan. Also, a worker with *intra-firm general* skills is less likely to suffer unemployment from the introduction of new technology, and therefore is less resistant to the new technology, than another who is trained for a narrowly defined task. This consideration may explain why Japanese firms have been able to adopt new technologies rapidly since the 1960's. Finally, job rotation encourages workers to share knowledge and tasks among themselves, and such sharing enables them to cope effectively with local emergencies without the help of experts (Aoki, 1988).

Flexible job structures based on cross-training have existed in U.S. firms as well. Jacoby (1989), for example, reports that similar practices which were prevalent among some large firms in the late 1920's were part of the strategy to stabilize employment. However, U.S. firms in the postwar years have tended to emphasize narrow task specialization and sharp job demarcation, and these are the characteristics that make it difficult to train workers in a diverse range of skills.

Other evidence of flexibility is in Japanese collective agreements, which tend to be brief and even obscure (Hanami 1981, chapter 2). The brevity of contracts reflects the fact that the parties involved understand that contract terms can be modified readily in response to newly emerging circumstances. This understanding obviates the necessity to stipulate detailed contractual terms. In contrast, collective agreements in America are characterized by a precise and detailed description of the standards to be applied in every possible disagreement as well as a complete description of the rights and obligations of both parties. Japanese agreements accept that some unanticipated developments are bound to occur, and strive to establish mutual understanding and trust. As Hanami observed, "the detailed enumeration of specific contact provisions would be fatal to this flexibility" (Hanami 1981, p. 53).[3] Major decisions in Japanese firms are

---

3. For a related discussion on Japanese labor relations, see Sugeno and Koshiro (1987). The collective agreements between the United Auto Workers (UAW) and Diamond Star (a joint venture between Mitsubishi and Chrysler) and Mazda (a joint venture between Mazda and Ford) are brief: agreements at each company contain about 80 pages in contrast to the 1987 UAW agreements with the General Motors, which consisted of over 520 pages of national agreements and various local agreements--one local agreement had over 150 pages. The UAW obviously made extensive concessions in allowing flexibility in

(Footnote continues on next page)

made in close consultation with their enterprise unions, and management and labor depend on good faith interactions with each other to resolve disagreements and disputes.[4]

Joint Consultation, Consensus-Based Decisions, and Quality Control Circles

Management and labor in a typical Japanese firm spend much time and energy exchanging information and consulting both informally and formally.

(Footnote continued from previous page)

adjustments at these transplants. It is noteworthy that the national agreements with General Motors don't apply to its new Saturn Corporation, a GM attempt to compete with Japanese small automobiles; there, the agreements with UAW are spelled out in mere 28 pages! It is likely, however, that agreements at the Japanese transplants and Saturn will grow in size as these operations mature.

4. Even Japanese firms without unions make efforts to facilitate communications between management and labor. A president of a non-union medium-sized firm (about 800 employees) told me that his employees and officers frequently interact with one another on matters of concern through a "friendship club". Another motive appears to be to forestall a unionization of his workforce, consistent with Freeman's (1989) hypothesis that management opposition to unionization is responsible for the recent decline in the union density in Japan as well as in the U.S.

One formal process is the joint consultation system.[5] Joint consultation takes place according to regularly set schedules in some cases, and as need arises in others. Joint consultation exists even in non-unionized sectors, though it is more prevalent in the unionized sector.[6] According to a 1984 survey, of 1,802 unions, 1,068, or 59 percent, used joint consultation (Sugeno and Koshiro, 1987). Among unions in large firms (1000+ employees), the proportion of unions with joint consultation was 71 percent. Even among very small firms (29 or fewer employees), the proportion was 34 percent.

Joint consultation is designed to deal with such problems as recruitment, dismissal, transfer and promotion, changes in production techniques and in management policies, plant closing, industrial safety and the like (Shirai 1983, Hanami 1984, and Sugeno and Koshiro 1987).[7] In the

---

5. The joint consultation system has been rare in the U.S. Works councils (Betriesbräte) in West Germany and other European countries also use joint consultations.

6. According to a survey taken by the Ministry of Labor in 1977, almost 83 percent of unionized establishments and a little over 40 percent of non-union establishments used joint consultation (Shirai 1983, p. 143). For informative discussions of joint consultation, see also Koshiro (1983) and Sugeno and Koshiro (1987).

7. According to Sugeno and Koshiro (1987), joint consultation provides the parties with "channels for intimate communication with the result that many matters which might otherwise develop into shop floor disputes are agreed upon in advance and peacefully implemented." (p. 143). For some evidence of joint consultation's positive effects on firm performance, see Morishima (1989).

1984 survey mentioned above, eighty-six percent of unions listed expediting communication, and 83 percent listed promotion of harmonious relationships as the major objective of joint consultation.[8]

The joint consultation practice became prevalent in Japan after 1955, paralleling the development of the productivity enhancement campaign (*seisansei undo*), whose objective was to raise productivity and international competitiveness by importing modern technologies from the United States and Europe (cf. Section 3). In my view, this campaign played a significant role in spreading joint consultation and other modern industrial relations practices in Japan. Even if one were to subscribe to the historical continuity of institutional development, it seems reasonable to view the period after the late 1950's as being one of consolidation of what had been in progress before.[9] I argue that the productivity enhancement campaign, by promoting technical progress and productivity growth, raised the benefits of investing in employment relationships.

---

8. Other objectives mentioned are the maintenance and improvement of working conditions (77%), improvement of productivity (63%), participation in management activities (38%), and other (20%). This information is from Japan Ministry of Labor, The Latest Status of Labor Agreements, 1984, Table 5-3. A case study may be an effective way of appreciating the workings of joint consultations and grievance procedures. See an illuminating case study of the Japan Steel Corporation and the Postal Service by Sugeno and Koshiro (1987).

9. See Hashimoto (1990b, Chapter 3) for a historical perspective on many of the Japanese practices.

Another, less formal, process is consensus-based decision making. In this process, important decisions are made only after a consensus has been achieved by an extensive sharing of information and through the practice known as "*nemawashi*". *Nemawashi* literally connotes the practice of preparing for a successful transplantation, or for the bearing of abundant fruits, by trimming roots of a plant well in advance. The term has come to mean the taking of every necessary step to achieve a desired outcome, and the practice prevails throughout the economy rather than just in the unionized sector. The *nemawashi* practice is costly in time and energy. Since the practice has prevailed among many firms for many years, it seems reasonable to infer that the gains have been worth the cost. Joint consultation and consensus-based decision making through the practice of nemawashi are the cornerstone of the postwar Japanese industrial relations system. According to several American managers of Japanese automobile transplants in the U.S. Midwest, the time consuming process of consensus building is one of the major adjustments that Americans have to accept to work in the "Japanese-style" work environment.

The effectiveness of Japanese industrial relations practices may be inferred from data on labor disputes. I have noted elsewhere that there have been fewer cases of labor disputes, and the resulting productivity loss has been smaller, in Japan than in America (Hashimoto 1990b).[10] In 1981,

---

10. Japanese strikes tend to be short lived: They often occur at an early stage in the bargaining process, whether or not negotiations are deadlocked. Thus, strikes or other acts of dispute simply demonstrate that the unions

(Footnote continues on next page)

for example, there were 955 labor disputes in Japan involving 247 thousand workers. These disputes resulted in 554 thousand working days lost, or 220 days per 100 affected employees, or 14 days lost per thousand employees economy wide. In the U.S. there were 2,568 disputes involving 1.08 million workers, resulting in 24.7 million working days lost. The U.S. experience translates to 2,290 days lost per 100 affected employees or 276 days lost per thousand employees economy wide, much higher figures than for Japan.[11] What is noteworthy is that the number of days lost in Japan was rather high in the 1950's before the declining trend set in after 1960. Interestingly,

---

(Footnote continued from previous page)
disagree with the management (Matsuda 1983, pp. 193-195). Indeed, a distinguishing feature of the mentality of Japanese workers is their reluctance to cause any serious damage to the firm in which they work (Shirai 1983, pp. 135-140).

11. The same general conclusion holds for other years as well. After 1981, the U.S. data on labor disputes refer only to membership larger than 1,000 workers and are not comparable to the Japanese data. One word of caution is in order when interpreting the Japanese data. The data on disputes used here do not include more subtle forms of work stoppages, such as go-slow or work-to-rule methods. These informal practices are believed to be more widely used in Japan than in the U.S. Indeed, these practices are unpopular in the U.S. [See, for example, Hanami and Blanpain 1984, Part IV. by Hanami and Part V. by St. Antoine].

this trend pattern coincides with the increased prevalence of joint consultations and related practices starting in the late 1950's. It is clear that cooperative industrial relations in Japan are rather a recent phenomenon. In contrast, if anything there was an upward trend in the number of days lost in the U.S., consistent with the view that U.S. industrial relations tended to worsen during the postwar years.[12]

Quality control (QC) circle is another practice whose success requires low transaction costs. The Japanese QC circle was adopted from the concept of statistical quality control pioneered in the 1950's by the American named W. Edwards Deming.[13] The practice became popular after the early 1960's, and by the early 1980's there were about a million circles in Japan (Cole, 1979, Chapter 5 and Blair and Ramsing, 1983). Quality control circles in Japan are not limited to manufacturing; they exist among department stores, railways, retail shops, auto and television repair services, airlines, hotels, etc., and even among municipal governments

---

12. For example, Takezawa and Whitehill (1981) compare the results of their surveys taken in 1960 and 1976 in Japan and the United States. They infer from these surveys that Japanese management, unions, and workers have come to "share broad mutual goals for the attainment of which the parties are prepared to work together in spirit of cooperation" (p. 197). They infer that in the United States "workers' commitment to their enterprises has generally decreased; workers have increasingly rejected work as a way of life; and credibility in management has declined..." (p. 196).

13. See Cole (1979, 1980) and Blair and Ramsing (1983) for details on the history and practices of quality circles in Japan.

(Juran 1975). This practice has been "brought back" to the U.S. since the mid-1970's with apparently mixed results (Cole 1989).

Unlike joint consultation, the quality control circle typically involves direct participation of only a handful of production workers doing related work.[14] Instead of meeting in response to specific problems, a QC circle is a continuous study process involving the issues of quality and productivity (Cole 1980, p. 26). Usually, there is more than one QC circle within a firm, and each deals with productivity issues specific to a particular stage of production. Blair and Ramsing (1983, p. 492) notes that "Group cohesion and capacity for self control is encouraged through team building exercises, limiting group size (3 to 10), and usually choosing homogeneous membership." Since participation in the quality circle tends to be rewarded in terms of contribution to the company and self-development rather than in money, QC circles are likely to be more effective where there exists a longer-term employer-employee attachment.

It shouldn't be assumed, however, that quality control circles in Japan have always been successful. It is said that some firms experienced problems with them for a few years after their introduction. Workers sometimes felt they were coerced into QC circles, and the emphasis on productivity made the participants doubt the value to them personally of circles (Cole 1980). Moreover, there is no concrete evidence that quality control circles have had direct effects on productivity and quality in

---

14. Joint consultation involves both white and blue collar workers, not all of them doing related work, and deals with a much broader range of subjects than QC circles.

Japan. Since quality control circles are likely to work best when they are part of the overall emphasis on quality, it is understandably difficult to measure the contribution of QC circles themselves to productivity and quality. As Hayes pointed out, many firms already had a reputation for high quality by the time they adopted quality control circles (Hayes, 1981).

3. A Hypothesis on Private Sector Training in Japan

Training in Japanese firms is a long-term process for which the major input is time spent exchanging information and transferring knowledge among employees as well as between the management and employees.[15] Training occurs, for example, during joint consultation and consensus-based decision making as well as during more formal training sessions. Training that takes place in these activities entails costs, as these activities consume resources in terms of time and energy. Moreover, time investments in training take place even beyond the work place, as Japanese employees of various ranks, managers and non-managers alike, spend a great deal of time together "socializing" after work in restaurants and bars as if they were

---

15. The descriptions of various practices that follow apply best to larger Japanese firms. Therefore, one needs to be cautious in making inferences about the smaller Japanese firms. However, large firm practices tend to serve as the benchmark for other firms in Japan, and to the extent that other firms try to emulate large firm practices these descriptions are meaningful.

family members or close friends.[16] It is revealing in this regard that such socializing is considered to be more critical for younger employees than for those who already are in the management ranks.[17] These investments pay off by promoting smooth employment relations, which, in turn, raise productivity on the shop floor.

My research in progress, which involves numerous interviews with managers of Japanese automobile transplants in the United States, makes it clear that Japanese firms typically place a major emphasis on training investments. This research suggests, moreover, that, in thinking about the training issues, training should be thought of broadly to include not only technical training but also training in how to function effectively in a team, that is, how to communicate effectively with co-workers, how to teach and learn from them, and how to deal with conflict situations.[18] Such training continues throughout an employee's tenure in the firm. The critical aspect of the continuous training process in Japan is that senior

---

16. My Japanese contacts, both businessmen and an academic administrator, indicated that they tend to spend these resources especially when there is a need for producing a consensus. It is said that a typical salary-man does not return home until about 11:30 p.m. almost every evening. Most of these workers are salaried, and no overtime pay is involved in these activities.

17. See Valigra (1990) for an interesting account of a typical day in the life of a Japanese worker of management rank.

18. According to an executive of Toyota Motor Manufacturing, conflict management is one program that Toyota introduced in the U.S., but it is an unnecessary subject for training in Japan.

workers consider it their duty to teach younger, less experienced, workers. In fact, an important criterion for promotion in a Japanese firm is one's ability to teach co-workers. In a Japanese firm, a senior employee's value in the firm does not diminish if he should end up training his subordinates to be more knowledgeable than he. On the contrary, a successful trainee is a credit to the senior employee, who in turn is judged to be all the more valuable to the firm. Such an arrangement is sustained no doubt because in the "lifetime" employment environment in a typical Japanese firm, the newly trained worker does not pose a threat to the job security of the trainer.[19]

To understand the Japanese training practice as well as other industrial relations practices, let me adopt my recently formulated theory of employment relations in Japan (Hashimoto 1990b, c). That theory focuses on the transaction-cost environment, or labor climate in popular parlance, as the principal exogenous factor shaping the industrial relations

---

19. The relation between job security and the incentive to provide training has been discussed in the context of the American economy as well. Reagan (1988), for example, models the usual practice of layoffs by inverse-seniority as a device to encourage inter-employee training by guaranteeing job security of trainers. Parsons (1990) reminds us that early apprenticeship contracts addressed this problem by restricting the apprentice's right to compete with the master by specifying, for example, that the apprentice could not operate within a certain range of the master's own shop. These considerations suggest that the so-called "lifetime employment" practice (*shushin koyo*) and wages that are closely tied to the tenure in the firm (*nenko joretsu*), both of which reduce, if not eliminate, the disincentive to train coworkers, provide the key support for the training practices in a typical Japanese firm.

practices. Transaction costs in that analysis denote costs of communicating information between the employer and the employee as well as among the employees, including the costs of convincing the other party of the information's veracity. This approach resulted in a simple analytical framework for investigating how the transaction-cost environment affects the incentive to invest in the employment relations. The applicability of that theory to the issue of training is straightforward, as outlined in Figure 1.

See Figure 1 on page 183.

I postulate that the employer and employee invest in training in order to enhance their mutual well-being. It is informative to distinguish between two types of training: (1) training to enhance the employee's technical skills and (2) to increase the reliability of all types of information exchanged within the firm. In Figure 1, these investments are indicated in circles. These training investments together constitute the investment in the employment relations. The greater the training the more productive is the employment relationship. The benefits to investing in technical skills are obvious, and many authors writing on training issues have focused on this aspect. In contrast, the importance of reliable information exchange within the firm has not been emphasized in the literature. An employment relationship entails transmitting and verifying information among the parties involved as well as convincing one another of the veracity of the information. Improved quality of communication promotes quick dissemination of reliable information to the relevant parties, thereby reducing mistrust, disputes, and inefficient decisions, and promoting cooperative industrial relations and productivity.

The independent variables in my analysis are the costs associated with these investments (cf. Figure 1). The cost of training in information reliability is shaped by the transaction-cost environment, which reflects the degree of cultural heterogeneity of the workforce, its ability to function cooperatively as a group, management attitudes, worker propensity for mobility, and other "cultural" factors. Figure 1 indicates that the transaction-cost environment is influenced by formal education, as will be discussed below. The cost of training in technical skills is a function of how well basic education prepares students for training by imparting positive attitudes for learning as well as by teaching basic skills. I argued that there are more training investments in Japan than in the United States because the investment costs are lower in Japan (Hashimoto, 1990b).

Figure 1 indicates the role of formal (basic) education in training. Clearly, a solid education in the basic skills of arithmetic, reading, and writing is a prerequisite for a successful post schooling training in technical skills. In addition to teaching basic knowledge, the educational system in Japan instills skills and attitudes for effective group functioning and continuous learning on one's own. For example, school children are taught from early on to perform various cooperative chores in groups such as serving school lunches and cleaning the classroom at the end of the day. Also, as will be discussed later, Japanese employers rely greatly on self-study in training employees on technical know-how. This way, the basic education system helps shape the transaction-cost environment.

According to Figure 1, both types of investment feed back to each other. Thus, an exogenous lowering of the cost of training in information reliability increases the investment in such training, which, in turn, stimulates the investment in technical skills. As well, a lowering of the cost of investing in technical skills increases the investment in these skills, and in turn stimulates the investment in information reliability. An exogenous increase in the benefits of technical skills has a positive effect on the investment in information reliability, and vice versa. I also investigated how the interaction between the two types of investments affects the choice of contract type and found that an increased reliability of information is likely to lead to flexible contractual arrangements as prevail in Japan.

Figure 1 also shows that economic growth and technological progress can stimulate both types of investment. This prediction is noteworthy because it points to the link between training on the one hand and macroeconomic and industrial policies, on the other, which affect economic growth and technological progress (Hashimoto 1990a). Indeed, one might even go so far as to claim that the training incentive in Japanese firms was fostered in large part by the success of the macroeconomic and industrial policies in that country. Thus, it is not by coincidence, in my view, that Japanese investments in employment relations became pronounced in the 1960's coinciding with that economy's rapid technological change and accelerated economic growth during that period.

An important public policy initiative took place in the late 1950's in the form of the productivity enhancement campaign with the establishment of the Japan Productivity Center in 1955. This campaign contributed significantly to the encouragement of Japan's rapid economic growth.[20] The campaign helped guide private industries to acquire modern Western technologies, thereby contributing to the double-digit growth rate of the Japanese economy during the 1960's. The activities of the campaign included conferences and seminars in which top level industrialists, bankers, scholars, and bureaucrats participated; numerous visits by Japanese managers and unionists to the United States and Europe as well as visits by Western specialists to Japan;[21] and active information dissemination to the private sector industries.

To be sure, there initially was strong opposition to this campaign from labor unions and leftist politicians, who feared that modern technologies would displace labor and cause high unemployment. The campaign eventually gained the opponents' support after an agreement was reached on three principles; (1) to prevent unemployment of workers who would be made redundant by new technologies (the principle of job security), (2) to promote joint consultation between management and labor concerning the introduction of new technologies and related matters, and (3) to promote a fair sharing of the gains of new technologies among employers, workers and consumers. Job security and joint consultation have become firmly embedded in the Japanese industrial relations system. Job security, in turn, has

---

20. See Japan Productivity Center (1988) for illuminating historical discussion of this campaign.

21. Between 1955 and 1956, for example, forty-two missions involving 481 members were sent to observe various U.S. industries (Japan Productivity Center 1988, Chapter. 4).

helped sustain the incentive on the part of senior workers to train junior workers.

The subsequent high rate of economic growth in the early 1960's stimulated the investment in technical skills. The increased demand for technical skills raised the benefit from an increased information reliability, and this process was boosted by the low-transaction cost environment that prevailed in Japan. In turn, the increased information reliability further stimulated the investment in technical skills. The result of this process was a strengthening of the employer-employee relationship.

4. Discussion

Japanese workers invest more in on-the-job training, broadly conceived as an investment in employment relations, than U.S. workers (Hashimoto and Raisian 1989, Mincer and Higuchi 1988). I hypothesize that these differences reflect the differences in the costs of investment. Japanese industrial relations tend to incorporate measures for promoting cooperative relationships between the employer and employees. The flexibility of work organization and contracts in Japan results from the training made to improve communication as well as technical skills. These training investments are facilitated by the low cost of investments--because of the well-educated and disciplined workforce--in that country.

I have distinguished two kinds of training investments for improving an employment relations system, training in firm-specific technical skills and in information reliability. Japanese workers are trained not only in technical skills but also in skills in being effective team members, skills which promote information reliability. To maintain these skills, Japanese firms continuously retrain workers as required, and the skills are utilized flexibly within their own or subsidiary organizations. An often neglected aspect of Japanese training is that a significant portion of technical training relies on self-study by the workers involved. Workers are simply asked to study certain manuals on their own, for example.[22] Quite a few Japanese managers of the Japanese automobile transplants indicated to me that with the American workforce they cannot rely on self-study for technical training. The above phenomenon implies that total resources devoted to technical training relative to those devoted to training in information reliability are greater in Japanese transplants, or in American firms for that matter, than in their parent companies in Japan. This implication, in turn, may bear on the more cooperative industrial relations that exist in Japanese firms than firms in the United States.

    Private sector training was also instrumental in the development of skilled workforce in the United States. Thus at first, the Japanese experience would seem to parallel the experience of the United States. There are notable differences, however, between the two countries' experiences. Japan has relied primarily on a firm level, and on a worker level, strategy rather than on government programs, public vocational schools, and training institutions for the promotion of private sector training. Japanese workers develop and accumulate skills useful in the specific firms in which they are employed rather than in the economy at

---

22. It would appear, therefore, that the usual measure of training investments in terms of time spent on the job understates the total training resources devoted to the formation of on-the-job human capital in Japan.

large. Laws and public policies have played important roles, but the lead role belong to the private sector and to the workers in that sector.[23] Most importantly, the Japanese educational system has focused on ensuring the availability of educated and trainable new workers to all industries, leaving the provision of industrial training up to the individual firms.[24]

The cornerstone of the Japanese private sector training is the employee rotation system. As I discussed in section 2, this practice fosters the formation of intra-firm general, though firm-specific, skills. The resulting multifunctional aspect of workers promotes flexibility in job assignments. Also, since these skills are useful in many divisions within the firm, a decline in demand in one division does not necessarily lead to layoffs of affected workers. Obviously, such an arrangement promotes job security, which in turn encourages the employees to acquire firm-specific skills and to readily accept new technologies without resistance. Along with joint consultation and consensus-based decision making, job rotation has contributed to the harmonization of individual and organizational goals. The resulting bond between employees and their firm again increases the

---

23. In my view, Japanese postwar court decisions against blind applications of the employment-at-will doctrine, as well as policies to minimize layoffs and dismissals by providing subsidies to affected employers, have played a more significant role than the polices to promote occupational training in shaping the labor climate conducive to training in that country. For a discussion on Japanese public policies on training, see Takanashi (1990)

24. See Levine and Kawada (1980) for an informative discussion on the role of industrial training in Japanese economic development.

incentive to invest in the employment relation. In this way, Japanese training practices have contributed to low job turnover of skilled workers. The open labor markets that exist are limited to older workers, farm workers who migrate to the cities on off seasons, or unskilled and part-time workers, many of whom serve as buffer to the "lifetime" employees. The Japanese situation contrasts with situation in the United States, where the typical approach to training evidently has contributed to the high mobility of skilled workers among industries, firms, and occupations.

Finally, it is sometimes claimed that the racial and ethnic homogeneity of the Japanese population fosters harmonious industrial relations in that country. To the extent that population homogeneity leads to an environment of low transaction costs, this claim may have some validity. However, it is not the population homogeneity per se that lowers transaction costs. Rather, homogeneity in the attitude towards work, willingness to learn new skills and teach others, and the ability to function as a team member are the critical factors.[25] As an American manager at a Japanese automobile transplant observed, "managers in Japan share a common background with their employees so that they just have to

---

25. A Japanese manager at a Japanese automobile transplant stated, however, that the large difference in the physical size among American workers poses a challenge in installing machinery in such a way to minimize physical strains. In Japan, where the distribution of body size is compact, a given setting of machines is likely to be appropriate to a large number of workers.

point to the right direction and things get done. In America, managers have to do more to get the job done."

It is evident that firms in Japan and the U.S. face different constraints, and both have optimized given such constraints and have come up with different industrial relations and training practices.[26] The diversity in the U.S. workforce has had its payoffs, for example, in fostering individual creativity and independent thinking. My analysis does suggest, nevertheless, that the diversity of the American labor force has been a factor in discouraging investment in employment relationships, and in the tendency to emphasize technical training, in a typical American firm. Although training on the job may be largely firm-specific, the diversity factor would discourage investment in general human capital as well if, for

---

26. Japanese firms operating in the U.S. evidently engage in more extensive and lengthy interviews of job applicants than their parent companies do to create a low transaction-cost on the shop floor. A number of Japanese managers indicated that they couldn't engage in such an extensive screening lest they lose good job candidates to their competitors. It is interesting to note in this context that the Honda of America Manufacturing in Ohio was sued for having given hiring preference to workers from the Marysville area to the exclusion of the more racially mixed labor pool available in Columbus. The firm settled out of court in 1988 and paid $6 million to about 370 black and female workers. Honda now uses a computer to randomize applicants before selecting new hires, according to one of its managers. For related discussions on many of the Japanese transplants in the U.S., See Higuchi (1987) and Shimada (1988).

technological reasons, general and firm-specific capital must be obtained together in a tied fashion.[27]

Ultimately, one would hope to develop policy implications for the United States from studying other countries' training practices. The international competitiveness of the American economy is a critical policy concern for the United States. The key ingredients for an internationally competitive economy are the abilities of its labor force to adapt flexibly in an environment of continual innovation and to produce quality products in a cost effective manner. These abilities are fostered by training, and they appear to characterize Japan's labor force. It is no exaggeration to say that the stream of successful Japanese products in recent years owes much to the effective private sector training approach in Japan.

To develop policy implications for the U.S., it would be useful to study how the Japanese transplants in the United States are succeeding in adapting their parent companies' approaches to training and industrial relations. One of them, the Honda of American Manufacturing, is now exporting automobiles to Japan, and others will follow suit before long. These transplants appear poised, therefore, to contribute to the international competitiveness of the U.S. economy. Much more needs to be known about: (1) the extent to which these firms are succeeding in

---

27. Symmetrical to this argument, financial constraints or minimum wage laws that discourage general training also reduce firm-specific training. Thus, public policies to increase opportunities for young workers to obtain general training may also help with specific training. In the same vein, policies adopted to reduce transaction costs may encourage general training as well as specific training.

adapting their Japanese approaches to the screening of new employees, training, employee rotation, joint consultation, the just-in-time inventory system, quality control circles, the compensation system, job security, and other industrial relations practices; (2) the factors that limit the applicability of Japanese practices to U.S. workers, e.g., their high mobility, their heterogeneity, the level of their basic skills, and their attitudes towards work; (3) the trainability of U.S. workers as a factor in the location decision; (4) employees' evaluations of how the Japanese approach affects their outlook and productivity; as well as (5) some indication of time and money spent on screening and training new employees here compared to Japan. Such an inquiry will be the subject of my next study.

REFERENCES

Aoki, Masahiko (1988). *Information, Incentives, and Bargaining in the Japanese Economy*, New York and Cambridge: Cambridge University Press.

Blair, John D. and Ramsing, Kenneth D. (1983). "Quality Circles and Production/Operations Management: Concerns and Caveats," *Journal of Operations Management* 4: 489-497.

Cole, Robert E. (1979). *Work, Mobility, and Participation*. Berkeley: The University of California Press.

Cole, Robert E. (1980). "Learning from the Japanese: Prospects and Pitfalls," *Management Review* 69: 22-42.

Cole, Robert E. (1989). *Strategies for Learning*. Berkeley: The University of California Press.

Freeman, Richard B. (1989). "Business Labor Relations Goals and Practices Across OECD Countries," presented at the Japan MITI Conference, "Corporate Management and Labor Markets: Implications for International Competitiveness," January, 1989.

Hanami, Tadashi (1981). *Labor Relations in Japan Today*. Tokyo: Kodansha International.

Hanami, Tadashi (1984). "Conflict Resolution in Industrial Relations Relations," in Tadashi Hanami and Roger Blanpain eds. *Industrial Conflict Resolution in Market Economies*. Antwerp: Kluwer Law and Taxation Publishers.

Hanami, Tadashi and Roger Blanpain eds. (1984). *Industrial Conflict Resolution in Market Economies*. Antwerp: Kluwer Law and Taxation Publishers.

Hashimoto, Masanori (1990a). "Employment and Wage Systems in Japan and their Implications for Productivity," in *Paying for Productivity: A Look at the Evidence*. Edited by Alan S. Blinder, Washington, D.C. Brookings Institution, 1990.

Hashimoto, Masanori (1990b). *The Japanese Labor Market in a Comparative Perspective with the United States: A Transaction Cost Interpretation*. Kalamazoo: W.E. Upjohn Institute for Employment Research.

Hashimoto, Masanori (1990c). "Industrial Relations System in Japan: An Interpretation and Policy Implications," *Managerial and Decision Economics*, forthcoming.

Hashimoto, Masanori and John Raisian (1989). "Investments in Employer-Employee Attachments by Japanese and U.S. Workers in Firms of Varying Size." *Journal of The Japanese and International Economies* 3: 31-48.

Hayes, Robert H. (1981). "Why Japanese Factories Work," *Harvard Business Review* 59: 56-66.

Higuchi, Yoshio (1987). "A Comparative Study of Japanese Plants Operating in the U.S. and American Plants: Recruitment, Job Training, Wage Structure, and Job Separation," mimeo, Columbia University.

Jacoby, Sanford M. (1989). "Pacific Ties: Employment Systems in Japan and the U.S. Since 1900," University of California, Los Angeles, mimeo.

Japan Productivity Center, *Seisansei Undo 30 Nenshi* (The Thirty Year History of Productivity Campaign), 1988.

Jorgensen, Dale W., Kuroda, Masahiro, and Nishimizu, Mieko (1987). "Japan-U.S. Industry-Level Productivity Comparisons, 1960-1979," *Journal of The Japanese and International Economies* 1: 1-30.

Juran, Joseph M. (1975). "Quality Control of Service--the 1974 Japanese Symposium," *Quality Progress* 13: 511-514.

Koike, Kazuo (1984). "Skill Formation Systems in the U.S. and Japan: A Comparative Study," in *The Economic Analysis of the Japanese Firms*. Edited by Masahiko Aoki, Amsterdam: North-Holland.

Koshiro, Kazutoshi (1983). "Development of Collective Bargaining in Postwar Japan," In Tashiro Shirai ed. *Contemporary Industrial Relations in Japan*. Madison: University of Wisconsin Press.

Koshiro, Kazutoshi (1986). "Labor Market Flexibility in Japan--With Special Reference to Wage Flexibility," Working Paper, Yokohama National University.

Levine, Solomon B. and Kawada, Hisashi (1980). *Human Resources in Japanese Industrial Development*. Princeton University Press.

Matsuda, Yasuhiko (1983). "Conflict Resolution in Japanese Industrial Relations," In Tashiro Shirai ed. *Contemporary Industrial Relations in Japan*. Madison: University of Wisconsin Press.

Mincer, Jacob and Yoshio Higuchi (1988). "Wage Structures and Labor Turnover in the United States and Japan," *Journal of the Japanese and International Economies* 2: 97-133.

Morishima, Motohiro (1989). "Information Sharing and Firm Performance in Japan: Do Joint Consultation Committees Help?" Simon Fraser University Working paper.

Parsons, Doland O. (1990). "The Firm's Decision to Train," *Research in Labor Economics* 2: 53-75.

Reagan, Patricia (1988). "On-the-Job Training, Layoffs by Inverse Seniority, and the Incidence of Unemployment." Mimeo, Ohio State University.

Shimada, Haruo (1988). *Human Ware No Keizaigaku* (The Economics of Humanware). Tokyo: Iwanami.

Shirai, Taishiro (1983). "A Theory of Enterprise Unionism," in <u>Contemporary Industrial Relations in Japan</u>, edited by Taishiro Shirai, Madison: University of Wisconsin Press, 117-144.

St. Antoine, T. (1984). "Conflict Resolution in Industrial Relations," In T. Hanami and R. Blanpain, <u>op. cit.</u>

Sugeno, Kazuo and Koshiro, Kazutoshi (1987). "The Role of Neutrals in the Resolution of Shop Floor Disputes: Japan," <u>Comparative Labor Law Journal</u> 9: 129-163.

Tachibanaki, Toshiaki (1986). "Labour Market Flexibility in Japan, Europe and the United States," Working paper, Kyoto Institute of Economic Research.

Takanashi, Akira (1990). "*Shokugyo Kunren, Kakko Kyoiku To Rodo Shijo Seisaku* (Occupational Training, Schooling, and Labor Market Policies)," <u>Nihon Rodo Kenkyu Zassi</u> 370: 2-8.

Takezawa, Shin-ichi and Arthur Whitehall (1981). <u>Work Ways: Japan and America</u>. Toyko: The Japan Institute of Labor.

Valigra, Lori (1990). "A Day in the Life of an IS Manager," <u>Computer World</u>, A Supplement on Japan, August 13.

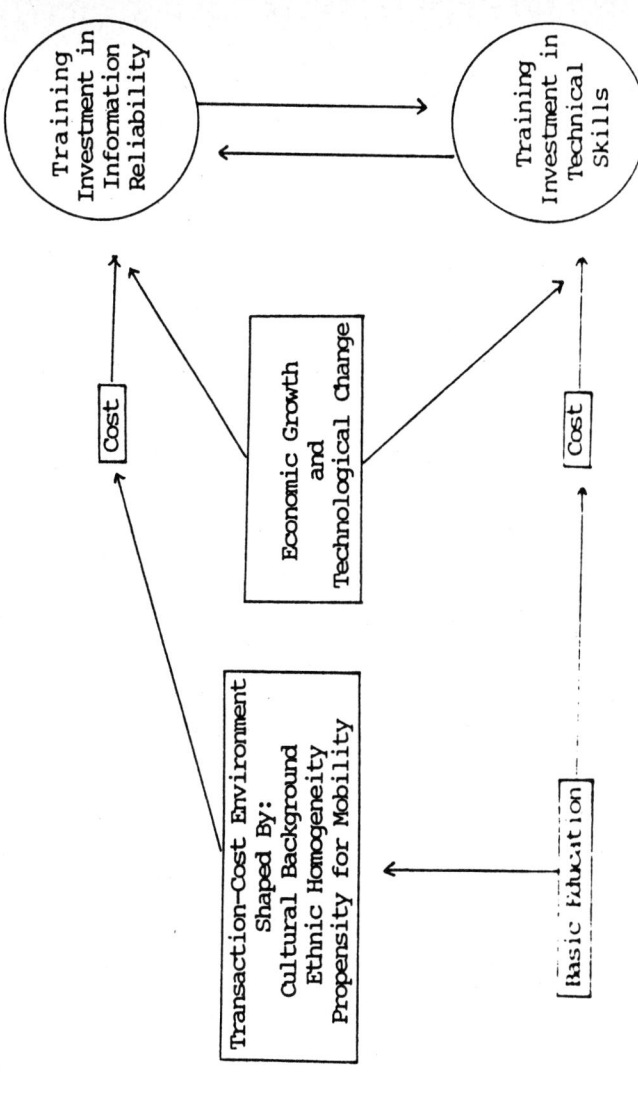

Figure 1: Outline of the Theory of Training Investments

MARKET FAILURE FOR GENERAL TRAINING AND REMEDIES

Jozef M.M. Ritzen
Robert M. LaFolette Institute of Public Affairs, University of Wisconsin, Madison/Erasmus University Rotterdam, The Netherlands
April 1989

Suggestions on this topic by Robert H. Haveman and Blake D. LeBaron are gratefully acknowledged.

1. Introduction

In this paper we will argue that the market fails to provide the socially efficient amounts of general training. We also discuss two different forms of public intervention aimed at the provision of the second-best optimal amount of general training.

Training is defined here as all forms of learning in which practical work experience forms an essential part. Training and workplace training or job training are used interchangeably in this paper. At present -both in the United States and in Europe- most of the supply and demand of training of adult workers takes place on private markets. The public role is mostly restricted to displaced or dislocated workers.
Training under the Job Training Partnership Act of 1982 is an example of such a program for the United States.

In Beckers's pioneering work on human capital (1964) the distinction was made between general and specific training.
Specific training only yields productivity gains in a specific firm. All the training which can be used in more than one firm is in principle general. Specific training will be provided by firms. Employers and employees will share the costs and the benefits of the training (Hashimoto and Yu, 1980). The firm is able to appropriate some of the influence on earnings than education and training from other sources[1].

General training is a heterogeneous commodity. It includes, for example, training in stainless steel welding as well as introductory mathematics, reading and writing. The heterogeneity may show up in differences in obsolescence rates of training and in the probability distributions of rates of returns to training. In the following this heterogeneity is ignored.

3. Uncertainty and Training

Training is a risky investment. The benefits to be derived for the individual from general training are uncertain in advance. The available information gives the probability distribution of the returns, not a single figure of the returns which applies to all. The impact of such uncertainty in the returns to training on the decisions of workers concerning training can be shown with earlier studies on the impact of risk on the education choice by Kodde (1986), Levhari and Weiss (1974) and Eaton and Rosen (1980).

The training choice is analyzed with a two-period model. Consider a worker with wage w_1 in the first period who has the choice to work full-time or to use part of the available time for general training. The amount of general training, s, can range from 0 to the maximum number of hours available for work in that period, denoted by T. The costs of training are the income foregone and the direct costs per hour of training, p_s. General training will enhance the wage rate in the second period: $w_s(s,x)$, where x is a stochastic variable which captures the a priori unknown states of the world. In the second period the worker is full-time employed. The maximum number of hours available for work is again: T. His or her wage income is:

---

[1] The positive effects of workplace learning on wages lasts 13 years, compared to 8 years in the case of learning in school (Lillard and Tan, 1986). This is not surprising. The greater efficiency of training results from the combination of practical and theoretical instruction, from the more recent date of the equipment, which often can be used in workplace training and from the availability of mentors in firms. Also workers are often more motivated for job based learning rather than learning in a school setting. But formal education definitely can play a role in providing the theoretical instruction associated with training and sometimes the training can be so general that the formal education system can better provide it.

$f(s,x) = w_2(s,x) \cdot T$

The function f exhibits the usual properties with respect to s of positive, but decreasing marginal returns. The life time budget constraint in this two-period model is then:

(1) $C_1(1+r) + C_2 = (w_1(T-s) - p_s + A_1)(1+r) + A_2 + f(s,x)$,

where the subscript i denotes the period (i=1,2);

C_i denotes consumption;

A_i denotes non-wage income;

and r is the fully certain interest rate (the rate of time preference).

The worker maximizes expected utility subject to the life time budget constraint by means of the choice of first-period consumption and investment in general training. The expected utility is additively separable over all states of nature in the von Neumann-Morgenstern fashion:

(2) $\max_{(C_1,s)} E(U(C_1,C_2)) = \max_{(C_1,s)} \int_{-\infty}^{\infty} U(C_1,C_2) \, dF(x)$

Here F(x) represents the distribution function of the states of the world. The utility function is monotone and concave in both variables. From the budget constraint we can write C_2 as a function of C_1 and s so that the condensed utility function has to be optimised with respect to C_1 and s only. The first-order conditions for a maximum are:

(3) $E(U_1 - U_2(1+r)) = 0$

(4) $E(U_2 f_s - U_2(1+r)(w_1+p_s)) = 0$

where U_j are the derivatives of U with respect to C_j and f_s is the marginal wage due to training.

Eq.(3) simply states that the ratio between the expected future and current marginal utilities of consumption equals the market discount factor. Eq.(4) can be written as:

(5) $E(f_s)/(w_1+p_s) = 1+r - \text{cov}(U,f_s)/[E(U_2)(w_1+p_s)]$

The covariance is negative if risk is multiplicative ($f(s,x) = x \cdot h(s)$ +constant as in Eaton and Rosen, 1980). In that case only the first-order term of the Taylor approximation is non-zero. The covariance can then be written as follows[2]:

(6) $\text{cov}(U_2, f_s) = U_{22} f_x f_{sx} \sigma^2$,

so that the risk premium which workers would demand above the rate of time preference in a decision to train for s hours is:

---

[2] Kodde (1986) uses a second-order Taylor approximation around E(x) and taking expectations with respect to x to show that the covariance between second-period marginal utility and the marginal benefits from training does not have to be negative under all circumstances.

returns to specific training since the training only yields returns to a worker if he or she remains in the firm of training. This is not the case with general training: workers can appropriate the returns to training by moving to another firm. It does not make any economic sense for the firm to pay for such training. Instead, the worker has an incentive to invest in general training (Becker, 1964, p.20).
A more extensive public role in general training is required, because of the financial risks for individual workers in investing in training. The financial returns to training are uncertain at the time the worker has to decide whether or not to invest. There is no insurance available for this uncertainty. As a result the investment in training will not be socially efficient: there is underinvestment in general training. This inefficiency may spill over in overinvestments in specific training in case the efficiency of specific training depends on the level of general training or if specific and general training are close substitutes (McMahon, 1988). Underinvestment in general training will lead to a loss in production and in welfare.

A public intervention could yield a second-best improvement if the uncertainty concerning the after-training wage is due to "private" as distinct from "social" risk, i.e. if the uncertainty is unrelated to macro-economic fluctuations. We elaborate here two proposals which aim at the reduction of the risk involved in training for the individual worker. There is a potential to reduce the risk, first, by what we have called an "inverse insurance"-scheme and second, by guaranteed extra wages to be earned after completion of training courses.

In the following section (section 2) we shall further consider the distinction between general and specific training, and discuss in this context some of the recent literature, wich attempts to explain why firms provide (and pay for) general training.
In section 3 a theoretical exposition of the effect of uncertainty on the training choice will be presented. Section 4 highlights data on training in the U.S. Although the volume of training is spectacular, we still make the case that there is not enough training.
Section 5 contains the proposals for a more extensive public role in training. Their theoretical justification is given in the appendices A and B. In the analysis it has been assumed that risk is multiplicative with respect to the wage. This paper concludes with a summary and conclusions (section 6).

2. General and Specific Training

From the definition of general training i.e. training which can be used in more than one firm, it follows that there is a large area of training which is general. Virtually all training in vocations and occupations is general rather than specific since it can be used in more than one firm. That would make specific training -as deliniated by Becker- a virtually empty box. But in practice the category of specific training can be defined to include all those types of training for which the excpected benefits of moving to another firm are not sufficient to offset the transaction costs of a move. The benefits are the extra earnings to be gained from the training over the foreseeable future. They depend very much on the time the training remains useful, in other words on the depreciation and obsolescence rate of the training over time.

By introducing transaction costs in the delineation of specific training we have made the specificity of the training dependent on circumstances other than the nature of the training alone. The training of welders of stainless steel in the north of Wisconsin may be more specific than the same training in the Chicago area, simply for the reason that the transaction costs required to use that training elsewhere are higher for workers in the north of Wisconsin, with relatively few industries which use stainless steel welding compared to workers in the Chicago area.
In the same vein, the argument can be made that the specificity of one and the same type of training increases with the size of the firm. A larger sized firm has a larger internal labor market. There are more chances that the firm can make competing bids to outside employers, thus reducing the financial gains to be achieved with a move to another firm.

This background is useful to explain why profit maximizing firms - contrary to Becker's deductions- do provide general training. There is ample evidence which shows that firms pay for general training.
A recent and -for this topic- very rich data set on training was compiled by Bishop (1988, see also Bishop's contribution to this volume). The data are on 1493 employers who hired someone after July 1980. The employers report on three essential variables:
- The degree of generality of the training, approximated with answers to the question: "How many of the skills learned by new employees in

this job are useful outside this company?". 59% responded "almost all", 13% responded "most" and only 7.5% answered "almost none".
- The productivity development of the typical individual hired in the job during the first two years of employment.
- The wage profile in those first two years.

The data show not only a prominent presence of general training within the training of firms, but also that the wage growth remains below the productivity growth, also in firms where the training is almost fully general. Hence, employers share in the costs of general training.

Bishop explains this by the transaction costs of moving. While this is plausible, it is not entirely satisfactory, since these transaction costs were not measured. Alternative explanations are possible, i.e. the (large) size of the firm (above) and the complementarity between general and specific training.

The complementary hypothesis as an explanation for firm investment in general training is forwarded by Feuer, Glick and Desai (1987, see also their contribution to this volume). They argue that firms can profitably invest in general training for their workers, as long as the wage derived from the shared return on specific and general training in those firms exceeds that of the full return to the general training in another firm. This is commensurate to assuming that general training enhances the efficiency of specific training. The hypothesis is tested with a sample of employees, some of whom enjoyed firm-sponsored general education and others who did not. Their empirical test, however, does not consider specific training explicitly. The Bishop model would most likely also have fitted their data equally well.

Although it is important to realize that firms do pay for general training, if defined in the strict sense of Becker, this says nothing about the degree to which this supply of general training conforms to a Pareto-efficient sypply: about the degree to which the market "succeeds". This will be the concern of section 4.

Why concentrate on general training, rather than education for adult workers? Certain types of general training and of vocational education are substitutes: the formal education system also can supply and does supply many of these courses, particularly for youngsters. We focus on general training rather than on education for adult workers, because for adult workers learning in combination with work is more efficient: Lillard and Tan (1986) find that workplace training has a more durable

$$bf_x f_{sx} \sigma^2,$$

where $b = -U_{22}/U_2$ represents the absolute degree of risk aversion. σ^2 is the variance of x, 'states of the world'.

An example might help to appreciate the impact of risk on the optimal training decision. For this example the following parameters have been chosen:

$w_1 = 1$, $w_2 = (1+s^{1/2}x)$, $T=1$, $f(s,x) = (1+s^{1/2}x)$, $p_s=0$, $U=C_1^a C_2^{1-a}$

The magnitude of the degree of risk aversion in second-period consumption, b, evaluated around the riskless training optimum is shown in Table 1. The degree of risk aversion increases with the preference for first versus second-period consumption and decreases with the compound rate of interest.

Risk can -depending on the degree of risk aversion- decrease the volume of training substantially as the example shows. The effect on utility is limited in these examples.

Insurance companies are not going to be involved in the insurance of human capital, because of moral hazard and adverse selection. In the absence of contingency markets in which the uncertainty on future earnings can be traded, there is no guarantee that the optimal training choice represents a Pareto optimum (Arrow and Lind, 1970). The private market will as a result not be efficient in producing training. There is a possibility that the results of the market can be improved upon by public intervention (see section 5).

To be sure: also investments by firms in specific training are risky. But firms have more possibilities to pool risks than individual workers have. Moreover firms can be assumed to be risk-neutral, so that the riskiness of investments in specific training does not warrant further analysis of public intervention in specific training. In contrast, since individual workers have few means to pool the risk in the returns to general training and because they are risk averse, a public role should be considered there.

4. The Failure of the Private Market

The overall annual dollar volume of training is high. Several sources are available to get an estimate of that volume in the United States. Table 2 gives a survey of those data which can claim a minimal degree of accuracy. These data include informal training. Much of the training is informal in the sense that it is fully intertwined with the daily work activities. There is no such thing as taking time off for training. In contrast, formal training activities require full time attention during the training periods and prohibit the use of that time for work activities. They reduce the workers productivity during the training time substantially and require in addition the outlay of costs for the formal training program.

In the estimates of both Mincer and Carnevale[3] it is assumed that the productivity of the worker is zero during the training period (Mincer, 1988a, p. 11). This exaggerates the estimate of the resources involved in informal training. At the same time the input of mentors in the training of others is not taken into account, which leads to an underestimation of the training costs. Using another data source we conclude that these estimates migh be too high[4].

Estimates of the dollar volume of formal training are somewhat more reliable, although they tend to suffer from selective non-response in surveys. Formal corporate training (including foregone earnings) is approximately between 30 and 55 billion dollar in 1987. At a wage bill of approximately 2.5 trillion dollars this makes corporate training a marginal activity in firms.

---

[3] Jacob Mincer presents estimates of the volume of informal training based on two different surveys, i.e. the 1976 University of Michigan's Panel Survey on Income Dynamics (PSID) and the 1982 Current Population Survey (CPS). The PSID contains information for the year 1976 on 1,200 male heads of households concerning the length of time of training required during the current job, as well as its learning contents. A supplementary survey collected information on the hours per week of training (Duncan and Stafford, 1980). The information on the length of training required is the answer of the individual worker surveyed to the question:"On a job like yours, how long would it take the average person to become fully qualified?". The Current Population Survey contains the incidence of training in its March 1983 survey; here training is measured form the answers of individual workers to the question: "What training was needed to get the current or last job and what training is needed to improve skills on the current job?". The estimates of Mincer are very rough, but agree well with a guestimate of Anthony P. Carnevale of the American Society for Training and Development. This guestimate is based on data of the Bureau of Labor Statistics concerning how workers get their training. These data include the ratio between formal and informal training. This ratio together with an estimate based on the Current Population Survey of 1983 on formal training (unpublished) yields the volume of informal training.

[4] Bishop (1988, Table 1) finds that in 1982 the productivity decrement of newly hired workers in the first quarter of employment due to training is around 25%. In order to arrive at the calculations of Mincer and Carnevale of informal training to be around 7 to 8% of the wage bill, new hires as a percentage of the labor force would have to be about 1/3rd of the labor force. This is an exageration of actual relative new hires. However, some training goes to experienced workers as well. Also the cost of training does include supervisors' and co-workers' time.

Inclusion of the training of dislocated, displaced an disabled workers, which is financed with public funds, hardly changes the overall picture.

From the existing data it is not possible to distinguish what part of the informal and formal corporate training is general and what part is specific.

The formal education system provides close substitutes to general training. To the best of our knowledge no data are available on the participation in vocational education by workers, once they have entered the labor market. Impressionistic evidence tends to show a relatively small participation.

The dollar value of training as displayed in Tabel 2 is huge. And yet, we conclude that there is too little investment in training. This conclusion is deduced from the following characteristics of training:

- Training yields -on the average- a substantially higher rate of return than other investment. Average rates of return were in 1982 - depending on the assumed depreciation rate- between 18 and 26% (Mincer, 1988a, p. 10). In this volume, Mincer's estimates vary between 8,7 and 37,5%. Mincer also shows how much these returns vary. This points to great uncertainty on the part of workers concerning the return to an investment in training.

- Training is highly concentrated in the early years of work. In 1976 41% of the training was concentrated on workers in the ages under 25 and 72% in the age group of 35 years or less (Duncan and Stafford, 1980). These age groups constituted 22% and 48% of the labor force respectively. Most formal employer-based training -68%- was in 1987 provided to employees between the ages of 25 and 44 years (Carnevale and Gainer, 1988, p. 18).

The concentration of informal training on the young does not make economic sense, if the depreciation time of training is relatively short, as it is most often estimated to be. Lillard and Tan (1986) estimate the annual depreciation rate of informal training to be between 15 and 20%. This would mean that training has to be renewed every 5 to 8 years, until retirement is near. If not, a potential source of profitable investment is left untapped.

In general, one notes that informal training is mostly focused on newly hired workers. It not only serves as an investment, but also as a screening and matching device for newly hired workers within the firm.

- Training is concentrated among the higher educated. Those with 8 or fewer years of education received in 1976 about 5% of all training (Duncan and Stafford, 1980), while they formed 11% of the labor force. Almost 50% of the training went to workers with some years of college or more education, while this group formed only 1/3rd of the labor force. We do not have the data to establish whether this is the result of the distribution of workers by age and level of education. It may well be that the concentration of training on higher educated workers is the result of the concentration of training in the early years of work experience in the firm.

If, however, the distribution of training does depend -keeping age constant- on the level of education, then this would also be an indication of over- or/and underinvestment. The evidence is that the rates of return to training do not differ between workers with different levels of education (Mincer, 1988b, p.25).

- Training is more prevalent in large than in small firms (Bartel, 1989, p. 6 and Bishop, 1982). There is as a result more underinvestment in training for workers in small firms than for larger firms. This finding is not surprising if one notes that the internal labor market of larger firms makes more training specific (see section 2). Another explanation for this finding is that larger firms have more possibilities to pool the risks of investments in training. Large firms might also be in a better position to preserve the value of specific training, because they are less likely to lose people.

These characteristics of the training effort lead us to the conclusion that there is underinvestment in training on the private market. The risks associated with the returns to general training provide a good explanation for this underinvestment. In almost all studies on the earnings expectations of human capital investors this uncertainty surfaces (see, for example, Leffler and Lindsay, 1979).

Risk may not be the only explanation. Another explanation could be capital market imperfections: the costs of training may be too high to finance by the worker out of savings or out of current income, while

there are no facilities to borrow for investments in training. In view
of the relatively low costs of training (compared to costs of regular
youth-time education, like college education) and because of the fact
that workers have a regular income, the explanation of underinvestment
by means of capital market imperfection carries less weight for
general training than for regular youth-time education. A third
explanation is the lack of an existing institutional structure for
general training, which takes by and large place within the firm, even
though the costs are borne partly by workers. This explanation lacks
conviction, since it begs the question why such a structure did not
evolve in the first place.

5. Remedies

In the presence of uncertainty and the absence of contingency markets
for its insurance, there is no reason to assume that the resulting
choices will be Pareto optimal. It might then be possible that public
intervention might lead to second-best improvements. Arrow and Lind
(1970) provide part of the analytical background for this position.
Two assumptions are essential for their argument:
- The returns from any particular investment are independent of other
  components of national income. Hirschleifer and Riley (1979) distinguish between "private risk" and "social risk", where the latter is
  related to general economic development. Arrow and Lind and
  Hirschleifer and Riley agree on the point that social risk should be
  treated in the same way in public as in private decisions.
- The benefits of the investment accrue to all tax payers[5]. They
  derive that then the present value of an investment should equal the
  sum of expected returns discounted by a rate appropriate for investments yielding certain returns. Government should behave as an
  expected value decision maker and use a discount rate appropriate
  for investments with certain returns. It is the risk-spreading
  aspect of government investment that is essential to this result:
  government distributes the risk associated with any investment among
  a large number of people. The per capita taxes, necessary for the
  financing of the project, approach zero when the number of tax-
  payers becomes very large.

---

[5] Arrow and Lind (1970, p 377)) mention for private benefits and
costs that these must be discounted with respect to both time and
risk, and exclude a government role if benefits are private.

The first assumption of statistical interdependence can be argued to hold reasonably well. A considerable part of the uncertainty on the returns to training is "private risk" and not related to general economic conditions. Uncertainty on future returns to training is determined by at least five factors:
- imperfect knowledge of abilities;
- uncertain life times;
- uncertain costs of search and timing of job offerings;
- uncertain rewards of general training;
- unknown future demand and supply conditions.

Only the last factor may be considered to be correlated with the development of aggregate income over time.

The second assumption is also satisfied if one considers the public role to pertain solely to workers, so that only workers pay the taxes for and receive the benefits from general training. In that case the benefits are still private, but they can accrue to all tax-payers.

Two schemes are considered here which could provide second-best improvements in general training[6]:
- subsidize the direct and indirect costs of training; this is called "inverse insurance" and elaborated in Appendix A;
- increase the certain part of the benefits from training, to be called "guaranteed wage increase scheme", the mathematics of the welfare improvement to be gained are presented in Appendix B.

In the elaboration of both schemes it has been assumed that risk is multiplicative.

"Inverse insurance"
The mechanism of inverse insurance is depicted in Diagram 1. In the first period a subsidy is available for training, while uncertain earnings in the second period are taxed on a certain rate, so that the amount of tax to be paid depends on the amount of subsidy and on the uncertain second-period wage rate. The Government (or some other collective agency, like employer or employee organizations) takes the risk for balancing the budget over time. The collective agency does

---

[6] The public role in training has been interpreted in many Western European countries to imply: paid educational leave, training funds to be financed out of contributions of employers and employees, or Government subsidization of training. In our proposals the public role is more limited, both financially and institutionally.

not have to take into account any private risks in this balancing, as the law of large numbers applies. In principle, the scheme does not require any separate financing, but can work with a revolving training fund. The subsidies for training are balanced against the taxes received.

Essentially, it is a form of a student loan scheme in which the payback of the loan depends on future earnings. Such schemes have been proposed periodically for loans for students who go to college (see for a recent proposal: Reischauer 1989). If applied to training, the certain subsidy and the uncertain amount of tax to be paid is likely to lead to a higher participation in training.

Appendix A shows how inverse insurance can yield Pareto improvements for a case where the subsidy per hour of training is independent of the number of hours of training, where the tax is proportional and where there are no limits on the amount of the subsidy (for example, that the subsidy should not exceed the direct and indirect costs). With a subsidy of $p_s s$ at s hours of training the tax rate in the second period is determined to be:

$$t = \frac{p_s s (1+r)}{E(f(s,x))} = \frac{p_s s (1+r)}{Tw_2(s,x)}$$

The effect of this inverse insurance scheme is straightforward. It reduces the risk premium the individual has to demand, to make training a utility maximizing option.

The uncertainty is completely eliminated if the subsidy is such that all of the uncertain income is eliminated. This result is due to the fact that no limit has been imposed on the subsidy per hour. This result is not very attractive, since adverse selection and moral hazard can be assumed to increase with the tax rate.
If a limit is imposed on the subsidy, the analysis shows straightforwardly that the optimal subsidy is the one at the limit (a corner solution). The risk premium to be demanded above the market rate of return decreases then from (see Eq(5)):

$$cov(U_2, f_s)/E[U_2]$$

to:

$$(cov(U_2, fs) - cov(U_2, f))/E[U_2]$$

This result follows immediately from the first-order condition for maximization of expected life time utility by means of first-period consumption (see Appendix A).

The results do not depend on the assumptions on the tax system employed or the constancy of the subsidy per hour of training.
They can easily be generalized to include subsidies per hour of training which depend on the number of hours of training (for example: a subsidy per hour of training which decreases with the hours of training) and to non-linear tax schedules (for example: a progressive tax).

The analysis might be extended to include the possible disincentive effects of the second-period wage-tax on the labor supply. The insight to be gained is, however, limited. The optimal subsidy-tax schedules will then depend on the assumptions made in the utility function with respect to the preferences for second-period income versus second-period leisure.

The scheme exhibits potentially two of the weaknesses which prevent the insurance of uncertain returns: adverse selection and moral hazard. Adverse selection can only be avoided if the scheme is compulsory for all workers who engage in training: they have to take the subsidy and to pay the tax afterwards. If the scheme were not compulsory, then only workers with low expected future returns of training might sign up, while workers with high expected future returns would not use the scheme. To balance the fund, the tax rate would then have to be increased, which would further drive out workers with higher expected returns.

The scheme compares favorably to an insurance plan as it might be possible to achieve required participation. But one cannot bar workers from participating in types of education, which are to some extent substitutable for general training. This kind of adverse selection can to some extent be countered by having separate funds for different types of job training. The expectations of workers considering a certain type of training in any one scheme should be as homogeneous as possible.

Moral hazards arises if workers, once they are trained under the scheme decide not to work as hard or as many hours as they otherwise would have done because of the tax. But then, others may decide to work harder for the same reason.

This scheme only provides insurance for socially diversifiable risks, and not for risks associated with major structural changes in the economy, like sudden changes in oil prices (Arrow and Lind, 1970 and Hirschleifer and Riley, 1979). Such shocks call for separate public funds for dislocated workers.

This scheme also addresses the capital market imperfections as a possible background for the market failure in general training, since it decreases the costs of an investment in training.
Capital market imperfections have been the main reason behind the proposals for income contingent loan schemes for college students. The preceding analysis is not only applicable to training; it also could provide the analytical underpinnings for income contingent student loan schemes.

The practical applicability of the "inverse insurance"- scheme for training, however, is much larger than income contingent loan schemes for college students for several reasons:
- The amounts involved (compared to the earnings) in training are smaller. Only part of the time is spent on training (while student loans cover full or nearly full-time education) reducing the opportunity costs and increasing liquidity for trainees.

Hence the resulting tax rates and their consequences for labor supply are smaller in the case of training.
- Compulsory participation in the scheme can be envisaged for training, while it is not a realistic option in student loan schemes.

Guaranteed Wage

The Guaranteed Extra Wage Scheme is depicted in Diagram 2. There is no subsidy involved in the costs of the training. But the training is certain to generate at the least a predetermined wage raise.

There is now a subsidy for those workers who end up -after the training is completed- with less than the minimum wage raise.
They receive a supplement from a fund on their wage such that the minimum wage raise is achieved.

The sources for the fund are the taxes paid by workers who earn after the completion of the training more than te original wage plus the predetermined wage raise. These workers pay a tax on the difference between their earnings and the minimum. The tax is -as with the "inverse insurance" scheme- paid into a revolving fund in which the taxes finance the subsidies. Taxes, paid balance with the subsidies. Appendix B shows for an example with the same parameters as used for Table 1 and with additional assumptions on the distribution of the risk, that the guaranteed minimum second-period wage, as a percentage of the expected wage, -if left open to choice- decreases with the number of hours spent in training. It hardly depends on the compound interest rate. Second-best welfare improvements can be achieved under this scheme. But also if the guaranteed minimum is fixed beforehand on a non-optimal level, it can be easily shown that such welfare improvements are possible, since the resulting optimal (welfare maximixing) choice for training exceeds the one at a zero guaranteed minimum wage.

Adverse selection and moral hazard are also problems for this scheme. Adverse selection problems are avoided if the scheme is made compulsory, and every worker who has completed a certain general training pays a tax on the income above the minium. As for the other scheme, moral hazard need not be a major obstacle.

The inverse insurance scheme has two advantages over the guaranteed minimum wage. First, it also helps to cover the investment. Second, the guaranteed minimum wage scheme is more susceptible to fraudulent behavior. Employers could be enticed to substitute part of the wage they normally would pay for workers -who have completed training- for the subsidy from the fund by awarding a wage under the minimum[7]. Also workers could convince employers to exchange wages for fringe benefits and escape the tax in this manner.

There is, however, serious reason to consider the guaranteed income scheme in those cases where wage profiles over time are strongly determined by seniority. In those cases, differences in training between workers of the same age have little or no impact on their relative wage rates. Such differences could be integrated in the contracts which regulate the wage-age profiles.

---

[7] Note however that there is a countervailing power. Workers would have the incentive to bargain for the highest possible wage after the completion of the training. Every dollar earned above the guaranteed minimum still translates into an amount of one dollar minus the tax per dollar.

6. Summary and conclusions

This paper has reviewed evidence of market failure in general training. The notion advanced by Gary Becker in 1964 that workers would purchase for themselves the socially efficient amounts of general training is not supported by the available evidence. First, it is found that firms play a substantial role in the provision of general training. This is not consistent with the notion that the returns to general education cannot be appropiated by firms. Second, the rates of return to training (specific or general) turn out to exceed substantially (on the average) the market rate of return, pointing to underinvestment.

The main theoretical explanation for the underinvestment by workers in general training, which is advanced in this paper, is the uncertainty concerning the future returns to training. Based on this explanation, two proposals for public intervention in general training are presented which yield second-best optima.

In one proposal, workers receive a subsidy for participation in general training and pay a tax on the after-training earnings, more or less after the model of the proposals for income contingent loan schemes for college students. Since the subsidy and the tax rate are certain, the risk premium workers have to demand for training above the market rate of return decreases under this system compared to the present situation. In fact, the optimum subsidy is the maximum one, implying a post-training tax rate of 100%. This result is due to the omission of any constraints on the amount of the subsidy. If such constraints are imposed, then the utility maximizing solution still is clearly Pareto superior over a situation with a zero subsidy. Adverse selection can by and large be avoided by making the scheme compulsory. Moral hazards need not be a serious problem, as long as the subsidy does not exceed the full costs of the investement in training.

A second proposal quarantees workers a minimum wage raise after the completion of training. Earnings above the minimum are taxed. The taxes are used to supplement the wages of those workers who end up earning less than the quaranteed minimum. In an example, it is shown that the optimal quaranteed minimum, as a percentage of the expected wage, decreases with the amount of training and is hardly affected by the interest rate.

The scheme is definitely welfare improving. Adverse selection can also for this scheme be avoided by a compulsory system, while moral hazard will also be contained under optimal guaranteed wage raises.

The bottom line is that -from the point of view of the uncertainty involved in the returns to general training- a more extensive public intervention should be seriously considered.

References

Arrow, Kenneth F. and Robert C. Lind, 1970, Uncertainty and the Evaluation of Public Investment Decisions, AER, Vol.60 , pp. 364-379

Bartel, Ann P., 1989, Formal Employee Training Programs and Their Impact on Labor Productivity: Evidence from a Human Resources Survey, This Symposium

Becker, Gary, 1964, Human Capital, New York: National Bureau of Economic Research

Bishop, John H., 1982, On the Job Training in Small Business, Washington D.C.: Small Business Administration

Bishop, John H., 1988, Do Employers Share the Costs and Benefits of General Training?, Center for Advanced Human Resource Studies, Cornell University, Working Paper #88-08

Carneval, Anthony P., 1987, Testimony before the Subcommittee on Education and Health of the Joint Economic Committee, U.S. Congress, October 29

Carneval, Anthony P., and Leila J. Gainer, 1988, The Learning Enterprise, American Society for Training and Development/U.S. Department of Labor

Duncan, G. and F. Stafford, 1980, "The Use of Time and Technology by Households in the Unites States", Research in Labor Econonmics, Vol. 3

Eaton, Jonathan and Harvey S. Rosen, 1980, Taxation, Human Capital and Uncertainty, AER, Vol. 70, pp. 705-715

Feure, M., H. Glick and A. Desai, 1987, Is Firm-Sponsored Education Viable?, Journal of Economic Behavior and Organization, Vol. 8, pp. 121-136

Hashimoto, M. and B. Yu, 1980, "Specific Capital, Employment Contracts and Wage Rigidity", Bell Journal of Economics, Autumn

Hirschleifer, J. and John G. Riley, 1979, The Analysis of Uncertainty and Information- An Expository Survey, JEL, Vol. 17, pp 1375-1421

Kodde, David A., 1986, Uncertainty and the Demand for Education, RESTAT, Vol. 68, pp. 460-468

Leffler, Keith and Cotton M. Lindsay, 1979, How Do Human Capital Investors Form Earnings Expectations, Southern Economic Journal, Vol. 46, pp. 591-603

Levhari, David and Yoram Weis, 1974, The Effect of Risk on the Investment in Human Capital, AER, Vol. 64, pp. 950-964

Lillard, G. and H. Tan, 1986, Private Sector Training, Rand Corporation, R3331, March

McMahon, Walter W., 1988, The Economics of Vocational and Technical Education: Do the Benefits Outweigh the Costs?, International Review of Education, Vol. 34, pp. 173-194

Mincer, Jacob, 1988a, Human Capital and the Labor Market, xerox, Columbia University

Mincer, Jacob, 1988b, Job Traning, Wage Growth, and Labor Turnover, National Bureau of Economic Research, Working Paper no. 2690

Reischauer, Robert D., 1989, "HELP, A Student Loan Program for the 21st Century" in Laurens E. Gladieux (ed.), Radical Reform or Incremental Change, New York: College Board

Rosen, S., 1976, "A Theory of Life Earning", Journal of Political Economy, Vol. 84, pp. S45-67

Training Magazine, May 1988

TABLE 1

The Impact of Risk on the Training Decisions

A. The Degree of Risk Aversion (b)

	Compound Interest Rate	
Preference for First Versus Second-Period Consumption (a)	$r=1$	$r=2$
.25	.11	.08
.5	.32	.24
.75	.96	.73

B. The Impact on Training (for a=.75)

	$r=1$			$r=2$		
variance (σ_2)	0	.5	1	0	.5	1
training (s) in % of first period time	6.25	5.00	4.06	2.80	2.47	2.20
$\frac{\Delta s}{s}$		→ 20%	→ 19%		→ 12%	→ 11%
U1)	191	43	3	8	7	6

1) for $r=1$: $(U-1.057)10^5$; $r=2$: $(U-1.02)10^5$

TABLE 2

COST OF TRAINING PROVIDED BY EMPLOYERS

SOURCE	YEAR	ESTIMATED AMOUNT (BILLIONS OF DOLLARS OF 1987)
INFORMAL TRAINING		
MINCER/PSID	1987	296
CARNEVALE	1987	180
FORMAL CORPORATE TRAINING		
CARNEVALE	1987	30 (ONLY MEMBER ASTD)
TRAINING MAGAZINE	1987	32 (ONLY FIRMS 50 EMPLOYEES AND MORE)
BARTEL	1986	55
JTPA FEDERAL BUDGET	1988	3.8

SOURCES:
BARTEL (1989), CARNEVALE (1987), MINCER (1988) TRAINING MAGAZINE, MAY 1988

DIAGRAM 1

INVERSE INSURANCE

TIME

COSTS OF TRAINING TO   BENEFITS FROM TRAINING
THE WORKER   TO THE WORKER
    + OPPORTUNITY COSTS
    + DIRECT COSTS

    - SUBSIDY   - TAX
       | ↓
   ↰ ← — ← — FUND — ← — ← ↲

SUCH THAT

SUBSIDY = TAX = TAX RATE X EXPECTED BENEFITS

DIAGRAM 2

GUARANTEED EXTRA WAGE

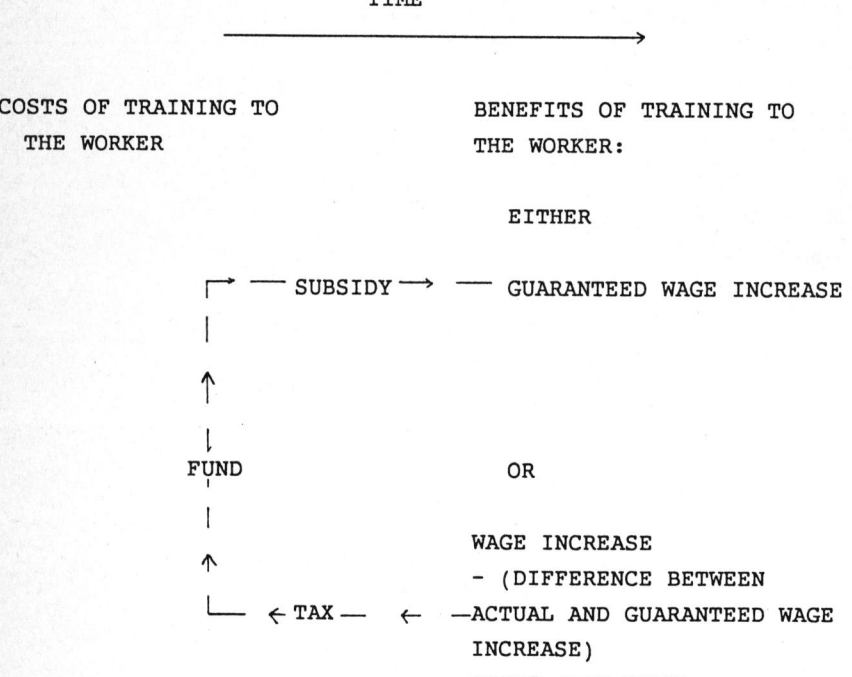

SUBSIDY = TAX = TAX RATE TIMES DIFFERENCE BETWEEN ACTUAL AND GUARANTEED WAGE

MARKET FAILURE FOR GENERAL TRAINING

Appendix A   INVERSE INSURANCE

Consider the introduction of an ex-ante given tax of

$$t = \frac{p_s s(1+r)}{E(f(s,x))} = \frac{p_s s(1+r)}{Tw_2^*(s)}$$

where t is the tax rate, $p_s s$ is the subsidy at s units of training and $w_2^*(s)$ is the expected wage rate in period 2. The subsidy per hour of training is constant.

This changes the budget constraint of Eq (1) as follows:

(A-1) $C_2 = -C_1(1+r) + \{w_1(T-s) + p_s s + A_1\}(1+r) + A_2 + f(s,x)\{1 - \frac{p_s s}{Tw_2^*(s)}(1+r)\}$

The subsidy schedule is set so as to maximize utility. The first-order condition for an optimum is:

$$E[U_2(s(1+r) - f(s,x)t/p)] = 0,$$

This implies that the aim of the subsidy schedule is to force the covariance between the second-period wage and marginal consumption to zero:

(A-2) $\text{cov}[U_2, f(s,x)]/E[U_2] = 0$

The first-order condition for maximization of expected life time utility by means of first-period consumption (i.e. Eq. (3)) is not affected by the introduction of the inverse insurance scheme. The marginal after tax second-period wage is the difference between marginal wage after tax and the marginal tax

$$\frac{\delta}{\delta s}[f(s,x)(1-t)] = f_s(1-t) - f(s,x)[\frac{p_s - p_s s}{w_2^*} \frac{\delta w_2^*}{\delta s}] \frac{(1+r)}{w_2^* T}$$

The first-order condition for training becomes now:

(A-3) $E[U_2 f_s (1-t) - U_2 f(s,x) \frac{p_s(1+r)}{Tw_2^*} + U_2 f(s,x) t \frac{\delta w_2^*/w_2^*}{\delta s}] =$

$E[U_2 (1+r)(w_1 - p_s)]$

After rewriting Eq. (A-3), using $E[U_2 a] = E[U_2]E[a] + \text{cov}(U_2, a)$ we find, using Eq. (A-2):

(A-4a) $E[f_s](1-t) - \frac{\delta t}{\delta s} E[f(s,x)] = (1+r)(w_1 - p_s) + $

$-(1-t)(\text{cov}(U_2, f_s))$

or

(A-4b) $E[f_s] = w_1(1+r) - (1-t) \text{cov}(U_2, f_s)/E[U_2]$

This result shows that a full subsidy such that t approaches one would yield the lowest risk. This result is consistent with Eq. (A-2) as we will show by taking a first-order Taylor series approximation around the mean of the covariance in Eq. (A-2).
This yields:

$$U_{22}(f_x)^2 (1-t) \delta^2 = 0$$

This result had to be expected since at t=1 the stochastic term disappears from the budget-constraint.

Appendix B   Guaranteed Minimum Wage

Let us consider a guaranteed minimum wage in the second period of w^1. For convenience we drop in the notation the subscript for the second period and the dependency of this wage rate on the level of training. We assume that the probability distribution of the second period wage is symmetric with respect to the means. The expected subsidy involved with the guaranteed minimum wage is for each level of training s:

$$S = -\int_0^{w^1} (w-w^1) h(w) dw = -\int_0^{w^1} wh(w)dw + w^1 P_-$$

where P_- is the probability that $w \leq w^1$, or

$$P_- = \int_0^{w^1} h(w) dw$$

The subsidy is raised by taxing proportionally the wage in excess of the minimum. The tax base, A, is then

$$A = \int_{w^1}^{\infty} (w-w^1) h(w) dw = \int_{w^1}^{\infty} w\, h(w) dw - w^1 P_+$$

with

$$P_+ = \int_{w^1}^{\infty} h(w)\, dw$$

The tax rate, t, is defined as the ratio between the subsidy and the tax base:

$$t = S/A$$

so that the net proceeds from the uncertain wage, as a proportion of that wage, are:

$$1-t = (w^* - w^1)/A$$

where $w^* = E[w]$. We demand that $t \leq 1$ so that $w^1 \leq w^*$

The second-period wage is now:
$$w^1 P_- + [w^1+(1-t)(w-w^1)]P_+ =$$
$$w^1 + (1-t)(w-w^1)P_+$$

The optimal distribution of life time income over first and second-period consumption -determined by Eq. (3) - remains unchanged.

To consider the optimal guaranteed minimum it will be useful to have the following derivatives:

$$\frac{\delta P_-}{\delta w^1} = -\frac{\delta P_+}{\delta w^1} = h(w^1)$$

$$\frac{\delta(1-t)}{\delta w^1} = \frac{-1}{A} + \frac{(w^*-w^1)P_+}{A^2} = (-1 + (1-t)P_+)/A$$

The first-order condition for the optimum minimum wage is, after some reorganization, for a given level of training:

(B-1)
$$\frac{\int_{w^1}^{\infty} wh(w)dw - w^* P_+}{[-P_+ + P_+^2 \frac{(w^*-w^1)}{A} - (w^*-w^1)h(w^1)]} + (w^*-w^1) = -\text{cov}[U_2,w]/E[U_2]$$

The right-hand side immediately makes sense: the larger the (negative) value of the covariance the bigger the difference between the mean and the minimum wage. This effect is reinforced since for $w^* > w^1$ the numerator of the first expression at the left hand is positive for a distribution which is symmetric with respect tot the mean, since

$$\int_{w^*}^{\infty} (w-w^*) h(w)dw > -\int_{w^1}^{w^*} (w-w^*) h(w)dw$$

and the denominator is negative. The negativeness of the denominator follows from the negativity of the marginal net proceeds rate for the guaranteed minimum:

$$\frac{\delta(1-t)}{\delta w^1} < 0$$

Let us consider wether the trivial solution of $w^1=0$ satisfies the optimality condition. For $w^1=0$ this condition reverts into:

$$w^* + \text{cov}[U_2,w]/E[U_2] = E[U_2, w]/E[U_2] = 0$$

This is only the case for a zero wage. A minimum wage of $w^1=w^*$ conforms with a situation where the covariance between second-period wage and the marginal utility for second-period consumption is zero: the case of a certain wage.

We shall now simplify the problem by assuming that
$$w^1(s) = \alpha w^*(s)$$
where α is a certain fixed factor $0 < \alpha < 1$.

The first-order term of a Taylor series expansion of the covariance around the mean is:

$$U_{22} f_x^2 (1-t) P_+ \delta_2$$

To establish the optimal training effort we now require the following derivatives:

$$\frac{\delta P_+}{\delta s} = - h(\alpha w^*) \alpha \frac{\delta w^*}{\delta s}$$

and

$$\frac{\delta(1-t)}{\delta s} = \frac{\frac{\delta w^*}{\delta s}(1-\alpha)-(1-t)[\int_{w^*}^{\infty}(\frac{\delta w}{\delta s} - \alpha \frac{\delta w^*}{\delta s})h(w)dw + \int_{w_*}^{\infty}(w-\alpha w^*)\frac{\delta h}{\delta s} dw]}{A}$$

The optimal training effort is now determined by
(B-2)
$$w_1(1+r) = \frac{\delta w^*}{\delta s}[\alpha+(1-t)P_+(1-\alpha)] + (1-t)P_+ \text{cov}(U_2, \frac{\delta w}{\delta s})/E[U_2] +$$
$$+ [P_+\frac{\delta(1-t)}{\delta s} + \frac{\delta P_+}{\delta s}(1-t)]^*$$
$$* [w^*(1-\alpha) + \text{cov}(U_2, f)/E[U_2])]$$

This equation says that the opportunity costs of training in the first period should equal the discounted beneftis. These benefits are the marginal guaranteed minimum ($\alpha \frac{\delta w^*}{\delta s}$) and the after tax extra wage $(1-t)P_+\frac{\delta w*}{\delta s}(1-\alpha)$. Training may increase the wage rate and it may effect the probability of earning more than the minimum. These two effects are also included in Eq. (B-3).

To illustrate this, we use the parameters of the example of Table 1. We now also need information on the distribution of x. This distribution of x is assumed to be rectangular with

$$g(x) = 1/2 \text{ for } 0 \leq x \leq 2$$
$$g(x) = 0$$
so that $\delta_2 = 1/3$

The distribution of the difference between the first-period wage (w=1) and the second-period wage is then (with $w \geq 1$)
$$h(w-1) = \frac{1}{2(w^*-1)} \text{ for } 0 \leq (w-1) \leq 2(w^*-1)$$
$$h(w-1) = 0 \text{ otherwise}$$
or
$$h(w) = \frac{1}{2(w^*-1)} \text{ for } 1 \leq w \leq 2w^*-1$$
$$h(w) = 0 \text{ otherwise}$$

The guaranteed minimum wage is $w^l = a(w^*-1)+1$ with $a<1$ for a given level of training, so that
$$P_- = a/2 \; ; \; P_+ = 1 - a/2$$
$$S = (w^*-1) a^2/4$$
$$A = (w^*-1)(1-a+1/4a^2) = (w^*-1)P_+^2$$
and
$$1-t = \frac{1-a}{P_+^2}$$

Eq. (B-1) can now be expressed as follows:
$$\frac{(1-1.5a)(1-.5a)}{1-a} = b[w^*-1] \, 1/3$$

The optimal a is schedule is given here for a relative preference of .75 for two different values of r for the training levels which are relevant in view of Table 1:

	r=1	r=2
s=.06	.639	---
s=.05	.641	---
s=.04	.645	---
s=.03	---	.652
s=.02	---	.655

The higher the training level, the lower the guaranteed minimum (expressed as a percentage of the mean). The higher the interest rate (at a constant "a"), the lower the degree of risk aversion and the higher the guaranteed minimum.

NONMARKET FAILURE IN GOVERNMENT TRAINING PROGRAMS

W. Lee Hansen[1]
Department of Economics
University of Wisconsin-Madison
Madison, Wisconsin 53706

Introduction What is the rationale for the public to finance and provide job training and retraining? This question may seem out of place in light of this country's 30-year history of federal support for training and retraining programs. Yet, the checkered history of these programs--reflected by their changing purposes, shifting organizational structures, and at best mixed results--leaves a residue of concern about them. This concern is heightened by what appear to be mounting political pressures to expand federal training programs. These pressures stem from increased attention to the collective good attributes of training and renewed emphasis on the social costs of worker displacement. For these reasons, the rationale for public support of training and retraining programs needs to be clarified.

The thought process used to explore the question entails a sequence of steps, each of which constitutes a section of this paper. The paper begins by reviewing the evolution of public sector training and retraining efforts. The next section examines the rationale for these programs, drawing on the theory of market failure which has been applied extensively to another form of training, namely, formal schooling. This presentation leads directly to a discussion of nonmarket or government failure in job training and retraining programs. The final section of the paper contrasts market and nonmarket failure and their effects in considering how much public support is to be allotted to training and retraining programs.

A Brief Review of Federal Labor Market Programs Public support for employment and training programs is relatively recent in origin, building on an array of earlier programs designed to improve the functioning of labor markets. Perhaps the most important of these earlier efforts was the unemployment insurance program which sought to reduce the impact of worker layoffs resulting from seasonal and cyclical fluctuations. This program originated in Wisconsin during the early 1930s and in

---

[1] Prepared for Symposium on Market Failure in Training, La Follette Institute of Public Affairs, University of Wisconsin-Madison, May 11-12, 1989.

the late 1930s was expanded into a national state-federal program. Unemployment insurance provides a replacement wage for laid-off workers who are obligated to search for new jobs as a condition of receiving benefits (Hansen and Byers, 1990). Funding of UI programs, however, has been provided through a tax on employees.

Several other programs sought to improve the quantity and quality of information about the labor market. By contributing to a smoother functioning labor market, unemployment should as a consequence be reduced, which would as a by-product minimize unemployment (Lester, 1966). In the 1930s Congress established what is now the Job Service to help match job seekers with job vacancies. After World War II the Department of Labor began on to publish information regularly on the current state of the labor market by region, occupation, and industry. Periodic employment projections by occupation and industry were also released to inform the public--both employers and workers--about the future supply and demand for labor and the need for particular types of education and job training.

The federal government first ventured into the provision of job training in the early 1960s as a result of growing concern about structural unemployment (Ginzberg, 1980; Levitan and Gallo, 1988). Initially, the identification of growing numbers of long-term unemployed in the nation's depressed areas (e.g., Appalachia) stimulated by this concern. This led to passage of the Area Redevelopment Act in 1961 which, in addition to trying to reinvigorate the nation's depressed areas, provided a modest funds for retraining-relocation of long-term unemployed workers in these areas. By the early 1960s the focus of political concern shifted to structural imbalances, reflected by the persistence of higher unemployment rates among less-educated workers and to anticipated job displacement because of increased automation. These developments led to a concerted push for job training and retraining programs as a way to reduce unemployment and contribute to the nation's economic growth. Congress responded with the 1962 Manpower Development and Training Act (MDTA), whose major purpose was to provide retraining for displaced workers.

With the beginning of the War on Poverty in 1964 concern shifted dramatically from the problem of reducing unemployment to reducing poverty, which was to be achieved by altering the distribution of earnings (Council of Economic Advisers, 1964). In the short run, transfer payments would ease the difficulty. In the long run, increased education and training opportunities would permit people to earn their way out of poverty. Under this approach, Congress through the 1964 Economic Opportunities Act created a variety of new training programs designed to help people, especially the hard-to-employ, acquire basic job market skills. These programs included the well-known Job Corps, Neighborhood Youth Corps, and other community-based training programs. Still other programs were activated in the late 1960s.

As the difficulties of the task became more apparent, the view developed in the early 1970s that manpower programs--training and job creation--could be more responsive and effective if their management was shifted from the federal to the state-local level but with continued federal funding (Ginzberg, 1980). To effect this change, Congress enacted the Comprehensive Employment and Training Act (CETA) of 1973. Growing concern about youth unemployment in the mid-1970s led to passage of the Youth Employment and Demonstration Projects Act (YEDPA) of 1977. In still another attempt to deal with unemployment and training issues, Congress passed the New Jobs Tax Credit of 1977 to help expand employment and then the targeted Jobs Tax Credit of 1978, which gave employers special incentives to hire specifically targeted population groups. Meanwhile, the 1978 reauthorization of CETA focused greater attention on the disadvantaged and hard to employ. As a result of this flurry of activity, funding for CETA and related programs reached more than 2.3 percent of all federal spending.

With the change of administration in 1981 and growing public disillusionment with federal employment and training programs, still another transformation occurred. Funding for CETA programs was initially cut. Shortly thereafter the program itself was scrapped. Out of the ashes emerged the 1982 Job Training Partnership Act (JTPA) whose purpose was to develop increased public-private cooperation in providing training and retraining. It offered a variety of assistance to dislocated workers, poor youths, special groups such as migrant workers, and so on.

How can we sum up the experiences of the past three decades? The record demonstrates a considerable willingness to experiment with various approaches and to spend substantial sums on employment and training programs--a cumulative total of $64 billion by federal year 1979 (Ginzberg, 1980). Notwithstanding these efforts, there is little evidence that these programs made any substantial dent either on the level and structure of unemployment rates or on individual earnings and poverty rates (e.q., Hollister, *et al*, 1984; Betsey, *et al*, 1985; Levitan and Gallo, 1988; Barrow and Aron, 1989).

The reasons for the disparity between expenditures and results has been the subject of much discussion. It is clear that these programs have been plagued by numerous problems. Some experts describe them as associated with the politics of unemployment--the formulation, administration, and reformulation of public policy (Baumer and Van Horn, 1985). Others put emphasis on the difficulties of policy implementation-resistance, imperfect convergence of interests, and disorganized interests (Levin and Ferman, 1985). Still others focus on key issues--program scale, program elements, eligibility standards, delivery systems, oversight and control, and coordination (Ginzberg, 1980).

These different ways of describing why training programs have not worked effectively indicate that public efforts to remedy failures in private markets leave something to be desired and may raise questions about the wisdom of public intervention.

The Rationale for Federal Job Training Programs The rationale for this array of legislation evolved over time in response both to changing national concerns and feedback on the effect of the resulting programs. The legislative language and popular descriptions of these programs began by stressing the objectives of reducing the costs of unemployment by helping unemployed workers qualify for new jobs through retraining. By the late 1960s, the emphasis had shifted to that of reducing the number of poor people by equipping them to become productive members of the labor force. The evolution continued, so that by the end of the 1970s these programs also came to be justified for their help in achieving a broader set of economic goals, including full employment, economic growth, and economic security (National Commission on Employment Policy, 1980, 1981).

Economists, meanwhile, were trying to sharpen the rationale for these programs (e.g., Weisbrod 1966, 1968a). Weisbrod argued that public investment in job training made good economic sense because such investment could not only increase allocative efficiency, but could also help achieve distributional equity. These two concepts proved to be highly useful in structuring the evaluation of public programs, with the first leading to a focus on benefit-cost analysis, and the second highlighting what these programs do for their target populations, such as the unemployed or the poor.

As training programs developed, labor economists took a lively interest in them for a variety of reasons. Perhaps most important was the provision under MDTA, including funding, for the evaluation of these training and retraining programs. The gradual acquisition of administrative program data, on individual and program performance, and later, panel survey data, greatly expanded the possibilities for assessing the effects of these programs. Thus, began a long and continuing series of manpower program evaluations.

The record of these programs in achieving their goals remains quite mixed and contrasts sharply with the optimism of those who proposed these programs. It soon became evident that programs which increased efficiency could not necessarily be counted on to promote equity, and vice versa. Moreover, programs that simultaneously produced greater efficiency and were rare. Thus, despite high hopes for employment and training programs, their successes have been less than overwhelming. Why they have not lived up to expectations remains a subject of considerable dispute.

What seems to have gained little attention in the evolution of manpower training programs is the nature of the market failures which provide justification for government intervention. The hope or assumption that government programs--through direct or private provision with public funding--could overcome private market failings has strong roots in economics. By minimizing or better eliminating private market failures, so the argument goes, economic efficiency and sometimes equity could be increased (Haveman, 1976).

What kinds of failure occur in the training market that warrant federal action? Economists traditionally identify the following sources of private market failure: (1) pure public goods, (2) externalities, (3) market power and economies of scale, (4) inadequate information, (5) resource immobility, and (6) the unequal distribution of income and wealth (Wolf, 1979, 1988).

Of these six sources of market failure, only four seem pertinent to training: (2), (4), and (5), with (6) being more problematic. By way of illustration, training may yield some externalities, (2), that cannot be captured by individuals who pay for their own training or by firms which pay for the training of their employees. As a result, there will be private underinvestment in training. Inadequate information, (4), about available training opportunities may limit the ability of young people to obtain the appropriate training as they prepare to enter the labor force. Immobility, (5), implies that individuals may not be able to take advantage of better job opportunities elsewhere. The result is that labor resources are not distributed as efficiently as possible. Finally, the unequal distribution of income and wealth, (6), means that low earning power of many untrained workers limits their possibilities of obtaining the training they may need to fill available jobs.

In what sense do markets "fail" in actually providing job training and retraining? One view implicit in the work of economists, such as Becker and Mincer, is that markets do not fail (Becker, 1962, 1964; Mincer, 1962, 1974). Firms do not provide general training because there is little chance of recapturing the costs of that training. Firms that do provide general training face the prospect of having their newly-trained workers lured away by other firms which are willing to pay workers for the value of this additional training. If fact, general training in the form of schooling is typically subsidized heavily by government, thus making it uneconomical for any firm to think of providing such training.

Firms do, however, find it in their interest to provide specific training, because, according to Becker (1962, 1964), and Mincer (1962, 1974), they can capture the benefits of such investment in the form of increased worker productivity. Since specific training is of value only to the employer providing it, the incentives for other firms to poach trained employees is negligible. Employer provided training ranges from formal classroom instruction to on-the-job learning , with most it thought to be specific rather than general.

To the extent that training is some mixture of general and specific training, firms can avoid foregoing the value of their training investment by the structuring of their compensation systems. If training is partly general and partly specific, firms will find it advantageous to push the costs of the general training onto their workers, for example, by offering lower starting wages while training occurs. In such cases, firms can be viewed as having two operations, one producing the particular goods and services in which they specialize and the other producing training which ranges from fully specific to partly general. (Firms that produce only training would be described in this context as schools.)

Still other institutions exist to provide job training, some of which is subsidized (Carnavale, 1989; Tan, 1989). In the public sector there are high school vocational programs as well as those provided by postsecondary educational institutions. In the private sector apprenticeships are typically supported by industry and sometimes by unions. In addition, of course, there are training programs in proprietary institutions which are not subsidized.

What is the justification for subsidizing these latter programs, i.e., educational programs? The typical response is that general education and training provide benefits for everyone (Weisbrod, 1963; Bowen, 1977; Haveman and Wolfe, 1984). At one level, the benefits of a better educated society resulting from general education and training can be viewed as a public or collective good because these benefits are available to all and are not diminished by anyone else's consumption of them. At another level the subsidization of these activities is justified by the externalities produced. Because individuals cannot capture the full benefits from their education, the amount of education privately demanded is less than that which would be optimal from society's viewpoint. The difficulty with this position is that these external benefits remain elusive, defying easy identification and measurement. To the extent these external benefits are small relative to the private benefits of education and training, the externalities justification for these public subsidies is considerably weakened. A further complication arises because whatever externalities are produced may accrue not to the general population but rather to a more limited group, such as all college graduates in the case of college attendance (Hansen, 1974). This would argue for having college graduates rather than the general public subsidize college students.

Streeck (1989) and others (Ritzen, 1989) advance the interesting idea that job training can be viewed as a collective good because it enhances the flexibility of a nation's labor force in adapting to technological and related changes. Streeck goes on to argue that because job training is an inseparable mixture of general and firm-specific training (a joint supply problem), firms will invest less than the optimal amount in specific training because of the difficulties of recouping their investments from workers who quit to take jobs which reward them for the general training acquired from the firm. Based on these two lines of argument, Streeck claims that market failure occurs, thereby bolstering the case for public subsidization of job training within firms. His argument gains strength by the claim that general training, which is provided by firms as part of a program of specific training, will be more effective than general training provided in a formal (school) setting. If this is so, then the case can be made for reallocating existing subsidies away from general training provided through formal schooling to a combination of general and specific job training provided by individual firms.

Several observations can be made about the Streeck position. First, his argument ignores the likelihood that employers will push the costs of any general training onto workers by such devices as lowering their starting wages. Second, even if specific training provided by employers carries with it an inseparable general component, that general component of training may still be specific to the industry. Such a situation might call for industry-wide rather than federal provision and/or financing of training, with firm-specific training still provided by individual employers. Why more training is not provided on an industry-wide basis is perplexing. Finally, if there are collective-good elements of job training, it would be interesting to see the evidence of their existence and the potential magnitude.

Labor economists concerned with training programs have had surprisingly little to say about the importance of private market failures as a justification for public sector involvement. They seem to have either taken these failures for granted or not thought about bringing them up, perhaps because market failures are of much greater concern to public finance than labor economists (Ginzberg, 1980). More recently, however, the concept of market failure has penetrated manpower policy discussions, but the focus of these discussions has been limited largely to problems of transitional unemployment resulting from plant shutdowns. For example, Cyert and Mowery (1987), in their report on innovation and economic growth, cite the social costs of unemployment. They state that "plant shutdowns and large scale layoffs occurring without advance notice appear to impose substantial additional costs on both workers and the public sector by comparison with situations in which notice is given." They describe these effects as "externalities" because the "costs imposed on individuals and society . . . are not borne by the firms closing the plant or laying off the workers" (p. 156).

Ehrenberg and Jakubson (1989) make much the same point, highlighting the "important externalities [that] exist when workers are displaced." They focus on the divergence between the private and social costs of plant closings, contending that "employers do not bear the full social costs of plant shutdowns, both because unemployment insurance is imperfectly experience rated and because the costs shutdowns impose on communities are not taken into account by them" (p. 7). This leads the authors to conclude that "efficiency considerations suggest the need for federal . . . rules" that would in effect "tax" plant closings (p. 7). Much the same kind of argument is made by Creticos and Sheets (1989).

Whether these externalities are real or pecuniary is crucial to the discussion. It should be noted that plant shutdowns are largely the result of unforeseen changes in competitive forces in a world where unemployment insurance exists to help cope with unanticipated unemployment. The consequences of unforeseen events is hardly a real externality; rather, it represents a pecuniary externality (Weisbrod, 1968b) that does not necessarily merit public subsidy. It remains true that local communities may bear some additional costs because of worker displacement but, again, these are pecuniary rather than real externalities. For these several reasons, it is difficult to accept assertions that plant closings give rise to real social costs.

The Cyert and Mowery (1987) report goes on to suggest another form of externality, one that occurs because "displacement may cause workers to make career decisions based on defective or incomplete information" (p. 156). The upshot of this analysis is to call for more job training and retraining and for other labor market policies that can ease the social costs of unemployment resulting from job displacement. The criticism that workers may be misled because of defective or incomplete information is difficult to accept as a basis for the report's policy recommendations. Labor market information is almost always defective or incomplete. Providing more training without better information is unlikely to lead to improved outcomes. In any case, most labor market information is already supplied by the federal government, at little or no cost to the individual!

Aside from these few examples, most reports and studies argue for job training and retraining on more pragmatic grounds. For example, the Committee on Economic Development (1987) calls for a combination of private sector and public policies, among them private sector "support programs that allow people to shift to new opportunities . . . ", and a public sector "commitment to job training programs . . . ." The most recent of a string of reports, that of the Commission on the Skills of the American Workforce (1990), advances a comprehensive proposal that would utilize the entire array of educational institutions and several new forms of schooling-training institutions to assure mastering of basic skills and the acquisition of higher worker skills required for workers who do not need college degrees.

Suppose there is evidence of market failure. What then? Obviously, any number of options exist for enlarging the number of trained workers and for deepening the training of these workers, as exemplified by the variety of approaches employed over the past several decades. At one extreme government can publicize and make information available about training and retraining opportunities available in the private sector while at the same time regulating the providers of such training. At the other extreme it can mandate that employers provide training for their workers. There are numerous other positions along this spectrum. Government can finance and provide training, or it may choose to finance but not provide training. In either case, the demand for training can be increased by subsidizing workers who purchase training through the use of vouchers, tax credits, or tax deductions, or by subsidizing the training provided by employers. Which of these various options is likely to be most effective in dealing with market failure remains unclear.

<u>Nonmarket Failure</u> Why have government programs not been more successful in dealing with private market failure? If new training and retraining programs are to be introduced to deal with continuing private market failures, what is the likelihood such programs will be more successful than past programs? These difficult questions arise at the very time proponents of public programs are attempting to reshape public opinion about the need for more training and retraining and to improve the effectiveness of such programs (Bluestone and Harrison, 1988; Osterman, 1988; Levitan and Gallo, 1988).

Assistance in answering the first question, about why job training and retraining programs failed to produce more positive result comes from focusing on nonmarket failure--why government responses to perceived private market failures may go awry. This approach requires us to draw explanations for nonmarket failure and then to apply these explanations to training programs. The concept of nonmarket failure is a relatively new theme in economics, having evolved in the late 1970s and early 1980s. Its development occurred partly as a result of the disappointing experience with many Great Society programs launched in the late 1960s, chronicled so well by Aaron (1978), and partly as a result of the emergence of the public choice approach in economics, described by Gwartney (1976).

Perhaps more than anyone else, Wolf (1979, 1988) set out the concept of nonmarket failure as a direct parallel to the concept of private market failure. For each type of private market failure there is an approximate counterpart in nonmarket or government failure. This juxtaposition suggests that government activity to offset private market failure may be undercut by the prevalence of nonmarket failure. Whether nonmarket failures more than offset the effects of government programs is an empirical question.

The conditions under which nonmarket failure can exist and indeed flourish need to be reviewed before describing the various types of nonmarket failure, . The supply side characteristics include difficulties in defining and measuring not only the units of output but also their quality, centralization within a single agency of the responsibility for providing output in an environment not subject to competitive forces, and the absence of a price mechanism to discipline the market for the particular output. The demand side characteristics include an increased public concern about private market failure which has stimulated requests for corrective public programs, the possibilities for politicians to gain political support by favoring corrective programs even if these programs are not implemented effectively, and inadequate attention to determining whether government can be effective in correcting private market failures.

Wolf outlines four classes of nonmarket failure. Two more are added here to parallel the more extended list of private market failures. Consider first the case of public goods whose counterpart is what Wolf calls "internalities and private goods." Because of the peculiar nature of public goods and the rules governing the organization and operation of public bodies, decision makers in these organizations are prone to what are often referred to in markets as the principal agent problem, that is, they act for their own benefit rather than that of the public. This proclivity leads these bodies to concentrate on increasing the size of their budgets and then using their resources for new and complex projects that appeal to their own constituents. As a result, producers of what are presumably public goods produce benefits that are essentially private in nature though paid for by the public. This means that program costs are unnecessarily high.

Consider next the case of externalities and its counterpart, "derived externalities." Public programs are typically designed to achieve certain goals but in the process often produce unexpected side effects. The affects may impinge upon the welfare of other individuals or may conflict the operation of other government programs. In the latter case, these effects are likely to be negative rather than positive because each program is planned and executed in isolation from other related programs.

Still another nonmarket failure arises because of the concentration of market power. When government becomes the sole provider or financier of some program, the absence of competition combined with weak incentives to simulate the desirable aspects of private market behavior gives no assurance that resources are allocated efficiently. Moreover, the pressures that arise for uniformity in the amount of services provided or in the level of program expenditures further increases program costs.

Finally, the unequal distribution of power and prestige replaces the distribution of income and wealth as a source of failure, a point that hardly needs elaboration.

Two other sources of nonmarket failure must be mentioned to round out the story. Lack of information among the public as consumers and among workers as producers has its counterpart in public employees who typically have no strong incentive to gather the pertinent information that will help them provide the mix of goods and services, or of jobs, that the public wants. And just as individuals may be relatively immobile, public programs typically become rigid and unable to respond rapidly to changing circumstance.

The Conditions for Nonmarket Failure in Job Training Programs How is nonmarket failure related to job training and retraining programs? It is helpful to begin with the supply and demand characteristics of the market for training programs.

On the supply side, no agreement seems to have been reached about what are the outputs of training programs. This is exemplified by the evolving experience with the 1982 Jobs Training Partnership Act (JTPA) (National Commission on Employment Policy, 1987) and the problem reporting requirements for its training programs. What kind of information is to be reported and thus used as a basis for assessing program effectiveness? Is it program completion, placement, increased earnings levels, reduced welfare benefits, or something else? A closely related question concerns the time span over which the effects are to be monitored. Is followup data for the first year or even the first two years adequate to permit evaluation of the effects of programs which are presumably viewed as long-term human investments rather than current expenditures?

Another continuing point of contention is with the focus on the quality of program outputs and their subsequent effects (National Commission on Employment Policy, 1988). What level of effects--program completion, placement, increased earnings, reduced welfare benefits--are required before programs can be judged as successes? What kind of a cost-benefit outcome is required to justify the continuation of a program? If the narrow cost-benefit outcome is unfavorable, what weight should be given to other less easily quantifiable benefits?

Finally, how effective are the Department of Labor's regulations governing the multiplicity of providers of training (Sheets and Stevens, 1989)? Do the institutional conditions under which training is provided effectively focus the efforts of providers, or do they serve as constraints that limit the creativity of providers? How can providers be rewarded or penalized for their performance so as to simulate some kind of "bottom line" concept?

The demand side for training is characterized by similar difficulties. Growing pressures to expand public training programs reflect the powerful personal drama surrounding the impact of plant closings, layoffs, and the like. Many politicians find it easy to support training and retraining programs, knowing that the effectiveness of their implementation cannot be judged for years to come (Levin and Ferman, 1985; Baumer and Van Horn, 1985). And finally, the question that remains to be answered is how effective, job training and retraining can be in dealing with the problems of unemployment and poverty (Blalock, 1990).

This brief review indicates that the characteristics of job training and retraining programs open the way for nonmarket failure. This conclusion is hardly surprising in view of the numerous reports on how these programs need to be improved. This is simply another way of stating that these programs have failed to live up to the expectations surrounding them when they were initially proposed.

Nonmarket Failures in the Provision of Training Programs How do these characteristics manifest themselves in nonmarket failures? Which of the nonmarket failures are most prevalent in public training and retraining programs. A preliminary set of judgments follows.

The public goods-internalities failure is pertinent if the purpose of job training programs is to produce a better trained and more flexible labor force. This flexibility has not been achieved. The "internalizing" behavior of the organizations involved in overseeing and providing job training has obviously played an important role. The practice of "creaming," i.e. selecting into programs those individuals who are most likely to meet program performance standards rather than benefit directly from program participation may enhance the measured "success" of programs without doing much to increase work force flexibility.

Efforts can be made to counteract this behavior by writing tighter eligibility criteria so as to assure more effective targeting of programs their own ends. The natural resistance of program operators to tight eligibility standards and performance criteria is hardly surprising. Their reluctance to agree to outside evaluations of their program's effectiveness is also indicative that the programs may serve providers more than trainees.

The easiest item to handle is the externalities-derived externalities failure, with its emphasis on unintended side effects. A program to provide training to recently unemployed workers may be good one, but it cannot work effectively if it conflicts with some existing program. For example, the unemployment insurance program requires newly unemployed workers to continue their job search or face a cutoff of their UI funds, thus, effectively precluding them from entering job retraining programs (Hansen and Byers, 1990). Also, the benefits provided under retraining programs may not be substantial enough to induce potential participants to give up other public benefits when the rules prevent receiving both sets of benefits.

The issue of costs due to monopoly control is one about which less can be said. Obviously, government exercises its "monopoly power" in defining program goals, implementing programs, and evaluating program effectiveness. By design, its regulations and operating procedures downplay the use of incentives that might otherwise operate to limit program costs, especially administrative costs. Moreover, the incentive structures are often too weak to ensure that the appropriate level and quality of training is produced. Though the decentralization of CETA was seen as a step to reduce costs and increase effectiveness by breaking the monopoly of control exercised by the Department of Labor, another administrative structure and pattern of disincentives arose that created a different set of problems. The push toward further privatization under JTPA is further evidence of the difficulties of operating outside the structure of a market system. It also reveals the problems of monitoring the activities of many providers.

It is worth noting here that these three types of nonmarket failures are often discussed as "management and performance" problems Virtually all reports on past and present programs have offered recommendations for improving program management as an essential ingredient in improving the performance of programs and their participants (King, 1988; Creticos and Sheets, 1989; Blalock, 1990). The focus on management and performance issues, while not unexpected in the context of the bureaucratic environment, always offer hope that the difficulties programs are experiencing can be overcome and that success may indeed be achieved.

Last on Wolf's list is the matter of the distribution of income and power. The 1960s emphasized retraining, whereas the early years of CETA focussed on job creation programs. As redistributive concerns gained strength in the 1970s, and especially after Carter's election in 1976, greater emphasis was given to serving the poor and disadvantaged. With the 1970s, job training programs were scaled back and linked more closely to the private sector. These twists and turns reveal how different political constituencies rise and fall. In a sense, training programs reflect the continuing tension between who or what groups will benefit and who or what groups will pay. Thus, there is perennial concern about how to target job training programs, i.e. to what extent should they focus on the easy versus the difficult cases? There is also concern about how employers may be able to turn these programs to their own advantage by receiving public funds to provide training they would have been willing to provide anyway.

The additions to the list of nonmarket failures still need to be considered. The information available to guide government agencies operating or overseeing training programs is typically deficient. In trying to decide what types of training to offer or to recommend, reliance must be placed on analyses of current and prospective labor market conditions. If training and retraining programs are based on current labor market conditions, people may be trained for jobs for which there will be no demand when the training is completed. Gearing job training to prospective demand may produce similar problems, not only because employment projections are often so wide of the mark but also because these projections are not available for local labor markets. It is unclear if governmental agencies are capable of generating more accurate information about local labor markets than individuals living in these areas already possess. This means that figuring out what kinds of training to provide is no easy task.

The flexibility possessed by the public sector in adapting training programs to changing economic conditions is low. Even with the vast numbers of two-year institutions offering postsecondary vocational and technical programs, these institutions are ill-suited to provide training and retraining for newly unemployed workers. In large part the difficulty arises because they are geared up to the usual academic schedule and hence cannot respond quickly to local layoffs. Nor do they have available staff which are knowledgeable in the many possible areas of job retraining. Private providers under contract to provide retraining may be able to respond more quickly but may not be able to provide effective retraining for lack of adequate staff. Compounding these problems is the vast network of regulations and operating procedures which often prevent making needed and timely adaptations in local programs. Larger scale adaptations may require congressional approval which are difficult to obtain outside the four-year reauthorization cycle.

Before leaving this topic, it is worth noting that perhaps the most massive nonmarket failure occurs in our most fundamental training program--elementary and secondary education. To some extent, this failure precipitates many of the failures discussed here. The evidence of failures comes from reports on the weak performance of young people in the schools (Mullis, et al, 1990), as well as piecemeal remedies (Commission on Workforce Quality and Labor Market Flexibility, 1989), and more comprehensive proposals to integrate schooling and training (Commission on the Skills of the American Workforce, 1990).

Concluding Comments This paper offers a different perspective on the arguments for increased public financing and provision of job training and retraining programs. In reviewing the development of these programs over the past three decades, it sought to identity sources of private market failure which would justify public involvement. For reasons that are not entirely clear, the literature pays little or no attention to the existence of such failures. This omission is perplexing in light of widespread criticisms and acknowledged shortcomings of publicly supported training efforts.

A resolution is obtained by recasting the discussion in terms of a parallel set of nonmarket failures. The efforts to offset private market failures gives rise to public programs that are by their nature subject to similar and perhaps offsetting nonmarket failures. This symmetry leads to the inescapable conclusion that a balance must be struck, between (1) private market failures which result in suboptimal levels of training and retraining, and (2) government or nonmarket failures which can undercut the expected positive effects of training and retraining efforts by producing inappropriate types and amounts of training and at excessive cost. Though no accurate assessment of the relative strength of private versus nonmarket failures is possible, the extensive literature from policy researchers and analysts suggest that the problems of nonmarket failure are substantial, so substantial that private market failures cannot by themselves serve as an argument for public programs (Levin and Ferman, 1985; Baumer and Van Horn, 1985).

The current emphasis in job training programs is to locate them within a private employment setting. This new approach, while appealing in many respects, also suffers from difficulties arising because of the complex interplay of public and private interests. A major task for economists, policy analysts, and job training experts is to rethink the issues of private market and nonmarket failure, figure out what kinds of nonmarket failures are likely to occur, and devise ways of minimizing the strength of these failures. Once that is done there can be a more realistic assessment of the probable success of job training and retraining programs. Only then will it be possible to decide whether training programs can improve allocative efficiency and distributional equity, which are the ultimate objectives of training programs.

REFERENCES

Aaron, Henry, *Politics and the Professors: The Great Society in Perspective*, Brookings Institution, 1978.

Barnow, Burt S. and Laudan Y. Aron, "Survey of Government Provided Training Programs", on *Investing in People: A Strategy to Address America's Workforce Crisis*, Vol.1, U.S. Department of Labor, September 1989.

Baumer, Donald C. and Carl E. Van Horn, *The Politics of Unemployment*, Congressional Quarterly, 1985.

Becker, Gary S., *Human Capital*, Columbia University Press, 1964.

Becker, Gary S., "Investment in Human Capital: A Theoretical Analysis," *Journal of Political Economy*, Supplement, October 1962.

Betsey, Charles, L., Robinson Hollister, Jr., and Mary R. Papageorgiou, *Youth Employment and Training Programs*, National Academy Press, 1985.

Blalock, Ann Bonar (ed.), *Evaluating Social Programs at the State and Local Level: The JTPA Evaluation Design Project*, The Upjohn Institute, 1990.

Bowen, Howard R., *Investment in Learning: The Individual and Social Value of Higher Education*, Jossey-Bass, 1977.

Carnevale, Anthony P. "The Learning Enterprise," *Training and Development Journal*, February 1989.

Committee on Economic Development, *Work and Change: Labor Market Adjustment Policies in a Competitive World*,. New York, 1987.

Commission on the Skills of the American Workforce, *America's Choice: High Skills or Low Wages*, National Center on Education and the Economy, June 1990.

Commission on Workforce Quality and Labor Market Efficiency, *Investing in People: A Strategy to Address America's Workforce Crisis*, A Report to the Secretary of Labor and the American People, U.S. Department of Labor, September 1989.

Council of Economic Advisers, *Economic Report of the President: 1964*, U.S. Government Printing Office.

Creticos, Peter A. and Robert G. Sheets, *State-Financed, Workplace-Based Retraining Programs*, A Joint Study of the National Commission for Employment Policy and the National Governors' Association, National Commission for Employment Policy, Research Report 89-01, January 1989.

Cyert, Richard M. and David C. Mowery (eds.), *Technology and Employment: Innovation and Growth in the U.S. Economy*, National Academy Press, 1987.

Ehrenberg, Ronald G. and George H. Jakubson, *Advance Notice Provisions in Plant Closing Legislation*,, The Upjohn Institute, 1989.

Ginzberg, Eli (ed.), *Employing the Unemployed*, Basic Books, 1980.

Gwartney, James D., *Economics: Private and Public Choices*, Academic Press, 1976.

Hansen, W. Lee, "Need Research on External Benefits of Higher Education," <u>Comparative Education Review</u>, 18 (February 1974).

Hansen, W. Lee and James F. Byers, "Unemployment Compensation and Retraining: Can a Closer Link Be Forged?"

Hansen, W. Lee and James F. Byers (eds.), <u>Unemployment Insurance: The Next Half Century</u>, University of Wisconsin Press, 1990.

Harrison, Bennett and Barry Bluestone, <u>The Great U-Turn: Corporate Restructuring and the Polarization of America</u>, Basic Books, 1988.

Haveman, Robert H., <u>The Economics of the Public Sector</u>, John Wiley & Sons. 1976.

Haveman, Robert H. and Bobbi Wolfe, "Schooling and Economic Well-Being: The Role of Non-Market Effects," <u>Journal of Human Resources</u>, Summer 1984.

Hollister, Robinson, Jr., Peter Kemper, and Rebecca Maynars, <u>The National Supported Work Demonstration</u>, University of Wisconsin Press, 1984.

King, Christopher T., <u>Cross-Cutting Performance Management Issues in Human Resource Programs</u>, National Commission for Employment Policy, July 1988.

Lester, Richard A., <u>Manpower Planning in a Free Society</u>, Princeton University Press, 1966.

Levin, Martin A. and Barbara Ferman, <u>The Political Hand: Policy and Implementation and Youth Employment Programs</u>, Perganon, 1985.

Levitan, Sar A. and Frank Gallo, <u>A Second Chance: Training For Jobs</u>, W. E. Upjohn Institute, 1988.

Mincer, Jacob, "On-the-Job Training, Costs, Returns and Same Implications," <u>Journal of Political Economy</u>, Supplement, October 1962.

Mincer, Jacob, <u>Schooling, Experience, and Earnings</u>, National Bureau of Economic Research, 1974.

Mullis, Ina V.S., Eugene H. Owen, and Gary W. Phillips, <u>America's Challenge: Accelerating Academic Development--A Summary of Findings From 20 Years of NAEP</u>, U.S. Department of Education, 1990.

National Commission on Employment Policy, <u>Sixth Annual Report to the President and Congress</u>, December 1980.

National Commission on Employment Policy, <u>JTPA Performance Standards: Effects on Clients, Services and Costs</u>, September 1988.

National Commission on Employment Policy, <u>The Federal Interest in Employment and Training</u>, Seventh Annual Report, October 1981.

National Commission on Employment Policy, <u>The Job Training Partnership Act: A Report by the National Commission on Employment Policy</u>, September 1987.

Osterman, Paul, <u>Employment Futures: Reorganization, Dislocation, and Public Policy</u>, Oxford University Press, 1988.

Ritzen, Jozef M.M., "Market Failure for General Training," Robert M. La Follette Institute of Public Affairs, April 1989.

Sheets, Robert G. and David W. Stevens, Refining the Use of Market Incentives in the Public Provision of Training and Related Services in the 1990s, National Commission for Employment Policy, April 1989.

Streeck, Wolfgang, "Skills and the Limits of Neo-Liberalism: The Enterprise of the Future as a Place of Learning," Work, Employment, and Society, 3 (1989).

Tan, Hong W., Private Sector Training in the United States: Who Gets It and Why, Institute on Education and the Economy, Teachers College, Columbia University, 1989.

Weisbrod, Burton A., "Benefits of Manpower Programs: Theoretical and Methodological Issues," in G. G. Somers and W.O. Wood (eds.), Cost-Benefit Analysis of Manpower Policies, Industrial Relations Research Institute, University at Wisconsin-Madison, 1968a.

Weisbrod, Burton A., "Concepts of Costs and Benefits," in Samuel B. Chase, Jr. (ed.), Problems in Public Expenditure Analysis, The Brookings Institution, 1968b.

Weisbrod, Burton A., "Conceptual Issues in Evaluating Training Programs", Monthly Labor Review, October 1966.

Weisbrod, Burton A., External Benefits of Public Education, Princeton University Press, 1963.

Wolf, Charles Jr., "A Theory of Nonmarket Failure: Framework for Implementation Analysis," Journal of Law and Economics, Vol. 22 (April 1979).

Wolf, Charles Jr., Markets or Governments: Choosing between Imperfect Alternatives, MIT Press, 1988.

Studies in Contemporary Economics

B. Hamminga, Neoclassical Theory Structure and Theory Development. IX, 174 pages. 1983.

J. Dermine, Pricing Policies of Financial Intermediaries. VII, 174 pages. 1984.

Economic Consequences of Population Change in Industrialized Countries. Proceedings. 1983. Edited by G. Steinmann. X, 415 pages. 1984.

Problems of Advanced Economies. Proceedings, 1982. Edited by N. Miyawaki. VI, 319 pages. 1984.

Studies in Labor Market Dynamics. Proceedings, 1982. Edited by G. R. Neumann and N. C. Westergard-Nielsen. X, 285 pages. 1985.

A. Pfingsten, The Measurement of Tax Progression. VI, 131 pages. 1986.

Causes of Contemporary Stagnation. Proceedings, 1984. Edited by H. Frisch and B. Gahlen. IX, 216 pages. 1986.

O. Flaaten, The Economics of Multispecies Harvesting. VII, 162 pages. 1988.

D. Laussel, W. Marois, A. Soubeyran, (Eds.), Monetary Theory and Policy. Proceedings, 1987. XVIII, 383 pages. 1988.

G. Rubel, Factors Determining External Debt. VI, 264 pages. 1988.

B. C. J. van Velthoven, The Endogenization of Government Behaviour in Macroeconomic Models. XI, 367 pages. 1989.

A. Wenig, K. F. Zimmermann (Eds.3, Demographic Change and Economic Development. XII, 325 pages. 1989.

J. K. Brunner, Theory of Equitable Taxation. VIII, 217 pages. 1989.

E. van Imhoff, Optimal Economic Growth and Non-Stable Population. IX, 218 pages. 1989.

P. S. A. Renaud, Applied Political Economic Modelling. XII, 242 pages. 1989.

H. Konig (Ed.), Economics of Wage Determination. XI, 373 pages. 1990.

C. Dagum, M. Zenga (Eds .) Income and Wealth Distribution, Inequality and Poverty. Proceedings, 1989. XIII, 415 pages. 1990.

A. J. H. C. Schram, Voter Behavior in Economic Perspective. X, 274 pages. 1991.

J. B. Woittiez, Modelling and Empirical Evaluation of Labour Supply Behaviour. VI, 232 pages. 1991.

R. Arnason, T. Bjorndal (Eds.), Essays on the Economics of Migratory Fish Stocks. VIII, 197 pages. 1991.

Ch. Czerkawski, Theoretical and Policy-Oriented Aspects of the External Debt Economics. VII, 150 pages. 1991.

D. Stern, J. M. M. Ritzen (Eds.), Market Failure in Training? VII, 233 pages. 1991.